Review Copy

Shifting Gears to Your Life & Work after Retirement

Carolee Duckworth &
Marie Langworthy

ISBN-10: 0984513612
ISBN-13: 978-09845136-1-1

D0018578

Library of Congress Cataloging-in-Publication Data

Duckworth, Carolee, & Langworthy, Marie
   Shifting gears to your life and work after retirement / Carolee Duckworth
and Marie Langworthy. New Cabady Press.
Includes index, URL table, references.
ISBN-978-09845136-1-1 (pbk) 2014
1. Retirement 1.a) Retirement—Planning   332.024
2. Career Change   650.14
3. Personal Living 3.a) Self-Actualization 3.b) Finance--Personal   646.79
HQ1062
I. Duckworth, Carolee & Langworthy, Marie
II. Title

DEDICATION

This book is dedicated to all of us Baby Boomers seeking to invent the new retirement. A special thanks to those who have gone before into the unknown waters of New Age retirement—the new frontier—and provided candid interviews illuminating the twists and turns.

And two particular dedications. One by Carolee to Dr. Wesley Walton, her dad by birth and Marie's by mutual adoption. Thank you, Dad, for being a true believer, and a major contributor well up into your 90s. You showed the way.

The second dedication is by Marie to Minnie (AKA "Sittoo"), her mom by birth, and Carolee's by mutual adoption, who with her unconditional and unrelenting belief that her children could become and accomplish anything they set their mind to, remains "the spur to prick the side of my intent."

ABOUT THE AUTHORS

Dr. Carolee Duckworth spent her long career working to empower people to become their own more complete and fulfilled selves. To this end, she co-created the *Common Cause Award* winning "Center for Re-employment Services," serving displaced workers, displaced homemakers, and 55+ career changers, stimulating their mental capabilities to prepare them to select and enter new careers.

Carolee also designed and redesigned courses and programs for Technical Colleges and industries in order to empower and increase critical thinking and technology-use skills and confidence. She created and launched College Online (*www.College-Online.com*) to increase access for students of all ages and life situations, enabling them to enhance their skills and advance their careers "any time, any place, any person, any pace."

Since she "*shifted gears*" herself, Carolee has focused on writing articles, courses and books to empower individuals of all ages to reach for their dreams.

Dr. Marie Langworthy, in her former life as an educator and administrator, derived her greatest satisfaction from hiring underachieving adults, empowering them, turning them loose, and watching them grow professionally. Now in her 21st century life she has created her new niche, straddling generations. While teaching the 55+ Boomer generation how to use basic technology tools, she also works with and supervises future teachers enrolled in a local university's graduate program.

Not one to shy away from multitasking, Marie has also "shifted gears" with her own web-based business, Super Writing Services, (www.SuperWritingServices.com), where she provides clients with web content writing, article writing, presentation design services, editing, copywriting, and business writing.

Table of Contents

SECTION I:
BRAVE NEW WORLD FOR RETIREMENT

CHAPTER 1:
Who Are We?

Behold the tsunami of data sweeping across America about "The Baby Boomer Generation." Just log onto amazon.com, where you'll find literally thousands of "how to retire," "where to retire," "when to retire," "why to retire," and "whether to retire" titles! The big question ahead for employers, service providers, businesses and government agencies alike is "What are the Baby Boomers going to do?" and "When and where are we going to do it?" We want to know the answers to these questions, too.

Whether we are talking about financial resources, projecting health conditions and needs, discussing personal relationships, planning career options, or anticipating the lasting impact on the culture, the data is conclusive and compelling. Our group of senior citizens, born any time between 1946 and 1964, and numbering more than 77 million, is a force to be reckoned with.

As a group, we will require and provide significant quantities of products and services. And, as we always have, we will contribute to and change the American landscape as no other generation has before. Constituting about 30% of the population, we will continue to exert substantive political, social, cultural, and economic clout.

Simultaneously, we Baby Boomers will find that, voluntarily or otherwise, we are being buffeted about by these same political, social, cultural and economic forces that we ourselves have contributed to.

WOW FACTOR
Beginning in 2011, and continuing for 19 years, about 10,000 Baby Boomers will turn 65 every day.

Early Boomers, Late Boomers

At the outset, let's divide Baby Boomers into two groups. A first cohort, the "Early Boomers," consists of those born in the first half of the period, between 1946 and 1955.

Those born in the second half of the period, between 1956 and 1964, are sometimes referred to as "Generation Jones." The "Generation Jones" nomenclature comes from the author and journalist Landon Jones, who coined the term "Baby Boomer" in his book, *Great Expectations: America and the Baby Boom Generation.*

How do these two Boomer groups differ? Although all Boomers are too young to have personal memories of World War II, early Boomers were born into families that were still feeling the recent impact of that war (*www.DemographicsNow.com*, 2010). And they do have personal memories of the Korean War. Generation Jones members' first war memories are of the outbreak of the conflict in Vietnam.

Early Boomers remember the Cuban missile crisis; the assassinations of JFK, Robert Kennedy and Martin Luther King Junior; the walk on the moon; the civil rights, environmental, and women's movements; the protests and riots; and Woodstock. In terms of key characteristics, the early Boomers as a group are: free-spirited, social-cause-oriented, experimental and individualistic.

Generation Jones Boomers came into awareness in time to remember Watergate, the Cold War, the oil embargo, raging inflation, and gasoline shortages. As a group they are less optimistic than early Boomers, tending to distrust government and lean towards cynicism.

Unprecedented Demands on Boomers

As the first generation to fully experience many profound changes, Boomers have arrived at life situations that would have been unusual, even highly unlikely, in the past, including:

- dual professional marriages
- late life parenthood
- serial singlehood
- globalization of work, home and family
- parenting the parents
- parenting the grandchildren

Dual Professional Marriages

Retiring Boomers have pioneered a new territory of dual professional marriages, where both husband and wife, having obtained stellar educations, go on to pursue professional careers. Many have run households in which there was neither a Mr. nor a Mrs. Mom to keep the home fires burning.

In these marriages, both partners were accustomed to a work life of challenges, engagement, and high demands that paid them regularly and well, both financially and in terms of recognition, advancement, and respect. In many cases, they both had the support of "staff" who carried out their wishes and to whom they were able to delegate tasks.

Theirs were the households of "all chiefs and no Indians", complete with business-related travel, regular professional development, and the excitement associated with addressing and meeting challenges with skill and even brilliance.

Late Life Parenthood

Many younger Baby Boomers, who started their families later in life, now find themselves approaching their 60's with children still in college. Given that college costs are soaring to nearly $50K+ annually, these members are facing a unique "sticker shock."

Because they bore their children in their early forties, these seniors now find themselves in the unlikely position of educating these off-spring as they themselves approach, or even enter, retirement.

Serial Marriages & Singlehood

Also, let's not underestimate the effect that divorce has had on "young" grandparents. Arrangements and rearrangements of marriages have resulted in family responsibilities that extend backwards and forwards, with blended families that include his children, her children and their children, as well as the offspring of all these children, not to mention an assortment of in-laws... parents, siblings, nieces and nephews.

The complexities compound exponentially with each new round of merged families, yielding an assortment of children and stepchildren, grandchildren and step-grandchildren, in-laws and ex in-laws.

Globalization of Work, Home & Family

Another highly significant phenomenon that Boomers have been the first to experience fully is the globalization of work, as well as home and family. This is the generation that not only left the farm, but in all probability left the city, the state, and in some cases, left the country!

Even if they continued to live close to their childhood roots, many Boomers have had opportunities to work and travel internationally. Some have lived abroad in one or multiple countries. Some have family members living abroad—children, siblings, parents.

Extended Parenting of Children and Parents

Boomers have been called the "sandwich" generation for good reason. In order to pursue an education, our children have been forced to remain home much longer than expected. Education-related financial constraints on parents due to prolonged dependencies of their children prevail not only through the college years, but afterwards as well. The reality—when new graduates fail to find suitable employment, they return home.

Meanwhile our parents are living longer, eventually needing more from us in terms of financial support, and sometimes personal care. Many of us have barely seen our children through college and out of the house on their own, before our parents have moved in to take their place.

These factors have caused changes in household makeup, with increased pressure on Boomers to meet our parents' needs as well as those of our children, in what can come to seem an almost perpetual generational cycle of needs and demands.

Parenting Our Grandchildren

Through an assortment of life's curved balls, some Boomers have found themselves, officially or unofficially, back in the child-rearing business—this time raising their grandchildren! Thus some Boomers are entering their retirement years with responsibilities for teenagers, young children, or even babes in arms. Their futures have come full circle, back to the perpetual demands to provide hearth and home, food and nurture, as well as the ever more expensive college education.

SNAPSHOT

Mary Lou and her husband Don worked hard, she as a college researcher, he as a carpenter. Don's passion was deep sea fishing, and after several trips to Costa Rica, Mary Lou and Don began to seriously look for retirement property there. Their plan was to move to Costa Rica, where Don would establish a small commercial charter fishing business.

But shortly before they were ready to retire, one of their sons went through a bitter divorce, then soon thereafter died, leaving behind his young daughter. So Mary Lou and Don suddenly found themselves back in the parenting business, as they assumed the guardianship of their granddaughter.

This placed their retirement plans on hold indefinitely. Once again, they had a child to raise and a college account to fund. Mary Lou has continued working, now as a tutor of high school students, while Don has become a prolific writer, sharing his experiences as a world-class deep sea fisherman.

Boomers Reach the Retirement Threshold

As Baby Boomers enter their 60's, they become the "Golden Boomers," retired or about to retire from their professions or occupations. Their average life expectancies are at an all-time high of 77.4 years, ranging continuously upwards the longer they live, to 88 years for women and 86 years for men who live past age 75. They may even live past 100, joining the burgeoning ranks of centenarians, now growing in number at more than 20 times the growth rate of the total population, and projected to number nearly 6 million by 2050 (*Aging*, 2009).

The economic impact of the Baby Boomers cannot be ignored. In the U.S. alone, over 50% of discretionary spending power rests with the Baby Boomers. We are responsible for over half of all consumer spending. And we are the vortex of a demographic shift that is causing many businesses to redesign their marketing strategies in order to capture the "gold" in what has been termed the "silver market phenomenon."

WOW FACTOR

In the area of health care, we as a group buy 61% of over-the-counter medications and an astonishing 77% of all prescription drugs. And we Boomers account for 80% of all money spent on leisure travel. *www.DemographicsNow.com*.

The combination of longer anticipated lifespans, entrenched patterns of consumption, and other factors, such as losses in retirement account funding due to the economy, has led many Boomers to consider post retirement as a "next phase" of life—work-wise, and otherwise.

SNAPSHOT

Stan held a job in the medical field for 36 years. Beginning his career in his early 20's, immediately after graduating college, he worked for the same organization for the entire duration.

As his later years progressed, he became increasingly disillusioned with his profession, found himself grudgingly going to work in the morning and becoming more and more cynical toward his colleagues and his clients. He finally came to the conclusion that he no longer wanted to work.

He was certain that, because of his seniority and his relatively lucrative retirement package, he would have no financial worries—that his retirement income was adequate and secure—that is, until he received a reality check about his medical plan. Because Stan was several years away from Medicare eligibility, his organization, while allowing him to remain under their medical umbrella plan, exacted a hefty contribution for family coverage, amounting to thousands of dollars a year.

Within a year, Stan was job hunting again. Although he did find part-time employment that he enjoyed, his new job requires that he travel much further from home.

Boomer Retirement Timing: Planned vs Actual

As a group, Boomers may hope and plan to work longer at their careers and retire later. But few, in fact, end up doing this. The pattern of planned versus actual retirement from long-term careers is striking.

According to surveys carried out by the Associated Press and _lifegoesstrong.com_, 42% of Boomers plan to delay retirement, and 25% claim they will never retire. You could call this a state of denial, or you could say that many Boomers still feel too young and full of life to start to think about being old.

According to the findings of the 2010 MetLife Retirement Readiness Index Study:

- 47% plan to retire _when_ they expected to;
- 46% plan to retire _later_ than they expected to;
- 6% plan to retire _earlier_ than they expected to.

Yet of those who have already retired:

- 33% ended up retiring _when_ they expected to;
- 3% ended up retiring _later_ than they expected to;
- 64% ended up retiring _earlier_ than they expected to.

What is most startling about these figures is the reversed pattern between retiring late and retiring early. While many hope to retire late (46%), only a few are able to do this (3%). And while very few expect to be ready to retire early (6%), a solid majority (64%) ends up doing just that, for whatever reason.

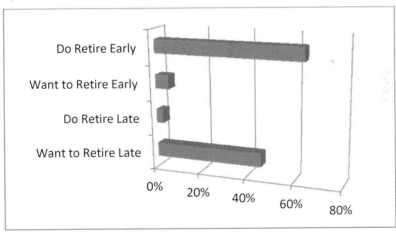

So Boomers Retire, Then UNretire

However, these figures do not paint the entire picture. Even if a majority of Boomers (64%) are retiring early from their long time career employment, as studies have shown, they are not entirely dropping out of the workforce.

A recent Merrill Lynch survey of Boomers found that more than 80% plan to continue to work even after they retire from their long-time careers. Fewer than 20% of Boomers see themselves as stopping work altogether.

Financial Positioning of Boomers

For many Boomers, plans to delay retirement have an economic basis. Around 60% of the Boomers have lost value in their investments due to the past decade's economic downturn. Other Boomers, who initially may consider themselves well-positioned financially to enjoy a productive, rich retirement, find themselves in for some major or minor shock waves that nudge them to reconsider.

Hidden, unexpected, costs lurk among the details of retirement plans. First, many retirees do not have a clear understanding of the additional medical costs they will need to assume upon retirement.

Next, retirees do not always factor in the impact that taxes will have on retirement incomes derived from IRAs and retirement accounts. Even those who are able to delay withdrawing funds from their IRAs and retirement accounts may be surprised to discover that as soon as they reach age 71, they will be required by law to "withdraw" annually a percentage of their previously sheltered retirement income, at which point that money will immediately become taxable.

Also, while we were working full time, not only did we have considerable *earning power*, in the form of raises, bonuses, promotions, career advances, but little time available to spend our earnings to enjoy shopping, the spa, the golf course, entertainment, or world travel. Now, in retirement, we have a luxury of time to spend what suddenly may have become a limited, fixed amount of money.

Hence, the paradox of having less money, with more time to spend it, and more ideas about how. These developments can become their own impetus to earn money again.

Other Reasons Boomers Go Back to Work

But financial readiness is only part of this picture. In addition to monetary needs and goals, of those 80% who plan to keep working at least part-time, 67% say they will do so in order to stay mentally active, and 57% in order to stay physically active.

There are many additional reasons to work that go beyond money, or even health. These include rewards that may be essential to a sense of well-being, social engagement and meaning.

Some Boomers plan a return to work in search of adventure or challenge. Others seek to continue enjoying the respect of colleagues and clients. Some still hope to have an influence... Or a way to be creative... Or a chance to use their expertise... Or an opportunity to help others.

Now What About You?

What may be an impetus for you to consider reengaging in work after retirement? Check any that apply. Then ask your spouse or partner, if you have one, to do the same.

- Money
- Adventure
- Challenge
- Respect
- Influence
- Social engagement
- Meaning
- A way to be creative
- A chance to use your expertise
- An opportunity to help others
- Intellectual stimulation

Medical, Health & Wellness Research Advances

In the past, our ancestors fell easy prey to the debilitating results of diabetes, hypertension, cancer, Alzheimer's and a whole array of related ailments and chronic illnesses. But with each passing day, through a combination of education, lifestyle change, preventive care, and advances in science and medicine, we are gaining more control over these and other diseases.

Advances in Disease Control

Even the heinous disease of diabetes is being controlled to degrees unheard of in the past. Progress in hypertension, and its villainous results in heart failure and stroke, is also making great strides.

Research provided by several studies under the sponsorship of the American Heart Association concludes that, because the medical community is experiencing increased success in treating hypertension, strokes have become less lethal and disabling over time. And let us not forget that weight, diet, activity level, and lifestyle habits all play an important part in keeping hypertension at bay.

Cardiovascular disease mortality also is in decline, as attested to consistently by study results (*http://hyper.ahajournals.org*, 2011).

Regarding the dreaded disease of cancer, types of therapy and treatment, the emphasis on prevention as well as cure, and millions of dollars being poured into research for both the causes and the cures for all types of cancer—these factors give us hope that this killer will continue to lose its momentum. In fact, we now seem to have turned a corner where most of us have more personal experience with family, friends, and acquaintances who have beat this dreaded disease than have succumbed to it.

The Baby Boomer generation's addiction to sun worshipping and smoking has unfortunately resulted in epidemic occurrences of skin and lung cancer. Additionally, our ignorance of the dangers of certain types of chemicals in the workplace also left many of us victims. But organizations such as the American Cancer Society have made major contributions in educating the public and creating changes in behavior and lifestyles that have decreased our exposure to elements that are dangerous to us.

Another dreaded condition is dementia (loss of brain function that occurs with certain diseases), and the particular form of dementia called Alzheimer's (affecting memory, thinking, and behavior, and worsening over time). But with every passing day, medical science is achieving more successful results, both in determining the causes of Alzheimer's and in warding off its consequences.

WOW FACTOR

A vaccine against Alzheimer's disease is in early testing. The mechanism for this vaccine is to block the buildup of the toxic amyloid protein that is responsible for destroying the brain. Early findings indicate that the vaccine is safest and most effective when administered before the protein buildup has begun.

Prevention of Disease

Our advances in disease control are paralleling our increased understandings of factors that underlie the development of diseases, the better to head them off. These advances include emerging knowledge of the role played by dietary and other lifestyle factors, such as regular physical and mental exercise, and the relief of stress.

We have made other significant health and wellness advances that enable the prevention of age-associated decline. One such development that promises major improvements, is our increased understanding of the role of age-related decreases in essential hormones and the health problems that stem from these developing deficiencies. This understanding has clarified the need to replace deficient hormones, and to replace them naturally using bio identical hormone supplementation, in order to maintain health and vigor, and even to reverse health patterns that otherwise could lead to disability or disease.

Other advances in understandings that impact our anticipated lifespans involve various environmental hazards. Here again, increased knowledge of consequences, combined with remedial action, has had the effect of protecting us from these risks.

These advances, collectively, are having a significant impact on our likelihood of living longer and healthier lives.

Longer Lifetimes

So ... the good news is that, through a combination of nature and nurture, many Boomers will be blessed with good health, the harbinger of a long, productive, active life.

It's true—because of all the progress and research in preventive medicine, as well as current and emerging advances in medical technology and diagnostics, a healthy 65-year-old male Boomer can expect to live 22 more years, while the average female Boomer can expect to live 25 more years (2010 _www.DemographicsNow.com_ report on Baby Boomers statistics).

The National Center for Health Statistics predictions are slightly lower, but still anticipate an additional 17 or more years for a 65-year old male and 20 or more years for a female.

In fact, in part because of continuing exponential advances in scientific and medical research, but also because of other changes such as our increased involvement in lively pursuits, our expected lifespans continuously increase with every additional year we live. Also, as female and male partners continue to live, the celebrated gap between their expected lifespans, women versus men, begins to close.

According to the *National Center for Health Statistics,* for those who live to age 50:

- A female can expect to live at least 32 more years, to age 82½.
- A male can expect to live at least 28 more years, to age 78½.
- The gap between male and female lifespans is four years.

For those who live to 65, these life expectancies increase by 2.5 years for females and 3.7 years for males, narrowing the sex gap from four years to three years.

- A 65-year-old female can expect to live at least 20 more years, to age 85.
- A 65-year-old male can expect to live at least 17 more years, beyond age 82.

Those who live to 75 see yet another increase in life expectancy, with a further narrowing of the sex gap to two years.

- A 75-year-old female can expect to live at least 13 more years, to age 88.
- A 75-year-old male can expect to live at least 11 more years, to age 86.

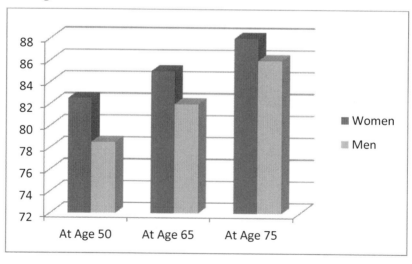

Many people will live even longer.

- A man who lives to age 65 has a 30% probability of living an additional 25 years, to age 90.
- A woman who lives to age 65 has a 40% chance of living an additional 25 years, to age 90.
- The possibility that at least one member of a 65-year-old couple will live past 90 is even higher—60%.

Beyond the 90-somethings emerge the centenarians, whose numbers are growing at a stunning rate, and will continue to do so.

WOW FACTOR

Numbering an estimated few thousand in 1950, the 100+ population escalated to over a third of a million worldwide by 2010, with highest concentrations in the U.S. and Japan (*Aging*, 2009).

And So...

There you have it. Boomers are reaching retirement age in torrents, and then are living longer. And, although many Boomers find themselves nudged (or propelled) into retirement from lifelong careers earlier than they expected, wanted, or could afford, their health is so good, and their drive to remain engaged is so strong, that the sum effect likely will be to return to work and to continue working well beyond the once traditional retirement age of 65.

In fact, 80% of all Baby Boomers plan to work at least part time after they retire, some forced by economic necessity, but others simply because they feel great and are not ready to let a number place them on the retirement shelf.

This means that *over 61 million of the 77 million Boomers* are in the "new" retirement position of seeking their next *work* after they are "set free" from their former "*day jobs.*" Of these, a phenomenal 40%—totaling upwards of *30 million people*—plan to work "until they drop" (Dream, 2011).

If you include yourself among the 80%, or even the 40%, and are not yet involved, reinvolved, or newly involved in post-retirement work you find challenging and rewarding, perhaps you need to "re-think" your remaining years, workwise and otherwise.

And that, my Boomer friends, is what this book is all about—figuring out what you plan to do with the rest of your life—a life that all signs indicate will be longer than you ever imagined.

To begin this process, the next chapter will examine the very concept of retirement, both as it was defined in the past, and how it is being redefined now as Boomers reinvent it.

CHAPTER 2
Retirement Paradigm Shifts

It has become eminently clear that the paradigm of retirement has shifted, and will continue to shift. The old retirement pattern—a long career of hard work, followed by no work and utter freedom to pursue leisure activities—is no longer typical, or even all that attractive. A point made repeatedly by many retirement authors, agencies, and researchers is that Baby Boomers are "reinventing retirement."

The Retirement Paradigm of the Past

According to the old paradigm of retirement, work ended at or around 65, at the close of our second life stage. At that point we were expected to withdraw from the world of work and "enjoy" a life of leisure.

Perceptions and Expectations

Since retired people were mainly defined by what they would NOT be doing rather than what they WOULD be doing, they were considered to be a relatively homogenous group. This perception was consistent with the industrial model that also was, and continues to be, applied to our children in their schools.

Old paradigm "retirees" were relegated to a life of reduced expectations in terms of social, professional and vocational contribution as well as of physical abilities and mental agility. Once they retired, seniors were defined by what they HAD BEEN in the past. "I *was* a teacher." "I *was* a doctor." "I *was* the CEO of a company." They were referred to, and referred to themselves, in the past tense.

SNAPSHOT

Walter was a hard worker and a wizard with anything and everything mechanical. He worked hard and long for a North Carolina carbon plant, arriving at work at 5:30 in the morning, and

---

staying until everyone else had gone home. He came home tired every night, usually falling asleep in the chair in the kitchen while his wife fixed dinner. He did grow a vegetable garden, but that was about it for sidelines or hobbies. His wife was a reader, but he never developed that interest himself.

And then he retired, or more accurately, was asked to retire. On his last day at work, his life work shifted precipitously from *all* to *none.* In just one day he went from being the mastermind and problem solver of choice—the one everyone came to first — to being a man with nothing better to do than to sit around the house waiting for his wife, who still worked at a highly engaging job, to come home.

He filled his first few weeks of retirement with the backlog of small domestic tasks he had formerly neglected. But then there he was, with nothing left to do.

Fortunately for him, his wife's brother appeared at the door one day and asked him to go fishing. This became his new "job"—his retirement "career." He devoted himself so completely to fishing as his next "job," his own refrigerator and freezer were soon overflowing. So he sought out other fish lovers with whom to share his bounty and his passion.

The Old-Style Retirement Industry

A large and thriving retirement industry grew up based on this old retirement paradigm. Every manner of goods and services were offered, designed to meet the wants and needs of those who were retired—for a healthy price, of course.

And what were those wants and needs perceived to be? Separate housing communities, for one thing, where yard and household maintenance were taken care of, leaving the retiree free—to do what??

Homogeneity for another. Retirees were seen to want "planned" communities where they were surrounded by others who were "just like them." Other lucrative businesses that targeted retirees were long-term and continuous care communities, where health and life needs would be provided for until the end of life.

Recreational and entertainment options comprised another large segment of services for seniors, focusing on pursuits and entertainments through which retirees could while away their bountiful "free" time —the ubiquitous bingo nights, golfing resorts, sing-alongs, and bus outings to outlet malls.

Outliers & Rebels from the Old Style Retirement

Of course there were outliers, even within the "old" retirement model. These individualists, in a sense, were the precursors of what was to come. When they accepted their "golden handshakes," they may have redefined themselves, but they did not "retire" themselves. They may have left the work that had consumed their lives, but they found other meaningful work or pursuits that engaged them and that filled their lives with meaning.

SNAPSHOT

For most of her adult life, Aunt Amanda had a high-powered job working for the civilian arm of the Navy on a major US Navy base. She was the epitome of diligence and devotedness to duty. For all those years, she lived at home with her parents, put her personal life on the back burner, and gave her all to her work.

When she was in her mid-50's, the Navy entered an austerity era, offering golden handshakes to anyone who had been employed for 25+ years. Aunt Amanda was ready. Tired of a long commute, sometimes in treacherous weather, weary with office politics, and bogged down with the responsibilities of someone in management, she jumped at the chance to "pack it in!"

"Horror, horror, horror," the family wailed. What will she do? How will she survive financially and psychologically? After all, Aunt Amanda was married to her work. How would she fill her time? Also, she had a history of spending far beyond her means. How would she subsidize her champagne taste on the beer allowance her retirement offer promised? Little did they know. It came to be a family joke. Within only a few years, Aunt Amanda's combined retirement incomes proved greater than the salary she had brought home during her employment.

And she became a social butterfly. She avidly arranged outings to New York and elsewhere—to museums, theater, fashion shows. She booked lunch dates, filling her calendar for weeks, and even months, ahead. She became the party planner of choice for all family occasions. And, most unexpectedly of all for someone who had rarely cooked during her "former" life, she became a gourmet baker—so much so that family members literally fought over her chocolate nut squares.

Her post-retirement became so full socially, that other family members, who were busy working full time and raising families, soon learned that if they wanted to include her in any type of social event, they *first* needed to consult *her* calendar. She would ask rhetorically, "When did I ever have time to work?"

If they laid aside the professional reading and specialized expertise that had consumed them during their former working lives, these Boomers found other sources of mental nourishment and renewal, challenge and learning. If they opted to enter retirement communities, they then set about to reform those communities from within. They presented lectures as well as attended them, authored books as well as read them, wrote and performed in plays as well as attended them.

SNAPSHOT

Dr. Wesley Walton was an educator at heart, and a true believer in the value of an education in every person's life. He set out on a vigorous and passionate career, removing barriers and establishing scholarship programs (*Sponsored Scholarships, National Merit Scholarships, National Arts Awards*) to open up to every person, whatever their age, the bounty of opportunity an education can provide.

Other projects he created included: *Horizons of Science* (a film series for school children starring scientists of the time, such as anthropologist Margaret Mead and botanist Roman Vishniac), and the *College Suggestor* (a precursor of computer-based college selection tools).

Given his passion for his work, Wesley seemed an unlikely candidate for retirement. He had no use for watching movies or television. He read expansively for his profession, but rarely just for pleasure. And he had no hobbies to speak of. His main side interest was astronomy, which he did continue to pursue with zeal after he retired. He also loved classical music; a musician himself when he was younger, he attended concerts whenever he possibly could.

When he retired, earlier than he had planned or wanted to, he immediately launched into what would become an extended "encore" career that lasted him well into his 90s. If anything, he was even more passionate about his encore career than he had been about his primary one. His retirement "career" led him into community and environmental leadership; long-range funding and programming for the Arts; illuminating and teaching the deeper connections between science and spiritualty.

At age 70, after years as a widower, he fell in love and remarried. At 75, he purchased leather-bound copies of all the great books, and began reading his way through them. And he guest conducted a concert by the Ocean City Pops. At age 80, he established a family foundation to support philanthropic projects that included the donation of collections of framed photographs taken by the Hubble telescope, as part of his mission to show the import of the Hubble images to the "life of the spirit."

At age 85, he co-authored a book, *Spirit of the Universe*, and began presenting lectures, and even "preaching" one sermon, on its contents. At age 90, he assigned each of his children and grandchildren a book to write that, according to him, *only* they were uniquely qualified to create.

Exit the Old, Enter the New Paradigm

The retirement paradigm has shifted, and is continuing to shift, in major ways. What once would have been an atypical retirement, as with the Dr. Wesley story above, is now becoming more typical.

The "encore" career is on the minds of many, if not most, retiring Boomers. Yes, we are leaving jobs that we once held well and energetically. But, no, we are not done yet. As we stand before our about-to-be-former colleagues, receiving our proverbial golden watch, or our silver Revere Bowl, our minds are racing with ideas about what comes next.

Boomers are "the most educated, most techno-savvy generation in our country's history," says William Frey, a demographer and visiting fellow at the Brookings Institution. "They will want to stay engaged in their work and be physically social." Ken Dychtwald, author of *Going From Success to Significance in Work and Life,* concurs, adding: "I think we are going to see adult education, re-careering and personal reinvention become a standard part of the later years."

It is almost difficult for retiring Boomers to read about the goods and services that were popular with earlier retirees, or to watch the ads that unwisely continue to promote them. "They can't be talking about me," we think.

Now that we are the ones being targeted, we view these offerings and shake our collective, and still well-functioning, heads. Few, if any, of us meet the earlier pattern of what retirement looks like or what goods and services were wanted or needed. As we arrive at what once was an endpoint, our eyes remain focused on the horizon, looking ahead.

The Retirement Industry Regroups

The "retirement industry" recognizes this extreme shift and is actively working to regroup. Many of the advertisements that worked so well in the past for those who came before us, are utterly unappealing, irrelevant, even offensive, to those of us now entering the retirement landscape. And many of the goods and services our predecessors flocked to purchase have completely lost their appeal, their usefulness, and thus their market.

In order to save their businesses, and continue to provide goods and services to the hundred million of us aged 55 or older, the retirement industry is struggling to redefine the market and figure out what we will want, and what to offer us.

The big questions are, "What are retiring Baby Boomers going to do?" "Where will they go to do it?" and "What goods and services will Boomers need or want to buy?"

What Are Retiring Boomers Going to Do?

For starters, Boomers want to look and act young. A projection by *Global Industry Analysts* anticipates that in the next several years, the market for anti-aging products, services and innovations will expand from $80 billion to more than $114 billion, thanks to burgeoning demands from Boomers. Everything from skin care products to exercise regimens to dietary supplements to wellness programs will likely be in increasing demand.

Secondly, Boomers want to stay connected and creative. Sites like *Eldergadget.com* note that those currently over 75 who use computers are highly active in *email, digital music and photo editing*. This trend will only increase as Boomers retire.

Thirdly, there's the "forever young" image factor. Have you noticed more white-haired sports car drivers on the road lately, with the top down, cruising off somewhere looking relaxed and happy in a powder blue convertible or a red Mazda Miata?

The list goes on. The sum total is well expressed by Varsity (*varsitybranding.com*), a product branding company offering marketing services to help "capture the mature market." The Varsity Team advises businesses to: "Remember that the mature market isn't acting their age, from their adoption of technology to their youthful glow."

WOW FACTOR

Builders of 50+ housing complexes may incorrectly assume that their buyers do not use the Web or e-mail. In fact, this group is very Internet-savvy. Increasingly, seniors expect and require that wi-fi hot spots be readily available, both in their community centers and clubhouses, as well as in the high-tech home offices in their new homes. [From *Nation's Building News*: *www.nbnnews.com/*]

Where Do Boomers Want to Live?

With 80% of us planning to work at least part time after retirement, and 40% of us planning to "work until we drop," where do we plan to live? According to the *MetLife Mature Marketing Institute*, 91% of pre-retirees ages 50-65 responded that they want to live in their own homes after retirement.

Of those Boomers who do plan to move, many are relocating not in order to *decrease* stimulation and involvement, but to *increase* it. One such migration pattern is the shift to urban living, with its cultural offerings and efficient public transportation systems. Other appealing options for Boomers are college towns, because of the vitality and intellectual stimulation that these communities offer.

WOW FACTOR

15% to 20% of older people living in the suburbs would like to relocate to urban areas. These moves are motivated by a lifestyle change, not by a real estate purchase alone. [Jane M. O'Connor, chairwoman of the *National Association of Home Builders.*50-plus New England Housing Network.]

Another emerging trend—more retiring Boomers are pursuing the ultimate travel experience of living abroad, full-time or part-time. Others design lives based around outdoor living, migrating to warmer climates in the winter and cooler climates in the summer, not just for greater comfort, but also to enjoy expanded access to outdoor activities—hiking or golfing, boating or swimming, fishing or biking.

Alternative housing models are gaining in popularity with Boomers in transition. One such model, inspired by projects in Denmark and other European countries, is termed "co-housing." These co-housing developments become deliberately tight-knit, with residents agreeing in advance to socialize with their neighbors "more than is usual."

In these complexes, the sense of community is fostered by clustering homes around large pedestrian-only areas with a shared "common house" where many of the social activities take place. Of the 119 co-housing developments completed so far, only three are for seniors only, while the vast majorities are mixed-age developments, by design.

What Retiring Boomers Are *Not*

For starters, Boomers are *not* a homogenous group. On the contrary, we are entering our retirements according to our own unique personalities, with our own lifestyle goals and intellectual and community pursuits—as well as our own travel, study and work plans. To describe one of us, is not to describe all of us.

Secondly, Boomers generally are *not* interested in a future dedicated entirely to ease and relaxation. Although we do want control over the work versus relaxation balance, even in terms of this balance, our designs for our third phase of life are marked by diversity, not sameness. Very few of us are likely to be interested in bus trips to outlet malls, senior sing-alongs, or bingo nights. But for some of us, having the time to read or study or garden or travel sounds blissful.

Thirdly, Boomers are *not* ready to set aside our lives of learning and adventure, engagement and contribution. In fact, we are more likely to be moving *towards* a full life than to consider ourselves to be *beyond* it. We are as likely (or *more* likely?) to be envisioning a retirement adventure of living in a major city, or even in another country, as we would consider a geared down life in a retirement community where all of our needs are met.

As a matter of fact, many, if not most, of us have an aversion to the prospect of having everything done for us, leaving nothing for us to do for ourselves—nothing to challenge us—nothing to learn. We may seek out, even enjoy, this type of helpless lifestyle on a 10-day cruise—complete with chocolates on our pillows and our bed covers turned down—but *not* as a permanent arrangement.

WOW FACTOR

The number of retirees living abroad, based on the number of benefit checks Social Security mails overseas, has skyrocketed from 396,000 in the year 2000 to 529,311 by 2012, showing a growth rate of 34%.

Many retire to Mexico, Central America, or the Caribbean. Growing numbers retire to Italy (19,600), Greece (13,882), Portugal (8,590), France (7,975), Spain (6,232), Croatia (948) and Malta (334). From *Retiring Outside the United States.*

What Retiring Boomers *Are*

Focusing on some major characteristics of retiring Boomers, they:
1. are energetic and vital,
2. are techno-savvy,
3. are entrepreneurial, and

4. are globally aware.
5. have more to offer,
6. have the desire and ability to offer it, and
7. have expectations of living for one or even two additional 15-year cycles beyond what was formerly common.

Because retiring Boomers are *energetic and vital*, we are far from the point of being ready to step aside. We may be more than ready to "retire" a *job*, but most of us are not yet ready to retire *ourselves*.

Because we are *techno-savvy*, we can and will remain connected and engaged for many years to come. The Internet has changed how people work, connect, communicate, and create. It provides many venues for work and creativity that are unaffected by age. We can and will avail ourselves of these barrier-reducing advances.

Because we are *entrepreneurial*, we can and will remain employed, either by working for others or by working for ourselves, long into the future. For many of us, our so-called retirement years will be our most creative and purposeful time of life.

WOW FACTOR

"Contrary to popularly held assumptions, it turns out that over the past decade or so, the highest rate of entrepreneurship activity belongs to the 55 to 64 group.

Increasing life expectancy suggests a blossoming of even older entrepreneurs. Today's entrepreneurial 60-year-old could be the 2020s entrepreneurial 70-year-old. Even more noteworthy is that startups with older work owners are more successful, at least as measured by their survival rates." From the *Ewing Marion Kauffman Foundation Study of Entrepreneurship*.

Because we are *globally aware*, through our work lives, our experiences, our travels, and our involvement, the scope of our retirement work can and will extend beyond our local neighborhood, and even beyond our state or nation, to include international venues. Again Internet technology, and the interconnectedness that it supports, makes all manner of retirement pursuits possible.

The global market for products and services provides us the opportunity to work abroad from home. Or we can make our home abroad and work either globally or locally from there. We can live in Jacksonville and work in Paris, or live in Paris and work in Jacksonville. The world, quite literally, is our domain, with all the opportunities this entails.

Because we *have more to offer of ourselves* after we retire, as well as *the desire and ability to offer it*, we bring to retirement a willingness to step out into the unknown, while carrying our strengths and passions with us. We are aware that we can make a significant difference with our lives, and we are willing to expend the energy, and even the resources, to make this happen. We may be tired of the commute and the job routines of our past, but we are not yet ready to come to a complete halt. And we don't need to stop. We are not done yet.

Because we *have the expectation of living* at least one, if not two, additional 15-year cycles of life, the gift of time is on our side. We can venture out into retirement work that matters to us. Or we can move forward into a life of leisure first, and then return to meaningful new work later, when we are ready to do so. We can move down one path, then back up that path and down another. We can do these things in any order, or we can choose several paths to pursue simultaneously.

We know that there is more that we hope to accomplish... and with the Internet, which most of us understand and are fully able to use... we have the option of structuring new careers that will suit us well and make use of our abilities—pursuits that will allow us to contribute and to remain engaged, both in work and in life.

It is an indication of the times, and also of our lives and futures, that the 2012 Academy Awards presented two awards to octogenarians. When Christopher Plummer bounded up the stairs to the stage at age 81 to receive his award as "Best Supporting Actor," his lively trajectory became a metaphor for our vision of our future selves.

Each of us has our own version of "stairs" that we fully intend to bound up, now and well into our 80s, or even our 90s. What will our own "stairs" be? That is the critical question that must be answered.

And So...

Given that Boomers are "the most educated, most techno-savvy generation in our country's history... and will want to [continue to] stay engaged in their work and be physically social," the idea of doing nothing for the rest of our lives is not an attractive option for many of us. We need to remain intellectually stimulated, to continue to grow as professionals, albeit, perhaps, in a direction totally different from the one we pursued in our former work lives.

In contrast to many previous generations, many, if not most, Boomers do not see a future where their work stops abruptly when they reach age 65 and their so-called "retirement" begins. Instead, many of us see on-again, off-again work mixed with periods of leisure. Some of us will continue to work because we need to financially; many others of us will continue to work because we just want to.

What do we hope to gain through our continued engagement in work? Some of us have high expectations of adventure. Others are dwelling on empowerment and professional enrichment. Still others envision a flexible agenda consisting of alternating periods of work and leisure. Many hope to supplement retirement income, expanding their possibilities as well as their dollars.

Many of us want to continue to work in some venue because work lends purpose and meaning to our lives. We like to—and choose to—rely on our current strengths, talents, capacities, and resources—our natural abilities, training, and experiences. And we will consider not just what we do particularly well, but also what we want to be able to do better.

As a start in this process, we will move ahead to focus on the larger picture of our lives so far—the ages and stages. This look back at the past will better enable us to plot our course ahead into the future.

CHAPTER 3
Boomer Retirement Landscapes & Timing

As we witness the many changes reflected by the lives of Boomers, including the dramatic increases in our expected longevity, we face a new retirement landscape, compounded by developments in our retirement timing. Mapping out the terrain of this new world of retirement is an essential step to navigating it successfully.

Three elements of our retirement futures that comprise the fuller picture are:
- *Where* we have come from—workwise and otherwise;
- *What* our current realities are—personal, financial and physical;
- *When* we retire—early, on schedule, or late.

Where Have We Come From?

Looking back at the passages of our lives, many of us will see that we have completed a full cycle about once every 12 to 15 years. These cycles have come together into three stages of our past—*Becoming*, *Being*, and *Redefining*, each comprised of two cycles.

I. Becoming	II: Being	III: Redefining
0-> 15 & 16-> 30	31-> 45 & 46-> 60	61-> 75 & 76-> 90

Stage I: Becoming

In the *Becoming* stage, we prepared ourselves professionally and personally for our lives of productivity. The *Becoming* stage was comprised of Cycle 1, from ages 0–15 and Cycle 2, from ages 16–30. Some of us spent considerable time during *Stage I: Becoming* collecting multiple skills, degrees and certifications that we carried forward into the *Stage II: Being* portions of our careers.

All this education and training may have enabled some of us to achieve success in a career that also brought us high levels of satisfaction, and in which we felt well utilized and highly engaged.

Stage II: Being

For most of us, *Stage II: Being* (Cycle 3, ages 31 to 45 and Cycle 4, ages 46 to 60) was what we came to think was the heart of the matter. Much of where we landed in *Stage II: Being* depended upon the academic and training opportunities that, through serendipity or hard work, we experienced and/or took advantage of during *Stage I :Becoming*.

Professionally, some of us settled into work about which we were passionate. Others of us found secure, steady employment at work that may not have been as fulfilling to us, but that did provide us with a respectable life style as members of the massive middle class workforce. Still others, in our *Stage II: Being* period, drifted from one job to another, never really finding our life's work niche, but managing to sustain ourselves economically.

There have been many additional variations within our *Stage II: Being* lives. For some of us, our *Stage I: Becoming* positioned us in the right direction and we found our way to a career we loved. But then some of us "veered off" to address the various specific demands of our jobs. Or as our employers discovered that we had an aptitude for technology or management or customer relations, we may have been pulled away, or pulled "ahead," from where we had felt the most engaged. The end result–we found ourselves going in a different direction where, although we were able to perform adequately or even exceptionally well, we knew that, in all truth, our hearts were not really invested. We may have loved our initial work, but not what evolved as we moved, or were pushed, up the ladder.

Yet another set of variations in our past work histories involves stories where our *Stage I: Becoming* years were cut short. For any number of reasons, we might have been forced to enter the world of work early, either because of financial needs at home or because we thought at the time that was what we wanted to do. We may have started school and stopped, or never figured out what we wanted to study if we did go to college. For whatever reason, we found ourselves "out there," hard at work and marching in place, long before we had a chance to prepare for, or even to know, what type of work we wanted to do.

Stage III: Redefining

Now we find ourselves entering the third stage, *Redefining* (Cycle 5, ages 61 to 75 and Cycle 4, ages 76 to 90+), where we are ready to take a new look at ourselves as professionals—who we are, who we want to become, where we want to go, how we plan to get there.

For many of us, this *Redefining* stage finds us more in control of our future than we were in Stages I and II. After all, in *Stage I: Becoming*, we were often too young, too immature, and too controlled by outside forces to self-determine our career destiny. And in *Stage II: Being*, life demanded that we concentrate on building the résumé, seeking the promotion, increasing the paycheck, and otherwise keeping our nose to the workplace grindstone.

Now in *Stage III: Redefining* we bring forward all the talent, skill and experience that have come before, to recombine them into our "what happens next." We are ready to ask ourselves, "What captures my mind, attention and efforts most fully, resulting in my total sense of losing track of time?"

Powerful assets that we developed over time from our earlier two stages, now inform our *Stage III: Redefining* adventure. They include:

- time,
- marketable professional/work skills,
- robust health,
- some degree of financial security,
- networking connections.

We differ not only in terms of what skills we developed, but also which of these skills we did or did not ultimately use during our work lives, and whether the skills we did use were ones we enjoyed. Did our work take us in the direction of our interests? Was the work meaningful to us, reflecting the underlying values that make us who we are? Did our work suit our personality type and temperament?

We will return to some of these types of uniqueness later to provide you an opportunity to clarify your own essence, and thus to ensure that your "you-ness" is incorporated into your own "new" retirement plan.

Now What About You?

You know best where your own past journey has taken you—where you come from. Take some time now to capture what your own progress has been so far through the stages and cycles of your own life. Include your own assessment of when and where (and if) your work life has been fully engaging for you.

Have you used the skills you developed during your own *Stage I: Becoming*? Did your work veer off, or otherwise become less meaningful to you? Or not? If you did lose your career compass, did you correct your course during some midlife, or mid-career crisis that early on propelled you into *Stage III: Redefining*?

What has your pattern been? Use the *Work Life Map* that follows to make notes about your points of origin and development.

My Work Life Map

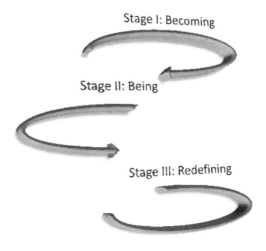

Stage I: Becoming

Stage II: Being

Stage III: Redefining

What Are Our Current Realities?

Not only does our diversity stem from our past, it also informs and defines us in terms of where we are now, and where we are heading next. What are the realities of our current and our future retirement situation: financially, physically, personally, and educationally?

Where Are We Financially?

What are our current financial resources, earned or put away during Stage II, inherited or created? Most of us have some assortment of sources and resources that we can personally rely on from this point forward. These are comprised of some combination of:

- Investments in property, stocks, and bonds
- Social Security
- 401Ks, IRAs, and so forth
- Earned benefits and pensions
- Royalties from publications, oil leases or other sources
- Ongoing income from property rentals
- Income from the ownership, full or partial, of a profitable business

To some degree, these accumulated resources will provide an income base for us that frees us after retirement to work at what we wish, not just at whatever earns the highest income. For some of us, initial plans to live solely on our retirement income will evolve into a realization that it would be preferable, perhaps even necessary, to earn more money after all.

Looking realistically at these combined income sources, and considering what we want and need financially for our life ahead, we fall generally into one of three groups. Take a moment to estimate where you are currently in terms of retirement finances.

☐ I need to earn more income.

☐ I want to earn more income even though I don't need to.

☐ I do not need or want to earn more income.

Where Are We Physically?

Yes, our collective health may be better, and our longevity may reach well beyond what earlier generations ever could have hoped for or even imagined, but the particulars of our health are diverse.

To personalize this reality, what is your own situation in terms of health, mobility, flexibility, and vitality? And how does your spouse or life partner measure in these areas? If one or both of you have experienced some decline in one or more of these areas over the years, to what degree can you, and will you, do what it takes to return to a healthier you?

We all know the drill. Eat well, but not overmuch. Get up from the recliner or couch every day and walk, bike, dance, work out, do yoga or swim. Sleep enough. Laugh enough. Intersperse into our days times of relaxation, or even meditation, to regroup and recover from the stresses of modern life. Exercise our minds as well as our bodies. Nurture loving relationships.

Some of us do better than others in following the prescribed drill. Many of us have every intention of making personal improvements. Where we are now varies. Where we could be given some renewed effort and focus may put us in an entirely different place.

What Is Our Personal Situation?

Again many variations exist, especially by this point in life. We now may be single, married, divorced or widowed. We may be remarried, perhaps more than once. We may be parents or not, with an empty nest or with children living at home, either young or grown.

Our parents may or may not still be living, either with us or elsewhere, nearby or at a distance. We even may have our grandchildren living with us, with or without having full-time responsibility for them.

If we live alone now, some of us may be considering a long-term extended family living relationship—sharing a household with a sibling, a parent, or a grown child. Or we may be thinking of moving in together with a close friend or a romantic partner.

All of these variations impact our retirement. But they do not preclude our taking charge and following through on what we want to do with the rest of our lives. Our families are significant factors in our lives, but so are we.

What Are Our Educational Assets?

Whatever we did or did not do during our Stage I years of *Becoming*, or our Stage II years of *Being*, our education has been a valuable asset. But it may not represent all that we would like to accomplish academically. Some of us already have degrees in something we love. For others, our degrees are in something we enjoyed once, but do not want to do anymore. Still others have yet to earn our first degree, but have always wanted to do so.

Whatever we have earned and learned to date, many of us find ourselves once more in search mode, exploring our best next alternatives for intellectual growth, either inside or outside the confines of a formal academic program. Degrees or not, certifications or not, credentials or not, most of us find ourselves at a juncture where our immediate questions are: "What do I know so far?" and "What do I want to learn next?"

As we shift gears into *Stage III: Redefining*, we can safely expect that whatever our retirement pursuits will be, they likely will come with a study list—books, classes, workshops, seminars, websites, research, even apprenticeships or mentorships. Become fluent in French? Learn to build stone walls? Master Internet Marketing? Study Brain Research? Become a bee keeper?

Education is not a terminal event. The continuum of what we know and what we need to know next can be broad and wide. This is good news. There is nothing more revitalizing than to set off on a new learning task, a "learning adventure" if you will, at any age—new laptop in your backpack—equipped with new notebooks and pens— with new questions in mind and new quests and challenges ahead.

Retirement Timing: "Later" Becomes "Now"

The so called "standard" retirement age in the US, at least in terms of Social Security, is 67. Nonetheless, by the age of 60 - 64, only 40 out of every 100 of us (43%) are still employed. By age 67, only 20 in 100 of us still work at our life-long jobs.

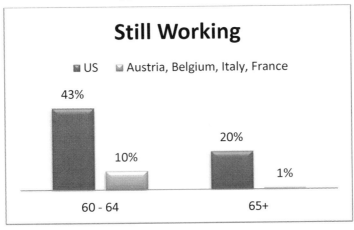

Although these employment numbers for American Baby Boomers may seem low, they are actually high compared to those of other developed countries of the world. In Austria, Belgium, France, and Italy, only 10 in 100 people work after age 60, versus 40 in 100 in the US. By age 65 in these same other countries, the employment rates drop to just 1 in 100—compared to 20 in 100 in the US.

Retiring: What We Want & What We Get

There has been much discussion about how the financial crisis would affect the retirement of the Baby Boomers. It seemed that certainly most of us would need and want to wait to retire later in our lives because of the impact the difficult economy has had on our savings.

While many of us may have felt the need to wait until *later* to retire, whether for financial or psychological reasons, many of us are not being given the opportunity to do so. Mass layoffs and budget cutbacks have led to an increase in retirement numbers.

As we mentioned in Chapter 1, although only a very few of us (6%) plan to retire *early*, almost 2 out of every 3 of us (64%) find ourselves doing just that. And although almost half of us (46%) plan to retire *late*, only 3% of us actually are able to do so.

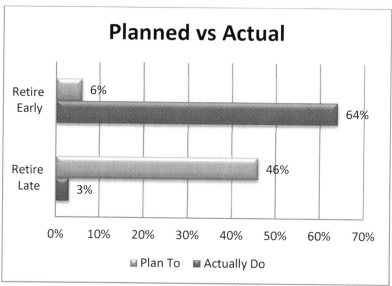

In other words, if you were to put **10** of us together in a room, **5** of us would say that we want to work *until* our expected retirement age, and **4** of us would say we want to retire *late*. Only **1** of us would say we want to retire *early*. But, as it turns out, only **3** of us will end up working *until* our expected retirement date, and rarely will even **1** of us end up retiring *late*. That means that the remaining **6** of us will end up retiring *early*, for whatever reason.

These are stunning figures. Looking at these discrepancies between what we want and what we get, we see that it is clear that if your own retirement countdown begins earlier than you wanted or expected, you are certainly in good company. But this is not the end of your story. What happens next at the point of your planned or unplanned retirement depends on your retirement countdown and your "new retirement" plan.

An Example

My own story precisely fits this unplanned pattern of retirement. Despite the fact that I was weary of teaching the same college courses over and over again, I had fully intended to continue to teach for at least five more years, up to and a little beyond my expected retirement age of 66. During this remaining five years before my retirement, I knew I was not yet prepared or ready to retire. Certainly I needed this remaining time to prepare financially. But even more compelling was the fact that I had not yet thought about or planned my next cycle of life and work, of social and mental engagement.

My college had other ideas. Suddenly, with barely eight months to prepare, I found myself facing a forced choice that would require either that I commute five hours a day, five days a week, to a campus 130 miles from my home, or that I "retire early." I chose the latter.

With my retirement countdown suddenly upon me, I found that I was ready, even eager, to retire my college teaching *job*. But I was *not* ready to retire *myself*. Although my retirement "ending" actually extended across a full year, it took me that entire year, plus an additional six months, to complete my retirement countdown process.

I know my story is not unusual. Many of us who cross the threshold to retirement, of our own volition or otherwise, need to, or want to, continue to work. Our future work may be radically different from the career field of our past. Our work may not even be at a "job," as we have come to understand that term.

Those of us who want to be engaged in work that is personally and professionally meaningful will find ways to continue on, possibly even doing work that more completely expresses our most essential selves. To the degree that we know ourselves fully, we will be able and ready to choose our own best next pathway. And to the extent that we recognize and respect the diversity of others, we will be able to be genuinely helpful to others who are hoping to do likewise.

The Retirement to Re-launch Timeline

Transitions from "retirement to re-launch" take time and creativity, particularly when that retirement comes upon us suddenly. Even for those of us who are fortunate enough to have been given the time and opportunity we need to plan ahead, once retirement is upon us, many of us find ourselves unready after all.

Retirement, even when it is long-anticipated, and certainly when it occurs earlier than expected, creates a void. What was, is no more. The world as we know it ceases at the stroke of midnight. Change of the most profound nature snatches us up like a great tidal wave and propels us, tumbling and gasping for breath, until it drops us into unfamiliar territory–the great unknown—dazed and confused, and perhaps even angry and a bit frightened. When our date of retirement is upon us, and then becomes a reality, many of us find that we have major creative work to do in the form of reframing our lives, focusing on the personal life and work we envision doing next.

According to the *Metlife Retirement Readiness Index Study*, although many of us have determined that we want and/or need to find our next work after retirement, only 54% of us have completed the steps to identify what we specifically want to do, and what options we have available. Even fewer of us have carried out the actions necessary to pursue the options that appeal to us once we have identified them.

Now What About You?

Take a moment now to complete *The Retirement Readiness Index* (by MetLife) as a first step towards moving towards your own next life and work adventure. Rate each item below on a scale from 1 to 4. [1 = Not at All to 4 = Fully Completed]

Your Retirement Readiness Index

WORK

I have decided whether to fully retire or to work part-time in retirement.	1	2	3	4
I have determined which of my skills could be easily transferred to a new part-time job.	1	2	3	4
I have looked into alternate career or part-time work opportunities for myself in retirement.	1	2	3	4
I have formulated ideas about how much work I would like to do in retirement.	1	2	3	4
I have explored what employment possibilities are available to me if I want to keep working full or part time in retirement.	1	2	3	4

LEISURE AND ACTIVITY

I have determined the proper balance between work and leisure time in retirement.	1	2	3	4
I have identified my personal goals in retirement.	1	2	3	4

RELATIONSHIPS

I have considered the importance of relationships with coworkers when making a decision to retire.	1	2	3	4
I have considered how the various aspects of my retirement might positively or negatively affect the relationships I have with my family & friends.	1	2	3	4

INCOME AND BENEFITS				
I have assessed whether full-time retirement would be financially feasible for me at this point in my life.	1	2	3	4
I have evaluated how changes in the economy will affect my pension, investments, and retirement benefits.	1	2	3	4
I have determined the steps necessary for me to receive the company, government, or other benefits to which I am entitled.	1	2	3	4
PLANNING				
I have determined the factors that are critical for a retirement that is personally satisfying to me.	1	2	3	4
I have developed an alternative plan that could get me through a considerable or unexpected setback in my retirement.	1	2	3	4
I have evaluated whether my retirement plans meet my needs, personal, social, and financial.	1	2	3	4

For all items you rated as 3 or 4, well done! For all 1 or 2 responses, these are the areas that you still need to address. Take a few minutes now to list those areas that still need your attention and effort.

TASKS YOU RATED AS 1 OR 2

_____

_____

_____

THREE TASKS RATED 1 OR 2 THAT YOU WILL WORK ON FIRST

1._____

2._____

3._____

And So...

Now that we have reflected on the diversity of Baby Boomers in terms of our backgrounds, our current realities, and when we actually will (or did) retire compared to when we expected, wanted or planned to... And now that we have this freedom and these resources... We might, paradoxically, have more questions than ever!

What do I want to be, to do, to see, to experience? How risk-averse am I? Have I basically remained the same person through all three Stages of my life, or have I morphed into someone who even I sometimes find unrecognizable?

Am I more tempered, more temperate, more deliberative? Do I have more "aim, aim, aim, fire" and less of the "fire, aim, aim, aim" of my youth? Do I have the drive, the "fire in the belly," I felt in Stage II, or have I mellowed, become less interested in tilting at windmills?

So many questions! So many options! So many configurations! Hopefully, as we move through the process in this book, we will begin to sort out some of these options and make them more concrete, less nebulous, more attainable.

Most importantly, the chapters ahead will:

- *Help you to draw a composite picture of the Stage III you, emerging from, but distinct from, the you of Stages I and II.*

- *Challenge you to reconsider and fulfill your real self—the "who am I and where am I going"— and to see your next work in terms of the work that most resonates with you.*
- *Show you the possibilities, including some you may not have considered.*
- *Stimulate and guide you in developing and/or carrying out your Stage III roadmap.*

As you will see, the possibilities are endless, growing broader each day, limited only by your imagination and will to act. This is your time —time to explore further your own future twists and turns, hopes and opportunities, as a co-pioneer in the *New Retirement* paradigm. We will work through more of this process together, beginning with the first of five steps toward your own best new retirement—*Step #1: The Retirement Countdown.*

The benefit of taking the time you need for your *Retirement Countdown,* and the four steps that follow in the "New Retirement" process, is nothing less than the rest of your life well spent—with vitality, engagement, purpose and enjoyment.

SECTION II:
5 STEP PROCESS TO YOUR
NEW WORK

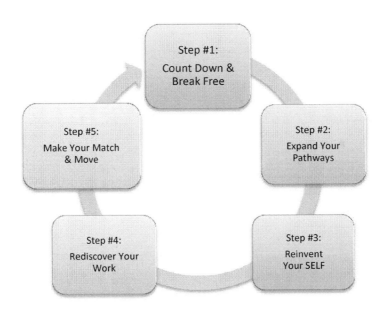

CHAPTER 4
Step #1: Countdown

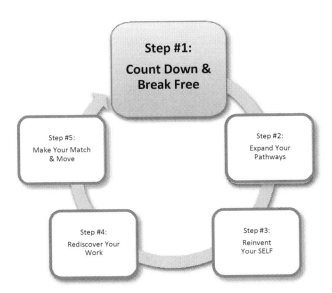

RETIREMENT HAPPENS! And sometimes it happens more suddenly than we expected—before we think we are ready for it. We still have so much to offer, yet suddenly we find ourselves shifted to the sidelines. The retirement countdown that we thought was far in the future is suddenly upon us.

For those among the 64% who have had retirement thrust upon us earlier than we had anticipated, there is no time to complete the countdown before arriving at that last and final day. Others of us, who are able to dictate our own retirement date, or for whom retirement still lies ahead, have the luxury of completing the countdown in advance, so that we are prepared for that final day of work.

Whether or not you have already retired or your retirement date still lies (or looms) ahead, the temptation may be to fill the vacuum immediately—with *something*. But therein lies a problem. If you skip

Step #1: Countdown (of the 5-step process), and move ahead too quickly, you may find yourself trapped on a path or paths that are not your best or most resonant choices. You may even find yourself piggybacking on someone else's life, while putting your own retirement life and aspirations on permanent hold.

To find *your* own next best work requires a letting go and a rediscovery process. Navigating through the full retirement countdown is necessary to bring your past work life to a close before attempting your next beginning. In order to change directions, it is necessary first to *stop* moving in the direction you are currently headed.

The momentum and focus of your earlier pursuits propelled you along a particular path. You have gone one way, and not the other, at each juncture. Your work life has entrenched itself in your every day and thought. This has been the life you have lived, mastered, and grown familiar with, possibly for many decades.

If you are one of those who did jump ahead to fill the void before you had your own next direction clearly in mind, return to accomplish those missed countdown tasks now. By doing so, you will release yourself from the past and be freed to rediscover yourself completely. As with most life changes of real importance, there are no shortcuts...and the outcome *does* matter.

The "what happens next" is all important, particularly when it is *your* life we are talking about. Give yourself the time and space that is essential for you to regroup and find your own best next direction.

Your Retirement Countdown

So let your countdown begin... You know the routine.

10...9...8...7...6... 5...4...3...2...1... BLASTOFF!

As a start, let's consider the full countdown sequence to see where it leads us Then we will discuss each count separately, with guidance about moving from one count to the next, all the way through to final BLASTOFF.

 Honor the Endings

Before the *"next"* can begin, the *"last"* needs to end. This is not an automatic, or a simple process. Begin your countdown by *ending* fully what has come before.

End your story well. Leave graciously, and, of course, burn no bridges. You may want to use some of your past contacts either as future clients or as links to future connections.

Be kind to yourself. Acknowledge that what you are going through is difficult and probably emotionally jolting. Spend time talking with friends and family. Take long walks. Plan a trip that will facilitate your exit from the entrenched habits and practices of your past life.

Take time to grieve and let go. Learn from the grieving process as it applies to other losses. Based on the work of Kubler Ross, this process has five distinct stages, leading up to acceptance. We may experience some stages of the process more or less intensely than others, depending upon the circumstances surrounding our retirement.

All five stages of the grieving process, leading up to acceptance, can apply to retirement. They include:

1. Shock and denial

2. Anger

3. Pain and guilt

4. Bargaining

5. Depression and loss

These five stages do not necessarily occur in order. We often move back and forth between stages simultaneously, one stage gradually diminishing as another seems to consume us. And as in dealing with the death of a loved one, when we experience the "death"—or end—of our career as we have known it, we spend varying lengths of time working through each step of a grieving process.

I speak from personal experience when I compare the process of arriving at our own retirement renaissance to the similar journey we go through when experiencing the death of a dear one. When I crossed the threshold into retirement myself, I truly went through these same stages, some less severe, but others surprisingly traumatic.

Depending on how wedded you were (or are) to your work, you, too, will identify with this comparison. You'll be nodding your head in agreement, saying, "Yeah, that's me, alright! How did you know?!"

Given the parallel between grieving the loss of a loved one, and enduring the loss of a lifetime career, you are assured of two realities. First—you will probably go through all of these stages, to lesser or greater degrees, depending upon the circumstances surrounding your retirement. Second—you will, yes you *will*, if you are basically of sound mind and body, *emerge whole*. Wherever you currently are in this process, trust me on this.

Let's look at these stages and observe how they mirror where you are on the continuum of "retirement grief." These stages are based on Julie Axelrod's article *The 5 Stages of Loss and Grief* that "paints a typical portrait of the emotional roller coaster we ride to arrive at this passage called retirement" (Axelrod, 2011).

Stage 1—Shock & Denial

The beginning of the process, the stage of *shock and denial*, will involve more passive inaction than positive action. This is to be expected, and it cannot be circumvented. We need this time of muddled inactivity.

Denial is a defense mechanism that buffers an immediate shock of some kind. Our instinct is to hide from the facts, to attempt to dismiss them from our minds.

In the context of retirement from work, we can end up feeling numb with disbelief. "My work defines me as a person—it is an integral part of who I am. It provides meaning and purpose to my life. This can't be happening to me. Where did this come from?" And, for those who retired voluntarily, "What have I done? What was I thinking?"

Stage 2—Anger

Anger is particularly powerful if our retirement has been unexpectedly forced upon us, either by internal political or economic forces, or by external health, family, personal causes. The pain of loss is very real. "How dare you suggest that I retire? After all that I've done for this company? How much of myself I've invested into this organization? How necessary I am to the successful functioning of this company?

With any early retirement, whatever the reason, we probably did not have the luxury of having the time we needed to take charge of our own destiny. As a result, we may not feel prepared—financially, personally, psychologically. We are angry because we have lost our sense of being in control of the process. And let us not forget that anger is generally a function of fear.

Depending on the catalyst that is forcing us to shift gears, we may direct our anger, justifiably or not, at ourselves, or at persons, places and entities outside ourselves. The organization, our boss, the current political/economic climate, our own confusion, perceived or real shortcomings, family, friends.... All of these can become potential targets of our anger. We are filled with a sense of helplessness, injustice, unfairness. How dare this happen to me?

Stage 3—Pain & Guilt

Even for those of us who were not "forced" to retire from a life-long position, we still may experience pain and guilt after it happens...a sense of work left undone. "How can they possibly manage without me there doing what I've always done? I am the one who developed these courses, or this program, or this product. I am the manager who knows best how to gain optimum performance from this team I brought together. Certainly I am indispensable. And if I am not, what does that mean about my value, not only now but in the past? I have always felt needed. Can it be possible that I am no longer necessary to the vital operation of the organization?"

For others, pain may not enter the picture of our transition, beyond perhaps a little nostalgia, and a twinge of sadness as we leave behind life-long friends, colleagues, and happy memories of a successful career. So too, we may not feel any guilt. Having stepped aside at the top of our game, and leaving behind a catalog of successes and accomplishments, we exit with a clear sense that the organization is in good shape–better, in fact, than when we initially arrived there.

Stage 4—Bargaining

Depending upon the circumstances of our leaving, bargaining can take several forms to "make it go away." If we were forced out of a position, or, as they call retirement in England, if we are "made redundant" (Imagine! What an insensitive, culturally offensive term–*redundant*!), we may attempt to negotiate an interim type of position, where we can remain with the organization on a part-time, consulting, work-from-home type arrangement.

Months later, when we look back on our attempts to survive the trauma of full retirement, we may come to realize that in most cases such a proposed solution was either not in our best interest, or even totally impractical. But, at the time of our impending separation, we were desperate. Any solution seemed preferable to "leaving forever."

Stage 5—Depression, Fear, Loneliness

In this stage, we finally realize the true magnitude of our loss, and it depresses us. Denial has given way to reality, and anger, pain, and bargaining are abating, making room for depression and fear of the unknown future ahead.

David Harris, in an article entitled, "Psychological Aspects of Retirement," says that, "Retirement is a normal phenomenon [where] ...some will experience mild symptoms of anxiety, as part of an adjustment reaction to late life. A minority will suffer a significant depressive reaction" (Harris, 1983).

Julie Axelrod talks about two types of depression. The first type is "a reaction to practical implications relating to loss. Sadness and regret characterize this type of depression...." In this first type of depression, we begin to question, to second guess, our decisions. What did I do wrong? Here's where the "woulda, coulda, shoulda" factors come into play. I "coulda" been more involved in office politics. I "shoulda" spent more time on projects A, B, C, I "woulda" had more traction, leverage, and credibility had I earned that advanced degree.

The second type of depression is more subtle, and, in a sense, perhaps more private. It is "our quiet preparation to separate." This grows out of the impinging necessity that we "separate ourselves from our professional comfort zone—all the daily employment routines and rituals that provided structure, gave meaning to our work and validated our professional existence." This separation is a challenging task that must be accomplished before we are free to move on.

At the end of the five stages of this grieving process, this honoring of the ending and loss, comes *acceptance*. When this is achieved, it is time to move to the next step in the countdown...

 # Recover & Renew

As we emerge from this time of grieving and separating, after we process and move through all the emotions that accompany any profound loss, we reach a point where we do begin to cope—to "accept" this change in our lives.

With this acceptance, comes a return of vitality and forward thinking, preparing us to move on through the recovery process. Sooner or later, a sense of quiet calm permeates our psyche. We gradually make peace with our status. We might not be happy with our current state. We may not have sought or chosen it. But it is what it is. We come to accept this new reality–to make lemonade out of what we perceive, whether accurately or not, to be the lemons of our current situation.

What strategies can we use to facilitate this state of acceptance? First, we need to admit our vulnerability. No one expects us to emerge just yet as a composite Gandhi, Wonder Woman, Iron Man. Secondly, we need to give ourselves permission to experience each and every stage of separation without feeling weak or inadequate. Thirdly, we need to allow our colleagues, friends, family to approach us with verbal and physical support. Believe it or not, we are not the first ones to undergo change, to experience the earth proverbially move beneath our feet!

When my late husband passed away many years ago, someone gave me the following advice, which I have never forgotten, and always share on appropriate occasions. In times of personal crisis or transition: a) don't make any major decision for at least a year; b) accept every social invitation extended your way; and c) be good to yourself by indulging yourself is small ways.

Yes, I think this advice holds equally true as we permanently leave our Stage II life and enter the acceptance and renewal part of the process. At this point, we at last are ready and able to get down to the business of moving forward to reimagine life as it will become, free from the shadows of our past life.

SNAPSHOT

Dr. Lynch Murphy was a Marcus Welby kind of doctor in the small town where he grew up, and returned to after completing his education and serving in World War II. He was beloved by his patients and deeply involved in the community. His practice was large and thriving. He had cared for the health and well-being of multiple generations of many families.

Dr. Murphy's work day followed a pattern that had become ingrained over 40 years of practice. He was up before dawn, followed by coffee and breakfast and a brisk half mile walk

---

over to his medical offices. On Mondays through Wednesdays... see patients in the morning, make rounds in the afternoon. Thursdays and Fridays, early morning surgeries, then see patients and make rounds. When Dr. Murphy sold his practice and retired, he still lived within walking distance of his office. And many of his patients understandably preferred to talk with him instead of the new "young" doctor who had purchased his practice.

Fortunately Dr. Murphy's wife, Lou, anticipated that he was going to have difficulty breaking free from his lifelong career as a physician. So she planned for the two of them to set off on a 3-month driving trip in France to break the pattern of Dr. Murphy's long entrenched lifestyle.

These months abroad were made all the more peaceful for him because he did not speak French. So Lou, who spoke fluent French and understood the French road system, did all the arranging, communicating and driving. Lynch, with his rudimentary skills in the language, was left free to observe, learn, enjoy, think, and otherwise decompress.

When they returned home from their trip, Dr. Murphy was refreshed and ready for his new life. As his retirement pursuits emerged, they took a much different direction than his lifelong career path. He became an avid reader and a student of history, emerging science, woodworking and photography. Over time he set up a full woodworking shop in his garage, and devoted himself increasingly to what once had been his hobby, spending countless hours happily designing and building one-of-a-kind cabinets and chests for his own home and as gifts for his children and grandchildren.

 ## Reorder...Make Room for What's Next

Even after you have honored the ending, your physical world may remain much as it always was. It is now time to:

- Remove the old,

- Reorder what remains,

- Welcome what is new, and

- Make room to focus on what is next.

You have your own personal legacy of priorities, people, time use and "stuff." There are the textbooks loading down your shelves from the courses that you taught over the past 30 years. Or the computer manuals. Or the medical journals. Or the building codes notebooks. Or the parts manuals. Or whatever made up the basis of your past career and expertise. Your file drawers are still filled with the grade sheets for all your past students, or the minutes from the committees you served on or the building specs you used as your roadmap. Box these up and store them for now.

There in your closet are the business suits, black, gray and navy, and your lineup of white and pale blue shirts or blouses. These stand as a constant reminder that you are not wearing them, and that you may never need or want to wear them again, except for that occasional wedding or a funeral. Out with them. Free up the hangers. Make Goodwill happy.

So, too, with your personal and professional people connections. Your LinkedIn, and perhaps even your Facebook, account may still be loaded with people you may or may not even like, but with whom you once needed to maintain strategic relationships as part of your former work. Trim these lists down to the people you choose to keep.

As you begin to reorder your world—priorities, people, activities, time and stuff—there will be something almost cathartic about removing the old in order to make room for the new. And as empty shelves appear... that's where you will put the books about France or writing or woodcarving or fishing or astronomy. And in your now uncluttered closet, you will hang the clothes that you love and that express the you who is about to break free.

Surprisingly, some of what may be the oldest on your shelves and in your files actually may make the cut of what you decide to keep. You may find that your next path loops you back to an earlier time in your career when you were more essentially engaged, and where you now are being drawn to return. You will know what needs to go, and you may be surprised by what you decide to keep. Some of your past pursuits, even passions, may have been set aside when your previous life and work intervened. These unexpected "keepers" may provide powerful clues to your "what comes next." Like a diamond cutter chipping away the stone, you may uncover a gem.

The physical evidence of what you choose to reject and dispose of, and what you retain, or even promote into a prominent place on your shelves and in your file drawers, is a map, of sorts, plotting the trajectory from your past career and life to your next one.

Now What About You?

Your personal reordering will take its own shape and reveal its own map. Its purpose is both symbolic and practical—to remove what binds you to past pursuits so as to free up the mental and physical space you will need for what will emerge as your Phase III adventure... namely, the rest of your valuable, and highly significant life.

Accomplishing this reordering task will require *action*. Remove from your shelves and files, your closets and address books, anything that you clearly know to be something you no longer need. As space empties, think ahead to what you will want to put there next. What will need to be brought down from the attic, up from the basement, in from the garage, retrieved from past thumb drives, repurchased or added new?

This winnowing process will feel freeing—even uplifting. Observing your ultimate choices may be highly illuminating in terms of clarifying what your future holds. Take a few minutes now to complete your own Reordering Map, listing what goes, what stays, and what will be added.

Your Reordering Map
What Goes?
What Stays?

> What is to be Added?

 ## Expand Your Pathways

With your new order established, your next pathway (or pathways) for retirement may be beginning to take shape in your mind. Perhaps these ideas have been on your mind for some time. The classic pathways of retirement have been:

1. **Life of Leisure:** Entertainment or hobby. Physical or mental. Skilled or unskilled. Engaging or merely amusing.
2. **Life of a Volunteer:** Artistic or political. Community or individual. Involved with people, data or things.
3. **Life of a Traveler:** Traveling as a visitor, as a "temporary local," or even as a part-time or full-time resident.

Now there are additional pathways of retirement open to you. Take the time *now* to expand your thinking to include at least these four additional paths, for a total of seven, as well as the various combinations thereof.

4. **Life of Engaging New Work:** Self-employed or for hire, online or in person, part or full-time, with many other variations.
5. **Life as an Entrepreneur:** Finding needs and meeting them, for profit or otherwise.
6. **Life in the Creative Class:** Creating for a living, or for pleasure, or both.
7. **Life of a Student:** Ongoing or periodic study, classroom or workshop, academic or artistic, online or in person.

You may end up pursuing one primary path, with others added to lesser degrees. Or you may combine two or more paths into a single future. *Life in the Creative Class* combined with *Life of a Student. Life as an Entrepreneur* combined with *Life of a Traveler. Life of Engaging New Work* combined with *Life of Leisure.*

We will discuss and consider these seven pathways further in Chapter 5. For now, at this point in your countdown process, take a moment to review the list and note your initial thoughts about what paths you may consider for your future life, and in what proportions. Determine what pathway you are leaving and what possible additional or different pathways appeal to you for this next phase of your life. For now, just attempt to sketch out your own rough *Pathways Map*.

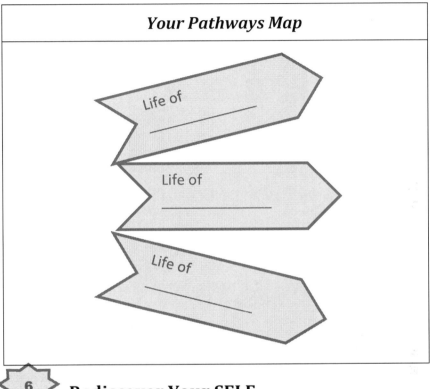

Your Pathways Map

Life of _____

Life of _____

Life of _____

6 Rediscover Your SELF

Next in the countdown, take the time you need to reinvent your SELF. With a pathway (or pathways) in mind, you may have a strong urge to jump ahead and begin your next life. This is entirely understandable. But forging ahead at this point can also be a mistake. The rest of your life is an important enough topic to merit your allotting the time and attention you need to get it right!

Soon after you retire, you will be presented with any number of pressures to choose a direction—any direction—and get on with it. These forces will emerge from various directions, appearing to be the single, simple solution to your retirement situation.

Yes, I know... Your grandchildren need to be picked up from school and watched until your son or daughter-in-law comes home from work. Your husband, who has not retired yet, needs someone to do the bookkeeping for his business. Your local library needs a volunteer to shelve books three days a week. Your former employer wants to hire you back part-time at reduced pay and without benefits, to continue doing what you already were mortally tired of doing.

Wait! Step back from all of these demands and possibilities until you first have arrived at your own short list of what *you* want to do with the rest of your life. In the meantime, protect your "space" and time. Nature may "abhor a vacuum," but you need to preserve yours, at least for now. Take the time to ponder and to decide: "Where do *I* want focus *my* time, talents and energy now? What more do *I* want to accomplish, for whom and how?"

To retire well, and in your own unique way, give yourself this gift of time to create a clear path *from* your past work that has been dictated by others *to* your future lifework that optimizes your personal gifts, hopes, values and purpose. Protect your time and space. Arrive at your shortlist. Play with your own mental images, projecting yourself into the future to experience in advance how you will feel about these visions and intentions. Let them "sit in your belly," as a wise Native American once said.

Now What About You?

Who are you and who are you *really*? To a degree, your past work life may have come to define you instead of the other way around. Return now to the question you struggled with 40 or more years ago: "*Who* do I want to be, and *what* do I want to do when I grow up?" The task of rediscovering yourself begins with finding, or re-finding your *voice*. What do you have to say with your life? Have you had the opportunity to say it yet?

We will return in Chapter 6 to complete the complex, and possibly surprising, process of rediscovering your unique and capable SELF— your validity and value. For now, at this point in your retirement countdown, just take a moment to begin thinking about yourself in all of your complexity, talents, natural gifts, values, and passions. Note any hidden aspects of yourself that immediately come to mind. Postpone being either selective or practical. Narrowing down to an actual plan as to what aspects of yourself will prevail will come later.

Begin with the ten questions in the *SELF Rediscovery Map* below, answering "Yes" or "No," then adding a comment.

Your SELF Rediscovery Map
1. Do you have a shadow side... an unlived life that was set aside for work or other reasons, but that still has the power to excite and interest you? ☐ Yes   ☐ No **Comment:**
2. Do you have a creative side that has gone unfulfilled? ☐ Yes   ☐ No **Comment:**
3. Do you have an entrepreneurial urge? ☐ Yes   ☐ No **Comment:**
4. Do you have humanitarian interests? ☐ Yes   ☐ No **Comment:**
5. Do you have an adventuresome streak? ☐ Yes   ☐ No **Comment:**
6. Do you have a curious nature? ☐ Yes   ☐ No **Comment:**
7. Is there an explorer in you? ☐ Yes   ☐ No **Comment:**

---

8. Is there a performer in you?
☐ Yes ☐ No
Comment:

---

9. Is there a teacher or guide in you?
☐ Yes ☐ No
Comment:

---

10. Is there a mentor or wise counselor in you?
☐ Yes ☐ No
Comment:

---

 5 ## Reenvision Your Purpose—Your WHY

As you envision what comes next, avoid being bound by images from your past. The *past you* may have been a doctor, but the *future you* may be a woodcarver. Why? Because you want to create and see the tangible results of your work.

Or in the *past you* may have been a woodcarver, but the *future you* may be a history tutor or a "bird guide." Why? Because your life purpose is shifting away from working with objects towards working with people.

This is a time to cast your nets far and near—a time to arrive at your own "short list"—your "bucket list"—of the goals and visions you want to realize in and for the rest of your life.

Resist whatever inclination you may have to censor your thoughts and goals based on so-called reality. Many things that may once have been impossible could be completely possible now. Control the urge to be overly "realistic" and self-censoring. You may still harbor negative mental habits or thoughts that once seemed useful and now continue to lurk just below the surface of your thinking, ready to insert barriers, and otherwise to ambush your goals before these positive possibilities even make their way onto your list.

More is possible than may be immediately apparent. If a goal is sufficiently important to be included on your short list, you will find ways to accomplish it. One of the challenges you will face is the need to see beyond whatever boundaries, either real or imagined, may have stood in your way so far—those voices, external and internal, saying "yes but." Your firm response could be: "If not me, *who*? If not now, *when*?"

Now What About You?

At this point the goal is to envision your future life and work purpose, however fuzzy the vision. Later there will be time to consider the specifics of the "how" and to adjust your plans to make all this happen. For now the task is to begin to figure out the "what" and its underlying "why."

Take a moment now to complete your *WHAT & WHY Short List* using the worksheet below.

Your WHAT and WHY Short List
WHAT appeals to you as your next life work or pursuit?
What is the underlying WHY—your purpose?

 ## Reconsider Your WHO

One given from your earlier work life was that the people with whom you worked and shared your days probably were predetermined. You may have had a role in hiring them. If they were your clients, you may have had a hand in acquiring them. But one way or another, the people in your work life primarily came with your job. Whether you liked them or not, and whether or not you wanted to work with them or otherwise to spend time with them, there they were. If you were like most of us, you enjoyed working with some of your colleagues, and others...not so much.

As you enter your retirement career, the colleagues you choose to work with, and the friends or family members with whom you elect to enjoy leisure pursuits, will be a deliberate choice on your part. Where once you were surrounded by people you might not have selected yourself, now *you* are the chooser. When you say goodbye to all of those people who once formed your daily circle, you will enter a life populated mainly by the people you elect to be with, to work with, to spend time with, to travel with.

This fact can be freeing and very gratifying. If you choose well, you will be rewarded with more companionable, and even more productive, alliances and associations. But now that you will be populating your own world, the other side of this coin is "no action, no people." As you listen to all the silence, and eat lunch alone for the third consecutive week, you may look up one day and wonder "where is everybody?"

Take time now, at this point in your retirement countdown, to put some deliberate thought into your WHO. From among your past colleagues, are there some with whom you wish to stay in contact, or even possibly to collaborate?

Some of your *"keepers"*–your intentional colleagues and associates—may be from your recent work. Others may be from your deeper past. You may need to track down and reconnect with this group. Or there may be new colleagues you will want to find, nearby or out in the world, face-to-face or online.

If your next direction of choice is to be a writer, you may want to find a writers' group, and possibly a writing mentor or teacher. Depending on your writing genre choice, you may want to consider partnering with a co-author. Or perhaps you know someone who has an important message to offer, but who needs a ghostwriter to get it into print. And you certainly will want to add an editor to your "intentional colleagues" base.

If you decide to take up painting again, you may need to locate a workshop and a life studies teacher, or join a "plein air" group and "paint under the sky" in the great outdoors. Or maybe you will want to team up with an enamel craftsman who can convert your work into "painted glass" to sell as decorative objects.

If the path you choose is a life of travel, who will be your travel partner? If you intend to get serious about improving your chess game, who do you know, or did you know, who plays well enough to challenge you? Or would you consider possibly joining a competitive chess club–online or local? If you plan to do more fishing, who will be your fishing partner—or mentor? What about your tennis partner, or golf group, or book club, or hiking club?

If you are married, or otherwise have a life partner, that person will undoubtedly be one of the major people in your retirement life. But there could be changes even here. Possibly your partner could assume an additional and different role in your mutual relationship. You may be surprised to discover activities and interests that you find you want to share, workwise and otherwise. Explore commonalities with your partner, new as well as familiar.

SNAPSHOT

James and Elena Conaway were a typical couple throughout their Stage II work life. As they prepared for retirement, they discovered that they shared an interest in having their own business, and that they both loved working with crystals.

The idea came to them that as a retirement career they would join together as business partners as well as life partners. Their joint mission would be to create and sell crystal art and jewelry, incorporating Swarovski crystals into their work. This was to be more than just a commercial enterprise for them, believing as they did that: "Crystals inspire our minds to embrace light, beauty, clarity, and our sense of awe. Since our energy follows our consciousness, crystals are a wonderful reminder to stay aware of the magical lightness of being and to be present in the light of the rainbow of love and peace."

Together they opened a shop called *The Crystal Underground (http://crystalunderground.com)* in their hometown in Maryland. Soon they added to their initial sales venue by developing a sales website, and also by joining the Renaissance Faire circuit, where they now offer their crystal, quartz, and gemstone creations to a broader audience.

The Crystal Underground is now a regular at the Arizona Renaissance Faire in February and March, the Colorado Faire in June and July, the Minnesota Faire in August and September, and the North Carolina Faire in October and November. They and greet their customers dressed in full renaissance garb,

---

> James in pantaloons and waistcoat and a velvet trimmed hat... Elena in gown and brocaded vest, draped in jewels. And they stay in character, addressing their clients in the language and style of "olde": "Yes, m'Lady." "May I be of assistance, m'Lord?"
>
> Adding to the "adventure" of this Renaissance-themed fair circuit , they camp out under the stars during festivals, using a popup trailer. Thus they enjoy total togetherness as a couple, and are in touch with nature during the loveliest season in each of four states. And since the same vendors return year after year to these faire venues, generally with their shops set up in the same spot, Elena and James have formed friendships with other like-minded, like-spirited, and similarly adventuresome missuses and gents.

Although now it will take effort and initiative to identify and engage the people who will be your associates in your new life—the people with whom you will spend time and communicate on a regular basis—the good news is that you will find yourself associating more with people you genuinely enjoy, value and admire. You may even discover on your WHO list someone with whom there may be exciting potential for an intentional partnership. We will be discussing this "partnering up" option more fully in Chapter 11.

Now What About You?

Think of the most exciting, energizing, enjoyable group of people you know. Be creative in your listings. Include people even if you have not been in touch with them for many years. Thanks to the Internet, you will be able to find them again.

Also, consider what your commonalities are. As you think this through, remove any preconceived boxes. Concentrate on their gifts and strengths beyond the bounds of the work roles and positions they held when you knew them.

You may have known Bill as an engineering instructor, but he could be more interesting and have more in common with you as an artist, playwright and poet. And, yes, Stuart may have been a computer scientist in his career, but he also created cellos by hand as a hobby. Chris may have been a beautician, but she also lived abroad for a number of years earlier in her life and thus would be an excellent resource for you as you plan to travel, or even to move overseas, and then write a book about it.

Think of your potential people in the broadest terms, selecting the facets that reverberate with you as you transform into your retirement persona and take up your retirement work.

Take a few minutes now to make some notes for yourself about your "intentional colleagues"–your WHO. Include both their names and the reasons you want to keep them in your life.

Who Are Your WHO?	
Who?	Why?

 Rethink Your WHERE

Again, the WHERE of your life was likely determined *for you* by your job and employer. Whether you found work close to home, or moved away from your hometown because of the demands of your work... Whether you then remained in one location throughout your career, or were asked by your employer to relocate, once or repeatedly... In all these cases, you were planted in a place by your work. Probably you never questioned this or tried to change it, settling and compromising for a variety of reasons.

Now, at this point in your retirement countdown, it is time for you to explore new horizons, and reconsider where *you* want to live. It may seem easier just to stay where you are. Moving is such a hassle. But don't sidestep this piece of your retirement puzzle. As with reconsidering your WHO, rethinking your WHERE may take effort and initiative. But giving this the thought it requires will yield gratifying results.

The place where you are living now may be your favorite location thus far—your own version of Utopia. Or possibly one of the past places you lived suited you better. You may have always wished you lived in a larger city–downtown where you could take in all its cultural and entertainment possibilities, and walk everywhere instead of always driving. Perhaps you have always dreamed of living abroad. You may wish for a more temperate climate, so that you could spend more of the year outdoors. Or you may even envision living in more than one place, migrating back and forth according to season, following the sun (or snow).

If you have a partner, the two of you will have areas of joint decision-making that will require serious discussion and thought. At this point in the retirement countdown, let those discussions begin, if they haven't started already. Jointly you may arrive at even more exciting possibilities than you ever could have imagined on your own.

The idea is to explore the full range of dreams and possibilities. Think beyond the "what is" to the "what could be." Then imagine yourself there and assess how you feel.

Now What About You?

Take a minute now to consider your own WHERE. If your own best WHERE is the place you live now, why is this exactly? If you are drawn to live elsewhere, what is driving this yearning?

For each WHERE priority you check below, write a brief comment that expands your thinking.

Where is Your WHERE?
☐ I want a different climate.   ☐ I want to have more of a life in the out-of-doors.   Comments:
☐ I want more access to cultural offerings.   ☐ I want to be nearer to family or friends.   Comments:

☐ I want to return to a place I lived before. ☐ I want to pursue a whole new place. Comments:	
☐ There are other lifestyle elements I am considering. Comments:	
How far does your new WHERE reach? (Check all that apply). ☐ Same town ☐ Another town ☐ Same state ☐ Another state ☐ Another region ☐ Another country ☐ Another continent Comments:	

Ask your partner to complete this worksheet too, preferably without seeing yours, so that he or she feels free to think independently. Once you have envisioned your WHEREs independently, compare notes and begin to envision your next WHERE together.

 ## 2 Refocus Your Learning

We have all heard the term "lifelong learning." This concept of continuing to learn throughout life is a powerful one, but one that requires thought and preplanning at this point in the countdown.

When you were in the *Stage I: Becoming* phase of your life, the entire learning task came with considerable pressure. Your education years were primarily geared to gain you entry into a career.

For many of us, these education choices were made on the fly or under duress. We had to declare a major when our college required it.

And our parents expected us to pursue a particular profession or trade. For others of us, our career path, and its educational requirements, was clear from the outset, and we followed a direct path from studies to work.

As you enter the "refocus your learning" stage in the countdown, note how your situation has changed. This time you will not hurl through a single-path education in order to emerge at the other end as quickly as possible so that you can check school off the list. This time your learning can be varied and self-directed. It can be exploratory, starting off in one direction, or three, then changing direction later, or adding directions, or combining several directions into an intriguing whole.

This time you do not need to choose among doctor, lawyer and Indian chief. You can begin by studying history, then add art and dance, then read about cultural differences, and learn a new language, then set off as a world traveler. You can master wood crafting, and study the physics of sound, then learn to play the cello and make your own cello by hand.

Learning, as always, is an invigorating, empowering, and challenging enterprise. It will introduce you to interesting people, including some who may turn out to be key additions to the gathering WHO list in your retirement life and work.

As you contemplate what you want to learn next, follow these five key guidelines...

- *First*, be wide open to ideas about what you want to learn.
- *Second*, become your own teacher, or find one, so as to have regular assignments and an expectation of effort, persistence and active participation.
- *Third*, adopt a "yes I can" approach to learning. If there is something you think you cannot learn, reconsider this! Whatever it is you struggled to learn in school, you can learn it now if you are so determined. It was never that you could not learn it. Rather it was that you did not have the right teacher or were not mentally receptive or developmentally ready to absorb the subject matter at that time. You are now in an entirely different place, with a mature mind and life experience to make your new learning more meaningful and thereby more attainable.

- *Fourth*, branch out to broaden, pull together to synthesize. Look for arms off the branch of what you know already, and what you are studying next, to see what else would give you more breadth and enable you to synthesize more comprehensively.
- *Fifth*, remember that, with learning, the journey itself is part of the pleasure. Experience the exhilaration and the "hard fun" of stimulating your mind and honing your talents.

Now take a moment to create your own list of *"What Have You Got to Learn?"* The sky is the limit... Logistics and follow-through will come later. Note why you want to learn these subjects or skills... Pleasure? Curiosity? Future work?

What Have You Got to Learn?	
Subject/Skill	**Why?**

 Break Free, then Blastoff!

With your endings honored... And after taking the time to recover and renew... Having reordered your life and space... And expanded your pathways... Then rediscovered your SELF... And reenvisioned your WHY, your WHO and your WHERE... And refocused your learning... What comes next?

As many times as we Boomers have watched rocket launchings, we know all too well the answer to this question. The final culmination of a countdown, including your new retirement countdown, is to *Break Free*, and then to BLASTOFF.

This breaking free and relaunch is the focus of the rest of this book. Exciting times lie ahead... Your times.

And So...

The retirement countdown does take time, but what comes next is fully worth this investment of time and energy. With your countdown completed, you will find yourself ready for, even excited about, breaking free from what came before to discover and relaunch into what comes next.

So what does come next? Read on to work through *Step #2* of the *5-Step New Retirement Process*. As part of this next action task, you will have the opportunity to complete the task that you began to think about in this chapter—to *Expand Your Pathways*.

Whereas your past life's work may have followed a single pathway, your new retirement career can, and probably will, be a combination of pathways. Contrary to what your mother always told you, you are entering a time when you actually may be able "to have your cake and eat it, too."

CHAPTER 5
Step #2: Expand Your Pathways

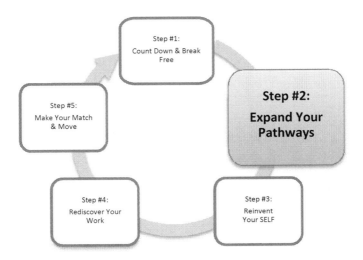

How many pathways do you have ahead? This may seem to be an odd question, since, at the point of our retirement, most of us are exiting work that was primarily devoted to a single pathway. Even for those of us who made significant career changes one or more times, we still are accustomed to lives where doing one thing, for the most part, meant *not* doing another.

From this point on, this is not so. Whereas your career may have followed a single pathway so far, your retirement career can and probably will follow a combination of pathways. As you design your own new retirement, it is time to exit the world of either/or, and enter the world of "not one or the other, but both or several."

As an essential part of the process of retiring well and remaining fully engaged and productive, take the time you need to look creatively at the particular pathways and combinations of directions that lie ahead for you. This is a new time for you, and new things are possible.

The groove of your old life may be a deep one, even entrapping. The challenge is to pull free of your past, and consider, then reconsider, the direction or directions of your new life. This process is worthy of our time and effort because it is so very important to get it right.

And even after you have arrived at an initial plan, you later may return to these pathways to do some rethinking, the better to expand your choices and recombine them in even more fulfilling ways.

Seven Pathways for What Comes Next

There are at least seven retirement pathways, as well as their many combinations. Three of these are fairly traditional. The other four are not so conventional. If you combine two or more pathways, you may enter them in sequence, or simultaneously.

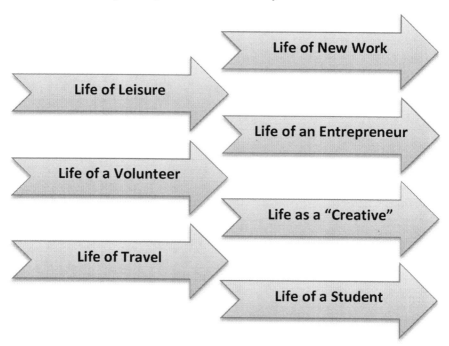

At first, some of us enter retirement thinking that we want to do *nothing*, at least for now. We may still feel the after-effects of being on the work treadmill.

So now we are eager to escape from the 9 to 5 or 8 to 6 or even 7 to 7 regimen. That's OK. If you identify with this scenario, you should, for the time being, do just that—*nothing*. BUT, in the event that you someday do tire of that activity, and you probably will, you might want to give some thought to what you really want to do with the rest of your life.

Perhaps you want to pursue a hobby full time. Maybe you've given some thought to volunteering. Travelling to places near and far has always been your dream. Or there's the possibility that you might want to combine leisure and some type of work. Let's explore each of these scenarios a little more in depth.

Three Traditional Retirement Pathways

Pathway 1: Life of Leisure

The life of leisure still appeals to many retiring Boomers. As a retirement pathway, leisure activities place higher in the priority list of daily living and take on new focus and importance.

Some of us choose to enjoy a hobby we have pursued before, or one that we have wished to pursue. These hobbies and other leisure pursuits can be combined with work, or even turned into work.

A one-time interest in fishing can turn into a passion for it, with an almost hunter/gatherer zeal to keep the freezer, and possibly all the neighbors, stocked with fresh fish. An interest in quilting can turn into a production line, sewing security blankets for the *Linus Project* so that each child who enters a homeless shelter will have one to snuggle. Or stitching red, white and blue quilts to be given to every injured service person as part of the *Veteran Project*.

The boundary between work and play can and does become blurred as we follow our passions with renewed energy and zeal.

SNAPSHOT

Tom was a CEO in a not-for-profit corporation. Over the course of his career, he had risen through the ranks to the top of the ladder, and had the corporate scars to attest to his arduous journey. Daily, weekly, monthly, he faced and flourished before a formidable firing squad of investors, board members, and subordinate staff.

> When the political winds brought major unsupportive changes in Tom's board, he interpreted these shifts as the time to leave the corporate world behind.
>
> Because of his extensive experience, his political instincts, and his proven success record, Tom was offered several lucrative positions as a consultant, trainer, and board member. When speaking of these "opportunities," he chuckles wryly. Morning meetings would interfere with his daily rounds of golf. And permanent commitments would interfere with his leisure travel agenda that has taken him throughout the world.
>
> Tom confesses that each morning, from one or another hole on the golf course, he looks up to see the daily freeway logjam and grins. As he reads the daily paper, he shakes his head at the all-too-familiar shenanigans he recognizes from those CEO days, long ago and far away.

What's the point of this story? One's performance during one's primary work life is not necessarily an accurate predictor of how we will spend the last third of our lives. Even if circumstances impelled or compelled us to leave our chosen avocation earlier than we had anticipated, this is no guarantee that we will want to re-assume a similar role, or any role, within the workforce.

In fact, the theory of "for every action there is an equal and opposite reaction" holds true here, too. It is not uncommon to find that those who leave the workforce after holding high-profile, high-powered jobs sometimes "drop out" totally from their demanding professional lives in favor of more mellow pursuits. No, I do *not* want to "stop by the office... have lunch with former colleagues... be invited to subsequent retirement parties... keep current on office gossip... send Christmas cards... Rather, I want to fade into oblivion from a work standpoint, never to be heard from again!

In our family, we had a standing joke to describe an aunt who never had any desire to leave the small hometown in which she was born. She looked with disdain and disgust upon those family members who travelled anywhere for any reason. "You've seen one mountain, you've seen them all!" was her famous comment. She wasn't into volunteering either! Her main retirement activities were shopping and LUNCH.

> ## Retirement Humor
>
> QUESTION: What do you do all week?
> ANSWER: Monday through Friday, NOTHING... Saturday and Sunday, I rest.
>
> QUESTION: How many days in a week?
> ANSWER: 6 Saturdays, 1 Sunday

Will You Want a Life of Leisure?

Will one of your retirement pathways be a life of leisure? Could you find contentment forevermore enjoying a hobby that you have always wanted to pursue? Is there a sport that you particularly enjoy, or a skill that you developed part time when time was at a premium, and now would like to develop more fully?

Perhaps you feel renewed being outdoors. Or seeing the products of your own hands. Or performing in community theater. You may not have had the time until now to even scratch the surface or plunge the depths of your passion. Now is the time. It's your turn. Go for it, even if this is only one of several pathways you will ultimately select.

It would not be an exaggeration to say that every one of us should cultivate at least a partial life of leisure into our "new" retirement. Train for that triathlon you've always felt you could complete. Get that aviator's license you've hankered to earn. Plant that English garden that you have seen and admired in someone else's yard!

Any of these pursuits, plus a myriad more, can and will easily bring you days and years of satisfaction, fun, and fulfillment! You've always wanted to learn to sail, to own a loom and weave exotic patterns, to write that memoire within you, to raise goats! Do it! Give yourself permission to follow your passion!

> ### SNAPSHOT
>
> Jewel and Harvey ran a lucrative business throughout their working lives, selling portable hot houses, with all the components necessary to germinate plants successfully in any climate. When they reached a point where they had earned as much money as they would ever need, and then some, they sold their business by posting an ad in the Wall Street Journal with the

headline." All the Money We Need..." After interviewing potential buyers until they found one they were *willing* to entrust with their business—their labor of love—they launched themselves into their next life—racecar driving.

At first only Harvey joined the racing circuit, both working on race cars and racing them. He bought himself a racecar of his own, and earned the title "Rookie of the Year." One of his most prized possessions was a photo of himself, seated in his racecar wearing his helmet, with fellow racing enthusiast Paul Newman leaning into the cockpit to talk with him.

Jewel soon joined Harvey in the world of racing, owning her own race car, of course. She was not interested in working on her race car, only in racing it. So Harvey set up a shop behind their Tennessee home and worked on both cars.

They both competed regularly in races until the year Jewell was in a racing accident. Another car rolled up over hers, crushing her hand as it grasped the steering wheel, leaving her in a cast and unable to race until her hand had had time to heal.

At that point, Harvey surprised Jewell with an all-expenses-paid trip to hike the Himalayas. Jewel claimed that the real reason Harvey gave her this incredible gift was that he felt guilty. Why? Because during the time she was out of commission, he had sole use of her racecar as well as his own. According to Jewel, "Harvey always liked my car better than his own."

Pathway 2: Life of the Volunteer

Volunteerism has long been a possibility for retired people. And now, as Baby Boomers retire in numbers, volunteer work has generally come to assume more meaningful forms. Beyond the envelope licking and phone answering stereotypes, meaningful volunteering options, and the capacity to match people to these options according to their own unique capabilities and interests, are plentiful and widespread.

To the degree that volunteering options are more optimally aligned with the individuals offering their time and services, volunteering takes on more of the engaging nature of employment. The new paradigm of volunteering requires a level of energy, deliberation and matchmaking formerly reserved for job hunting. Increasingly volunteers do not want to do "just anything," and agencies that enlist volunteers do not want "just anyone" to do it. We may be willing to work for free, but we are not willing to do work that is unfulfilling.

SNAPSHOT

Denise was a middle manager in a service organization for over 35 years. When she retired, she had no intention of leading a life of leisure. Financially, she had enough resources to live a comfortable retirement.

But socially and mentally, Denise had always needed to "be in the middle of the action." Even while still working full time, she had held several leadership positions within community and professional organizations.

After retiring, without missing a beat, Denise immediately became involved in her local school board, assuming the critical position of Finance Chair. By the time her term was about to expire, she was voted in as Chair Person. Additionally, Denise served as a member of the Board of Directors at her local hospital, later accepting the position of Chair of that board, too. Denise looks and acts younger than ever. She thrives on being active, doing good, and serving her community.

Will You Seek the Life of a Volunteer?

Will volunteer work be one of your pathways in retirement? Volunteerism isn't for everyone, but neither is travelling, or hobbying, or working. For those who are inclined to give of their time, their skills, their talent, their caring, volunteerism can be extremely rewarding.

WOW FACTOR

A University of Michigan study of adult males found those who volunteered their time, skills, and money to be happier and more positive about their lives, and to outlive their peers. *http://EzineArticles.com/6097038*

Volunteering has some great residual rewards too, as it:

- Helps you appreciate the mental and material riches you have;
- Sets an example for others;
- Provides structure, meaning and purpose to your life;
- Provides an opportunity to use and to hone your unique skills and capabilities in meaningful ways;
- Offers opportunities to meet and establish social contacts;
- Can lead to fulfilling paid employment.

If your choice is to follow a volunteering pathway, then Chapter 13 will be for you. There we will focus on carrying you through the process of designing and seeking meaningful volunteer work that is uniquely fulfilling to you—work to which you will bring your unique gifts and capacities that align with your life purpose—your legacy.

Pathway 3: Life of a Traveler

A large number of Boomers are globally aware and world-connected. Many of us have traveled, and even lived, abroad. When we enter retirement, we may have a bucket list of places we want to visit, experiences we want to have, and even locations abroad where we may consider relocating permanently.

WOW FACTOR

Nearly one in five of all Americans have thought about moving abroad. Among the college-educated, this proportion is even greater —about one in four.

The US State Department estimated in 2005 that around 6.6 million Americans lived abroad, in more than 160 countries, with over 1 million Americans living in Mexico, 688,000 in Canada, 224,000 in the United Kingdom, 169,000 in Italy and 102,000 in France.

Travel can be expensive. But moving abroad can be economical, and an excellent way to experience a different lifestyle. Some retirees are choosing destinations like South or Central America, where they can live more successfully on limited income. Others are choosing countries they are drawn to for a variety of other reasons—a sense of adventure, an interest in learning, a desire for a temperate year-round climate, access to culture and art, the appeal of an outdoor lifestyle.

Will You Want the Life of a Traveler?

Wait until you begin to explore the world of travel, if you have not already done so. So many options, so many places, so many adventures! Because so many Baby Boomers now have the time and the financial resources to travel, the entire travel industry has exploded with options of all types.

If you are a groupie who is more comfortable travelling with fellow Americans, and wants someone to do all the "leg work" for you, there are many companies that cater to your taste. The only physical exertion required on your part is to "show up" at the departure point! The rest is taken care of for you.

If you are the independent, adventurous, do-it-yourself type, who likes surprises, and doesn't get rattled by setbacks or unexpected glitches, you might want to research, plan and take trips totally on your own. Although this option requires a substantial investment of time and energy, it is by far the most satisfying way to experience your chosen destination's culture.

If you are somewhere in between these two extremes, there are excellent books and guides available (Rick Steves, Karon Brown, the Great Trips Series) that enable you to take an independent trip "as though you were traveling to your destination for the second time." These resources provide you all the guidance you need, but without the tour bus, giving you the best of both worlds—expert assistance and freedom, too.

Self-managed exploration has its own rewards. Negotiating train schedules, reading a menu written in a foreign language, shopping at the local street market, finding treasures in specialty shops away from tourist traps– all these experiences can be challenging, but such fun! And what a feeling of accomplishment, what a sense of self-empowerment and independence!

And then there is cruising. If you want to travel in a laid-back, serene, "far-from-the-madding-crowd" mode, there are all manner of cruises available, offering you comfort, relaxation, good food, entertainment, and fresh sea air–all this, and you won't need to repack your luggage constantly. It's like being at home—only at sea! In a lounge chair! With your own personal chef... and nightly entertainment. And each day you will wake up in a new exotic port of call beckoning to you to explore.

Cruises can explore the world one sea at a time—Atlantic, Pacific, Baltic, Mediterranean, Caribbean. They can be transatlantic or trans-pacific, with days upon days out of sight of land. They can meander along the great rivers of the world... The Rhine. The Danube. The Yangtze. The Nile. The Mississippi!

Perhaps you are an adventurer—a person who likes to travel off the beaten path, where no man or woman has set foot before. An entire industry now caters to those of us who want to travel to exotic destinations that can be reached only by two-seater plane, by local elephant, by zip line or on foot. A word of caution... These trips are not for the faint of heart, the naturally clumsy, or the couch potato. Be sure to read the fine print! If you read, "Physically Challenging; Requires Medical Immunization," you might want to reconsider, or, at the very least, be sure to purchase that optional trip insurance.

For those who love to learn while traveling, the offerings of *Road Scholar* (formerly *Elderhostel*) are a gold mine. Experience Christmas in Provence, or even in Finland, traveling north to the Arctic Circle to visit Santa's workshop or to ride a sleigh pulled by reindeer.

On an Elderhostel trip to France, you can: "Walk in the footsteps of Impressionists along the Seine, through Paris, Normandy, Provence and the beautiful Côte d'Azur. Discover the origins of these 19th-century painters and their groundbreaking brushstrokes as you study masterpieces in museums and explore the places, gardens and streetscapes that inspired them."

On an Elderhostel trip in Italy, you can: "Experience the best of Tuscan culinary traditions during intimate cooking classes at the International Academy of Italian Cuisine and visits to local markets, where you gather ingredients for your lessons, then enjoy the results."

Every year Road Scholar *(http://roadscholar.org/)* offers approximately 8,000 educational tours and programs in ninety countries and all fifty states. These programs combine the best of both worlds, bringing learning together with direct experience of the culture, art, music, and history you are learning about.

Smithsonian Journeys (*http://www.smithsonianjourneys.org*) is another educational travel resource, offering hundreds of fascinating tours, from "France Through the Ages" to "African Safari" to Mystical India" to "Costa Rica's Natural Treasures" to "Legendary Peru."

National Graphic Expeditions are yet another excellent option: *http://www.nationalgeographicexpeditions.com/.* By joining one of their many expeditions, you can circumnavigate Iceland on a small ship, or take a photography expedition to Alaska and British Columbia. You can traverse Russia on the Trans-Siberian Railroad, or step aboard the newly renovated *Palace on Wheels* in India, traveling to the fabled cities of Rajasthan, with their majestic forts and palaces, including the rose-colored city of Jaipur, and the Taj Mahal of Agra, sparkling by day and aglow at night.

Four Additional Pathways for a New Retirement

Beyond the standard retirement pathways of leisure, volunteer work, and travel, four additional pathways are becoming more probable, resulting in even greater diversity in terms of the actual paths that Boomers combine. These are:

- life of engaging new work

- life as an entrepreneur

- life as a "creative"

- life of a student

Pathway 4: Life of Engaging New Work

Many of us retiring Boomers, for a variety of reasons, will continue to work well past our expected retirement age. Likely, our work will shift somewhat, or even in the extreme, from what we have been engaged in throughout our careers. Whether we are working for ourselves or for others, using our same skills or new ones (or even old skills long set aside that we now find ourselves eager to return to), full-time or part-time, year-round or "gig by gig," many of us will assume the path of work as all or part of what we will do next.

We may not necessarily know yet what work we will do, or for whom. We may still need to determine how long we will work each day, for how much money, when and when not, and for how many years. If we do want to work, we will need to chart a course to make this new work *WORK* for us, given our emerging retirement lifestyle and vision.

SNAPSHOT

Bill worked a long career as an IBM executive engineer, engaging in highly technical and demanding work that escalated in terms of challenge. When IBM offered him an early retirement package, he was more than ready to accept. But although he had retired his corporate job, Bill was not ready to retire himself.

So what does a technology expert, with four decades of experience in corporate management, do next? The answer was surprising. *Sell birdseed.*

Bill went to work part-time at a local garden shop. Unlike his lifelong, high stress career in technology, selling birdseed was an absolute delight for him. He loved talking with customers, sharing his growing knowledge of birds and their habits, working with other nature enthusiasts. He loved everything about it.

"I would probably pay them to let me do this," he sometimes remarked wonderingly, "but even better that they pay me."

Are You Seeking a Life of Engaging New Work?

If one of your retirement pathways will be finding engaging new work, pause now to consider how many subpathways within this broader one will be available to you now that you have retired. The specific pathway you might think of first may be standard employment, working either part-time or full-time, for a small business or larger company. But there are other subpathways that could lead you in even more exciting and productive directions.

If you plan to continue to live where you live now, your concepts of what types of work will be available to you as a retired person may seem somewhat limited. But you need to think beyond your local area, where indeed your job options now may have narrowed, in order to explore the larger world of employment beyond traditional thinking. Much has changed regarding employment that you can put to your own personal advantage now if you decide to follow this pathway of locating engaging new work.

First, even in the realm of traditional jobs and careers, labor shortages are predicted as 77 million Baby Boomers retire and only 48 million Gen X employees are available to replace them. If you aspire to a job "out there" in the workplace, there will be options, including some you may not have considered yet. Chapter 10 will explore these traditional jobs "out there," including some areas of work that are particularly likely to be filled by senior workers. You will find that other employment opportunities can be pursued in nontraditional ways such as part-time or seasonal, or even structured as a job share.

Second, many traditional employers have shifted to outsourcing, in part as a response to a difficult economy. Outsourcing allows organizations to increase their innovation and productivity, while reducing their time-to-market by accelerating the development or production of a new product.

The contract talent that companies engage on a project-by-project basis, exactly when they need it, enables them to run leaner enterprises, yet ramp up when necessary to accomplish specific, potentially profitable goals. By outsourcing, employers are able to gain access to skills, knowledge and expertise that would be difficult or time consuming for them to develop in-house.

WOW FACTOR
Non-traditional contract workers make up more than one third of the US workforce. This segment is growing at twice the rate of the standard workforce.

The outsourcing movement is creating a flood of new contract-based work opportunities that may ideally match your skills, talents and interests. According to a report by ODesk (*www.oDesk.com*), more than 90% of US firms now use contract talent on a regular basis, and spend upwards of $120 billion annually on this type of expertise.

Third, online work is fast becoming a mainstream alternative to employment in the brick-and-mortar workplace. By online work we mean work that is actually done online for clients with whom communication and work exchanges take place without meeting "face to face."

According to the online employment report, a companion to the *Employment Situation Summary* issued by the US Bureau of Labor Statistics, a record 71,000 new online job opportunities were posted in the month of January 2011 alone, representing employee earnings of more than $13 million. By June of 2011, over 86,000 new online jobs were posted, showing an increase of 11% from the previous month and 81% from June of the previous year. By September 2011 almost 100,000 new online jobs were posted.

In Chapter 9 we will explore further the new retirement option of working online. If the pathway of engaging new work is one you are considering, read Chapter 9 before you decide on your own specific employment plan, and certainly before you take a position locally, to consider the larger picture of potential employers, including online, nationwide, or even worldwide.

WOW FACTOR

Your ideal work environment may not have even existed at the time of your last job search. And your ideal job may be in a field you haven't even heard of—yet.

If you have rejected the idea that work will be a pathway you will pursue, consider the "why" of your decision. You may be thinking in terms of an either/or lifestyle–either work OR travel, either work OR leisure activities. But the Web has transformed and translated work to be "anytime, anyplace, any person, any pace."

Whereas you may be finished with work that ties you down, dominates your days, and otherwise consumes you, you may find work where you control the *where* and the *when* to be exhilarating and engaging. Today, the Internet grants you the ability to work and have your freedom, too.

Pathway 5: Life as an Entrepreneur

Entrepreneurialism is a process of finding needs and meeting them, for profit. There are plenty of needs, both existing and emerging, that can become the backbone of a successful business. Such a business can contribute significantly in meaningful ways to the health, happiness and well-being of others–human, animal, plant, or environment. So we can balance our desire to earn money with our values and our goal to contribute something worthwhile to individuals in particular, as well as to society as a whole. Retiring Boomers are primed and ready to create such businesses and to make such differences. We bring considerable assets, know-how and energy, as well as a capacity to interact and communicate, to any enterprise we set out to create or co-create.

As part of our world view, coming of age as we did in the 60's and early 70's, we bring to the present a history of idealism that has long been our trademark as a generation. Back then we thought we knew what needed to be changed. We may still know, perhaps better than those who have come after us, how to make the world a better place.

WOW FACTOR

"Older entrepreneurs now lead the way in new business formation. The trend has continued during the past three years and spans even high-tech businesses once thought [to be] the sole turf of 20-somethings. What's even more noteworthy is that start-ups with older owners are more successful, at least as measured by their survival rates."

Phillip Moeller in US News & World Report, October 2010

Boomer know-how and vision translate globally as well, providing us competitive advantages when we carry our visions abroad. According to Kathleen Peddicord, in her article *How to Retire At Any Age:*

"As a citizen of the United States, you have a big advantage in the global arena. You've grown up in the world's most competitive marketplace. You have watched niches filled and businesses launched, and you have seen innumerable examples of entrepreneurial success and failure... Now imagine yourself in a much less developed environment. Being an industrious American, you can't help but look around and notice all kinds of market voids. And you may find yourself coming up with ideas to address them." *(http://money.usnews.com/money/blogs/On-Retirement/2010/08/30/how-to-retire-at-any-age).*

SNAPSHOT

Ann and Mike entered an early retirement with savings and retirement funds, expecting to have decades of healthy living ahead of them. They moved to Ambergris Caye, Belize, and built a house. But they wanted and needed to continue earning an income. So they looked for opportunities to fill a need and earn a living, but with time left to enjoy their island paradise.

The better they got to know the island, the more niches they saw needing to be filled. Among the ideas they considered were starting a restaurant, building a small hotel, opening a wine specialty store, running eco-tours, and finally, launching a fitness club.

Their final decision, to go with the health club idea, was based on two main reasons. First, they found that there were no fitness centers on the island. Secondly, and possibly even more important, they found the idea of starting a fitness center to be particularly exciting.

Cashing in their savings, they made the leap and launched the *San Pedro Family Fitness Club*, with tennis courts, a 250,000 gallon pool, and a workout facility. Their enterprise has been a great success—and it still leaves them enough free time to enjoy and explore their idyllic island.

Will Yours Be the Life of An Entrepreneur?

Will the entrepreneur pathway be one that you pursue during your retirement? If your immediate answer is "no," pause and rethink this, based on a broader definition of "entrepreneur." Many people think that entrepreneurship is defined as "starting a business." By this definition, a relatively small population of people are entrepreneurs. The United States Global Entrepreneurship Monitor (GEM) shows that less than 8% of the US population as a whole is actively engaged in starting a business.

Candida Brush, contributor to the *Forbes.com Entrepreneurs' Blog*, takes a broader view: "Entrepreneurship is a set of actions—it is identifying or creating an opportunity, marshaling the resources and providing the leadership and building a team to create something of value, either social or economic."

Have you identified a possibility, an opportunity you might create or explore? Before you answer this question, stimulate your thinking, by considering some of the examples from the popular television program Shark Tank (*http://abc.go.com/shows/shark-tank*). Even better, record and watch this program yourself to get a sense of what kinds of ideas solve problems and make a difference, while also generating income. Some entrepreneurial ventures include:

- **CHORD BUDDY**—A guitar learning system created by Travis Perry to encourage his 10-year old daughter to learn guitar, ChordBuddy allows you to start playing the guitar instantly. Buttons over the chord strings guide you, simplifying the learning process and giving you encouragement to keep going. As you gain skill, Chord Buddy can be adjusted so you progressively do more for yourself until you are playing entirely on your own. http://www.chordbuddy.com/
- **RENT-A-GRANDMA**—Rent-A-Grandmas are carefully selected mature women who are knowledgeable nannies, housekeepers, chefs, caregivers and personal assistants. Rent-A-Grandma has gained national attention through NPR and many news stories. http://www.rentagrandma.com
- **THE SWILT**—The Swilt is the sweater reinvented—blending the wearability of a sweater with the comfort of a quilt. With a few snaps, it transforms from a sweater to a full body cover, complete with pockets and a hood. The creators of Swilt are a husband and wife duo who launched the product in 2010, and soon had sold over a hundred units to people in their community, with no marketing http://www.theswilt.com.
- **READEREST**—Rick Hopper kept losing his glasses, and he knew he wasn't alone. So he took to his garage and created the Readerest, a magnetic and practically invisible patented clip that secures your glasses to your shirt wherever you go! This tiny product has already seen big results, and is now offered at Ace Hardware and Walgreens. http://www.readerest.com
- **DANCE WITH ME**—Billy Blanks Jr. has trademarked "Dance With Me" as a new take on "Zumba," taking fitness to a new level by incorporating dance and targeting all age groups. "It is currently being sold at WalMart, Target, amazon.com, and Best Buy. http://www.meettheblanks.com

What ingenious ways have you designed to solve a problem? Would you enjoy moving your ideas forward to the next level? There is more to it than having a great idea. But having a great idea is a start.

WOW FACTOR

Of those involved in early stage entrepreneurial activities, 18% are over age 55 and 9% are over 65."
(from the *US Global Entrepreneurship Monitor Report*)

Pathway 6: Life as a "Creative"

In the work life we are leaving, we may or may not have been part of what is now being termed the "Creative Class." But that may change as part of our "new" retirement plan. According to research on the nature of work, nearly 38 million Americans, 30% of all employed people, working in many diverse fields, now *create* for a living.

Richard Florida, in his book "*The Rise of the Creative Class and How It's Transforming Work, Leisure, Community and Everyday Life,*" describes what he terms an ongoing "sea change" that has had a huge economic impact on how the workplace is organized and what is valued.

Whereas feudal aristocracy derived power from the hereditary control of land and people, and the bourgeoisie from its members' roles as merchants and factory owners, the creative class derives its identity through their "ability to invent meaningful new forms."

Florida's claim is that the Creative Class now has become the dominant class in society--a key factor in our economy and culture. "We value creativity more highly than ever, and cultivate it more intensely."

"Core creatives" (as termed by Florida) are those who create art, design, or music as their life work. Now added to these are the broader group of creative professionals in business, finance, law, health care and other fields, who create new ideas, technology, content, services, and solutions to complex problems.

All of these, whether artist or engineer, musician or computer scientist, "share a common creative ethos that values creativity, individuality, difference and merit" (Florida, 2002).

WOW FACTOR

Over the 20th century, the *Creative Class* grew from roughly 3 million workers to its current size of 38 million. It has more than doubled since 1980 alone, and is now larger than the traditional Working Class (from Richard Florida's *Rise of the Creative Class*).

The key difference between the Creative Class and other classes lies in what they are primarily paid to do. Those in the Working Class and the Service Class are primarily paid to fit in and carry out established plans. Those in the Creative Class are primarily paid to create new plans, ideas, objects and solutions.

Norms are different for those in the Creative Class—individuality, self-expression, openness, celebration of difference. The Creatives are far less likely to base their identities or sense of self-worth on who they work for. They value being themselves, setting their own agendas, and doing challenging work that reflects their values and priorities. Although it is difficult to force Creatives to work, they are never truly not working. "Creativity cannot be switched on and off at predetermined times, and is itself an odd mixture of work and play" (Florida, 2002).

Creatives use time differently, tending towards long periods of intense concentration, punctuated by complete breaks in productivity when they need to relax and recharge, or to incubate ideas. They are self-managed and set their own hours, want the ability to learn and grow, shape the content of their own work, and express their identities through their work. And they are drawn to live in stimulating, creative environments where they feel free to express themselves.

SNAPSHOT

Winston was the son of a Mississippi judge. As may be expected, his father had a way of being very convincing. And so Winston found himself on a life course towards law school, to prepare himself to join his father's law practice. But Winston also was a highly talented musician. While in school, he supported himself by singing. An accomplished tenor, he frequently won competitions, even when competing against a tenor who later went on to fame and fortune performing with the Metropolitan Opera Company.

> At the turning point when Winston graduated from law school and passed the bar, he was tempted to pursue singing as his full-time career. But he had a young wife to support, and a child on the way. And so he set his course in the direction of practicing law.
>
> When Winston retired at the end of his long legal career, he joyfully returned to singing. His voice was still in surprisingly good form, despite its many years of neglect. He continues to sing for church services and memorials, weddings and other celebrations. On occasion, when he is feeling happy, he has been known to burst into song spontaneously, as when he serenaded a newly married couple while they danced their first dance.

Will You Want a Life in the Creative Class?

Whether or not you already have been part of what is now being termed the "Creative Class," this pathway may become an essential component of your "new" retirement plan.

Do you have a gift for creativity—whether through art or through problem solving? Are you among the "core creatives" who can paint, write, design, or compose music? Or are you a person who can create new ideas, new technology, new content, new services, and new solutions to complex problems? In either case, you may want to consider the Creative Class pathway, either on its own, or in combination with other options. Even if you have always considered the creative life to be impractical, rethink the possibilities now that your life realities have changed. What may once have seemed too impractical may be just the pathway that will suit and stretch you, and allow your singular gifts to flourish.

Pathway 7: Life of a Student

Studies can be a means to an end, or they can be a pathway in themselves. Some of us will choose the path of study, either alone or in combination with other pursuits. We will make diverse choices of what to study, and to what degree. We may also differ in our reason for studying—for the pleasure of it, to write a book, to shift to a new area of work, to become skilled at an art or knowledgeable in an area of interest. But all of us who choose this pathway will experience the benefits of studying and learning something new.

Clearly, study is good for the mind. It is stimulating and can be exciting. And as our knowledge and skill increase, we relish the rewards of advancing accomplishment. Learning something new, or even learning something old in a new or better way, is "hard fun." And hard fun is, well, hard. But it is also FUN.

Will You Want the Life of a Student?

Your learning quests can be driven by topics of interest or skills to be mastered. It can be a quest to learn *about* art as a subject, or about how to create it. You may want to learn how to *identify* birds or how to heal them when they have been injured. How to train dogs or horses, or how to breed them. How to understand human behavior or research it or write fiction about it or provide guidance and counseling.

Some of your current learning options are in fields of study and work that have changed dramatically, or that didn't even exist when you went to school. You may have been a Psych major, but how much do you know about the emerging area called "Positive Psychology"– the psychology of happiness and health?

Other sciences–Biology, Physics, Astronomy–have undergone fascinating developments within the past few decades, and even within the past few years. A lot has changed since you studied them in high school or college. You may have been a machinist or a drafter—expert at operating a lathe, a Bridgeport, or a slide rule. But now you are fascinated and ready to immerse yourself in learning all about CNC, EDM, and CAD/CAM technology. You may set out to become an expert genealogist, or study for your boat captain's license. Or you may, like one retired college professor, rent space in an expert potter's studio, to work side-by-side with him as guide and mentor, as you learn to throw a pot, glaze it, and fire it in a kiln.

Your new studies may assume the form of attending classes, either locally or online. Or attending workshops, possibly in interesting locations. What about a writer's workshop in Grass Valley, California? Or maybe a *Brain Research Seminar* in Jacksonville, Florida, providing you the excuse to escape the January cold at home and spend a week on lovely Amelia Island, driving island to island along the coast as you commute to sessions every day.

SNAPSHOT

Betsy attended secretarial school after high school and landed jobs that were never run-of-the-mill. Secretary to the college president. Secretary to the Coast Guard base commander.

When her children were fully grown, she went back to college to become a teacher, then returned again to graduate school to become a reading specialist. These educational "windfalls" allowed her to achieve her dream of working as a teacher and ultimately as a reading program supervisor.

After she retired and was widowed, she surprised her family and friends when she decided not to sell her husband's beloved cabin cruiser, but, instead, to learn to pilot the boat herself. So off she went to captain's school, learning about weather systems, navigation, and all the other essentials of being the captain. As "Captain Betsy," she was the only female boat captain to join the local Power Squadron, eventually serving as an officer of the group and even winning some key competitions, hands down.

Your own pathway of study may initially be reading-based. A good place to start is _amazon.com_, where it is possible to choose any subject or skill you want to add to your repertoire and do a search on it, yielding a wealth of results. Then select the top five books on your topic of choice and start to read them, taking notes and forming questions as you go. When you have read and absorbed five books on a subject, you will be more knowledgeable about that subject than the vast majority of people. The next five books you read and digest will draw you even closer to becoming an expert, giving you a sense of scope on the subject, and enabling you to formulate your own viable synthesis and command of your chosen topic.

Pathways Combined...

Many of us will choose some combination of these seven pathways, and perhaps others, creating balances among them. We may choose a life of work combined with travel. Or travel combined with volunteering. Or creativity combined with leisure. We may even select a pathway of extended travel, deciding to live abroad and do our paid or volunteer work from there.

SNAPSHOT

Stan's "play" passion was and is golf. As soon as the weather breaks in New England, he's out there on the golf course, looking for willing team-mates. Come winter, he heads south for a few weeks to play the links.

When Stan retired as a CPA, he could have turned to his play passion of golf. But he had always defined himself in great measure through his work. Also, he sensed that playing golf every day could and would eventually grow old, and expensive.

So In his first year after retiring, he restlessly searched the want ads, seeking employment. He didn't want to work full time. The ideal situation, he thought, would be to find something part time at which he could work 2-3 days per week. This would keep his CPA skills current, pay for his golf game, and give him a sense of accomplishment and satisfaction.

Three years passed, yet Stan had no luck finding part time employment. One day while he was sharing a drink at his favorite golf club, he heard that the club was looking for someone to work on ground maintenance. Stan, who grows an extensive garden in the summer, offered to fill the spot, on the condition that the club honors his request to spend one month during the winter golfing in a warmer climate.

Happily, Stan now works three days a week outdoors. He brags that he's getting his physical exercise while being paid, combining leisure and work in a balance that is ideal for him.

What Pathways Are Yours, In What Combination?

Which pathways among the seven we have discussed give you a feeling of excitement about what lies ahead? Would you want to combine more than one?

For each of the seven pathways, write down three or four ideas and why each idea appeals to you. If, at this point, you have ideas for only one or two of the pathways, that's okay, too. Later, after further thought, you may find yourself returning to expand your ideas.

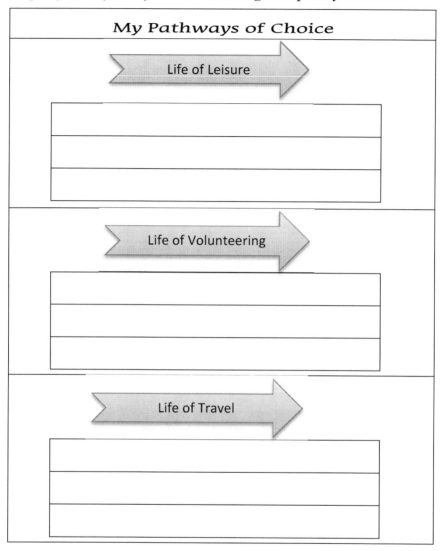

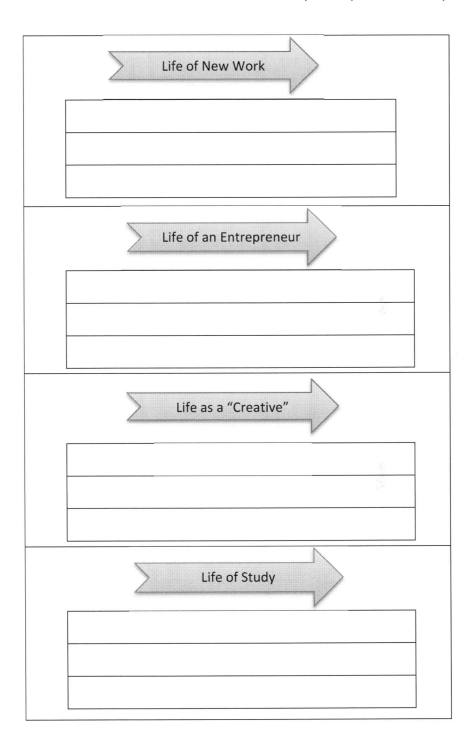

What Are Your Pathways EXPANDED?

Did you skip any of these pathways? Perhaps some courses of action are just not for you. But possibly a pathway that initially seems not to be your cup of tea, may look different to you after you break free and reinvent yourself. Even if you think an idea for a particular path may be only a remote possibility, take a moment now to go back and note it. We will come back to these notes later.

Surprisingly, you may find that some of the thoughts you added last are the most exciting to you. Yes, they may be outside your comfort zone now. Yes, it may take some creative maneuvering to make them happen. But when you begin to talk *visions* and *short lists*, these pathways could be the very ones that rise to the top.

What Are Your Pathways COMBINED?

If you picked two pathways to combine, what would they be? Would you add a third? Feel free to write down whatever comes to mind. We will return to this later for another attempt to refine and define your combinations.

And So...

You have begun to think now at a mega level—the big picture—about what pathways may form your engaging and fulfilling new retirement. Although you may have some initial ideas about what pathways appeal to you, maybe even excite you, you may have no specific plans in mind at this point. Specifics will emerge later.

Where do we go from here? With countdown completed, and pathways identified, "all" you need to do at this point is to rediscover and reinvent your SELF. The next essential step of the process of seeking and finding your own best new retirement is knowing your SELF well, then reinventing your life and work to be the fullest expression of that SELF.

To the degree that you give yourself the time and the open mindedness you need to accomplish this rediscovery of your SELF, you could be entering one of the best, most focused, productive, exciting, significant periods of your life.

CHAPTER 6
Step #3: Reinvent Your SELF

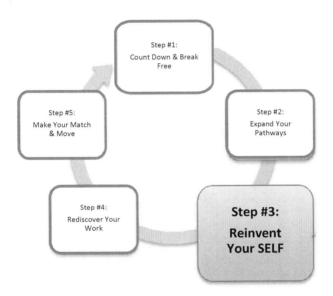

In order to arrive at your own renaissance and best next life—to determine what is (and is not) right as your unique sense of contribution and meaning—you first need to know your SELF.

"He who knows others is learned. He who knows himself is wise." So said Lao-Tzu. *"But the most difficult of all is to know yourself."*

As Step #3 in the *5-Step Process*, it is now time for you to focus on and complete the complex, and possibly surprising, task of rediscovering your unique and capable SELF—your validity and value.

Whatever pathways you follow in this next phase of your life, knowing yourself is essential. If you follow the pathway of leisure, what is it that you love and that will provide you a sense of engagement and completion? If you follow the path of volunteering, what will you volunteer to do and how will this reflect the essential YOU? If you follow the path of travel, where will you go, and who will you be when you get there? What YOU will you carry with you into other cultures through which you will connect and communicate in meaningful ways?

If you follow the path of new work, what will that work be, and how will it differ from what you have done until now? What is the essential work that is uniquely yours to do—your legacy work? If you follow the path of entrepreneurialism, what problems will you want to solve and how will you be uniquely able to solve them? If you follow the pathway of a perpetual student, what is it that you want to learn? And how does this fit with what and who you are?

Whatever you choose as your next pathway, knowing yourself is crucial to your setting off in this direction in a way that fulfills you rather than drains you. Knowing yourself allows you to determine not just the best way to fill time during your retirement, but the optimum way for you to express and engage your own unique self. In order to accomplish this, you will need to know your SELF extremely well.

Dr. Cecil Smith, a developmental psychologist at Northern Illinois University, in a talk entitled *The Long Weekend: Transition and Growth in Retirement*, described retirement as a long, gradual process—a beginning rather than an end—that is "a series of developmental tasks that must be recognized, negotiated, and resolved in order for the individual to find personal fulfillment."

In Chapter 4, as part of your retirement countdown, you made some initial notes about hidden aspects of your SELF. Review these notes now as we resume this exploration to identify the *fully defined you*. In the next chapter (Chapter 7) you will be asked to think about what you can *do*—your interests, values, skills, and traits—as part of redefining your work. But for now, the focus is on YOU, not on what you *can do*. To know clearly what you *want* to do next, you first need to explore your own personhood—your uniqueness—what makes the all-essential *you* thrive and flourish?

For you to be happy and fulfilled in the years ahead, you will need *enjoyment* and *engagement* and *meaning* in your life. All three of these factors are necessary, and all three are distinctive to you, based on your own unique self. Through the interactions and self-reflections of this chapter, you will have the time and opportunity to explore inward—to "mine for the gold." So now it is time to answer the question for yourself: "What has been simmering on the back burner of my heart and soul throughout my life so far?"

Who or What Is Defining Whom?

Retirement requires an identity shift. As such, it is a process, not an event. Although retirement promises to reap rewards, it also harbors challenges, and even hazards.

In her article entitled *"Emotional Aspects of Retirement,"* Elizabeth Holtzman points out that "In our society, work remains a defining feature of our daily lives and our identity." She adds that because of the sheer numbers of Baby Boomers who are retiring, "it is more important than ever that they retire successfully" (Holtzman, 2002).

To the degree that our past world of work defined us, keeping us certain and secure, our current (or future) status as retirees can be fraught with all kinds of uncertainties, including:

- **Financial:** Will I have enough money to live on?
- **Professional:** What will I do all day?
- **Social:** What will happen to all the friends I made at work?
- **Personal:** How will my relationship with my family change?

Yet it is these very uncertainties that open all kinds of potential windows—that offer us opportunities limited only by our level of risk tolerance and our self-allowance to dream and to explore. The transition that must occur at this point is a shift from *having our work define us*, to *having our SELF define our work*.

To rise to the challenge of discovering what the most essential *you* wants to do—what is uniquely meaningful and compelling to you—*you* will need to be the definer. You truly are now in a position to become the "master of your fate," the determiner of your destiny. At this point, it will be you who will craft your own happiness, one day at a time. And, yes, time is on your side.

> ### Journal Entry
>
> I've been thinking about the question "What is my calling?" I read that a calling–a sense of purpose–is "that which we bend to easily–that which comes naturally to us. All we have to do is pay attention."
>
> I found myself writing in response: "I want to empower people to make their lives better, fuller, and more meaningful." Speaking about talents, I wrote: "I have a special talent and passion for being a bridge–fully learning something myself, then translating and opening it up to others." This is a different, deeper vision of my calling than I had been aware of before."

Your SELF in All its Uniqueness

Another year older? You ought to be proud! You want to get boisterous, noistrous, and loud!

Just think of the things that you know how to do, the sorts of things no one can do except you.

Your brain's full of wherefores and who's whos and whys. You think someone else could be nearly as wise?

You're one-of-a-kind, you're uncommonly rare. You can't be replaced 'cause there isn't a spare.

You're another year older, I know that is true. But how many people can say they are you?! (Dr. Seuss)

Yes, you are one-of-a-kind, and uncommonly rare. But what are the particulars of your uniqueness? And how do those particulars come together into a full picture?

The four elements of your SELF to focus on here, and then to collect into a single profile are:

- What are you *like*? (your type and temperament)
- What *engages* you? (your interests)
- What has *meaning* for you? (your values)
- What can you *do*? (your skills and productive traits)

You may have ready answers to most, or even all, of these questions. But since the goal here goes beyond the obvious to a deeper level of self-renewal and personal reawakening, we will take the time now to return to many of these questions again, focusing in this chapter on the first of these four elements, "What are you like?" while addressing the other three questions in the chapter to follow.

As you re-examine your personal essential elements, your first goal is to arrive at a clearer understanding of your SELF. Your second goal is to expand your mindset and to *expect more* from your life ahead in terms of expressing and fulfilling the true you.

What Are You Like?—Your Personality Type

By now, you already know what your personality type is ... or *do* you?! Throughout your life, you may or may not have taken one or another of the many personality assessments that are available. Are you an extrovert, who is energized by talking and interacting with people, or an introvert, happiest when working on projects alone or with a few close associates? Do you tend to be a leader, organizer, or manager—a take-charge kind of person? Or do you prefer to follow directions and complete specific tasks that are assigned to you by someone else?

Do you take pride in being rational, and able to find logical solutions to problems? Or do you see your strength in being caring, compassionate, and nourishing, a good listener and encourager, aware of how people will feel as a result of a decision? Do you tend to be spontaneous, preferring to keep your options open? Or do you prefer to have a plan, and to reach closure as soon as possible?

One key to career satisfaction is the degree to which there is a match between your personality type and the work that you do. Whatever your type, you can find satisfaction and meaning in many fields. And even within a given profession or pursuit, there may be a particular aspect of that work that best suits you. At this juncture, as you enter your third phase, what matters most is that whatever you do next is based on a solid understanding of yourself.

A particularly illuminating assessment of personality types is the Myers Briggs, based on Carl Jung's typology. To determine your own personality type, you will be asked to complete a self-assessment based on the Myers Briggs.

This will yield a *4-Letter Type Code* that encapsulates your personality type—your foundational SELF. Knowing this code will illuminate your ability to move forward with your own best renewal and reinvention process. Later, you will have an opportunity to go online and take a short version of the test to confirm your self-assessment results.

"Wait a minute!" you say. "I've been there, done that. In my college psych courses, as prerequisites for specific jobs, for my own curiosity, I've taken either this or other similar types of personality profile tests. I already know what my personality type is."

Initially I thought so, too. But in the process of writing this book, I decided to re-take the test, to determine if I had changed in the 15 years since I had last taken the assessment. And, in one area, I had! According to Jung, changes like this are not unusual as we mature and develop what he called our "shadow side."

You, too, may be surprised by your new results. Even if your current results prove to be identical to your previous profile, what is most important is that you learn something new about yourself, or perhaps that you come to see the significance of one or more aspects of yourself in a new way. Besides—taking the test is fun!

Determine Your Type through Self Assessment

In order to assess your own type, you will be asked to select one of two preferences on each of four scales, using a self-assessment that is credited to Ross Reinhold of *Personality Pathways*:

http://www.personalitypathways.com/type_inventory.html

For each of the four scales that follow, ask yourself the question provided. Then read the descriptions and make your best judgment based on what you are *really* like, *not* what you think you *should* be like.

There are no "right" answers. You may return later to change your choices. And you will have an opportunity to confirm your selections by taking an online assessment.

The four scales are: Introvert versus Extrovert, Sensing versus iNtuitive, Thinking versus Feeling, and Judging versus Perceiving.

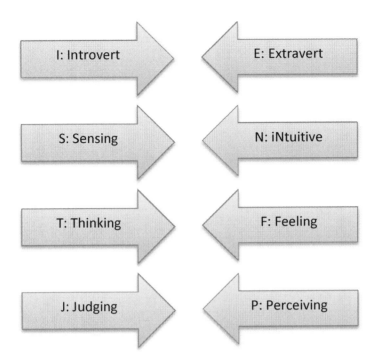

Extravert (E) or Introvert (I)

Question #1:
Which is your *most natural energy orientation*, Extraverted (E) or Introverted (I)?

Every person has two faces. One is directed towards the OUTER world of activities, excitements, people, and things. The other is directed towards the INNER world of thoughts, ideas, and imagination. While these are two different, but complementary, sides of every person's nature, most people express their innate preference for one over the other, particularly when they are tired.

Those who prefer *Extraversion* (E) are drawn to the outer world as their elemental source of energy. Rarely, if ever, do they feel "drained" by extensive amounts of interaction. To recharge their life force, they need to engage with people and activities in the outside world.

Those who prefer *Introversion* (I) gain their primary energy from the inner world of thoughts, ideas, and reflection. When circumstances require them to engage extensively with the outside world, they begin to feel drained, and need to retreat to a more private setting to recharge their batteries.

Extraverted Characteristics

- Act first, think/reflect later
- Feel deprived when cut off from interaction with the outside world
- Are motivated by the outside world of people and things
- Enjoy a wide variety of relationships with people

Introverted Characteristics

- Think/reflect first, act later
- Require "private time" to recharge their batteries
- Are motivated internally
- Demonstrate a mind that can sometimes be so active that it is "closed off" to the outside world
- Prefer one-on-one communication and relationships

Choose which best fits you:

☐ **Extraverted (E)**   ☐ **Introverted (I)**

Sensing (S)or iNtuitive (N)

Question #2:
Which way of *taking in information* is most automatic to you: Sensing (S) or iNtuitive (N)?

The *Sensing* (S) side of our brain notices the sights, sounds, smells and all the sensory details of the *present*. It categorizes, organizes, records and stores the specifics from the here and now. It is reality-based, dealing with "what IS." It also provides the specific details of memory and recollections from *past* events.

The *INtuitive* (N) side of our brain seeks to form, understand and interpret overall patterns from all the information that is collected, and records these patterns and relationships. It is imaginative and conceptual, and speculates on future possibilities.

While both kinds of perceiving are necessary, and we all do use both sensing and intuiting, we each instinctively tend to favor one over the other as seemingly more automatic or natural to us.

Those of us who prefer *Sensing* (S) as our means for taking in information, favor clear, tangible data and information that fits in well with our direct here-and-now experience. Our perceptions are focused on what we observe directly through our senses–what we can see, hear, feel, smell, or taste–to determine what is going on at the moment. We trust what can be measured or documented, and focus on what is real and concrete.

In contrast, those of us who prefer *iNtuition* (N) are drawn to information that is more abstract, conceptual, big-picture, and that represents imaginative possibilities for the future. We look for meaning in all things, trusting our inspirations and hunches. When we look at a situation, we want to know what it means, what its consequences might be, and how we might make it different or better.

Sensing Characteristics
- Mentally live in the now; attend to present opportunities
- Use common sense; create practical solutions instinctively
- Recall facts and past events in rich detail
- Do well when improvising from past experience
- Like clear, concrete information; dislike guessing from "fuzzy" facts

Intuitive Characteristics
- Mentally live in the future; anticipate possibilities
- Use imagination to invent new possibilities instinctively
- Recall facts and past events with an emphasis on patterns, contexts, and connections
- Do well when improvising from theoretical understanding
- Are comfortable with ambiguous data; guess at meanings

Choose which best fits you:

☐ **Sensing (S))**   ☐ **INtuitive (N)**

Thinking (T) or Feeling (F)

> **Question #3:**
> Which way of *making choices* is most natural to you: Thinking (T) or Feeling (F)?

The *Thinking* (T) side of our brain analyzes information in a *detached*, objective fashion, operating from factual principles to deduce and form conclusions systematically. It is our logical nature.

The *Feeling* (F) side of our brain forms conclusions in an *attached* and somewhat global manner, based on likes/dislikes, impact on others, and human and aesthetic values. It is our subjective nature.

While everyone uses both means of forming conclusions, each has a natural bias towards one over the other so that when we are given conflicting directions, one side is the natural trump card or tiebreaker.

Those who prefer *Thinking* (T) naturally prefer to make decisions in an objective, logical, and analytical manner, with an emphasis on tasks and results to be accomplished.

Those whose preference is for *Feeling* (F) make their decisions in a somewhat global, visceral, harmony and value-oriented way, paying particular attention to the impact of decisions and actions on themselves and other people.

Thinking Characteristics
- Instinctively search for facts and logic in a decision situation
- Naturally notice the tasks and work to be accomplished
- Are easily able to provide an objective and critical analysis
- Accept conflict as a natural, normal part of relationships
- Make decisions logically, through analysis

Feeling Characteristics
- Instinctively employ personal feelings and impact on people in decision situations
- Innately sensitive to peoples' needs and reactions
- Naturally seek consensus and popular opinions
- Are unsettled by conflict or disharmony
- Make decisions globally, based on values

> **Choose which best fits you:**
>
> ☐ **Thinking (T)**   ☐ **Feeling (F)**

Perceiving (P) or Judging (J)

> **Question #4:**
> What is your preferred way to *take action*: through Perceiving (P) or Judging (J)?

All people use both *Judging* (*Thinking* or *Feeling*) and *Perceiving* (*Sensing* or *INtuition*) processes to store information, organize their thoughts, make decisions, take actions and manage their lives. Yet one of these processes (*Judging* or *Perceiving*) tends to take the lead to determine the way we take action in relationship to the outside world.

Those who take action using a *Judging* (J) style, approach the outside world *with a plan*. They feel compelled to organize their surroundings, be prepared, make decisions, and reach closure and completion.

Those who take action using a *Perceiving* (P) style take a wait-and-see approach, accepting the outside world *as it comes.* They adopt and adapt, and are flexible, open-ended and receptive to new opportunities and changing game plans.

Judging Characteristics
- Plan many of the details in advance before moving into action
- Focus on task-related action
- Complete each meaningful segment before moving on
- Work best when able to keep ahead of deadlines
- Naturally use targets, dates and standard routines to manage life

Perceiving Characteristics
- Are comfortable moving into action without a plan
- Plan on-the-go
- Like to multitask, have variety, mix work and play
- Are naturally tolerant of time pressure
- Work best close to deadlines

- Instinctively avoid commitments that interfere with variety, flexibility, and freedom

---

Choose which best fits you:

☐ **Perceiving (P)**   ☐ **Judging (J)**

Your 4-Letter Personality Type Code

Record your *4-Letter Type Code* here, then read on to learn more about what this means about you and what suits you best, workwise and otherwise.

My 4–Letter Personality Type Code			
____ ____ ____ ____			
ESTJ	ESTP	ENFP	ENTP
ISTJ	ISTP	INFP	INTP
ESFJ	ESFP	ENFJ	ENTJ
ISFJ	ISFP	INFJ	INTJ

Once you have your *4-Letter Code* recorded, take a few minutes to read about your type. To accomplish this, go to the *TypeLogic* website: *http://typelogic.com/index.html*. Print out your type description and read it closely, highlighting important points, awarenesses and insights. The goal is to increase your level of awareness of *who you are*, including your prevailing strengths, traits and imperatives.

Ask yourself whether or not this description, based on the code you derived for yourself, resonates with you. If what you read does not sound like you, take the online version of the assessment, using the websites given below, to determine if a different profile emerges—one that more closely aligns with who you *really* are. Some of us are very close on one or more of the four personality continuums, and so may find ourselves more aptly described by a different code.

Determine Your Type Online

To confirm your self-assessment, use one of the sites below to complete an online version of the *Myers/Briggs Personality Profile*. Note that the tests and resources here are not the official Myers-Briggs Type Indicator (MBTI), but are adaptations of their original work. When you have completed the online assessment, check your results against what you earlier recorded as your *4-Letter Personality Type Code*.

HumanMetrics is one site offering a free assessment adapted from the Myers Briggs test, and providing immediate results:

http://www.humanmetrics.com/cgi-win/JTypes2.asp

NOTE: When answering questions, choose the one of two possible answers with which you agree the most. If you are not sure how to answer, then base your decision on your most typical reaction or feeling. Respond to all questions in order to get a reliable result.

Similar Minds is a second site that offers a short assessment adapted from the Myers Briggs test. After you indicate your sex, you will be asked to respond to 53 questions. Immediately after you submit your answers, you will receive your results.

http://similarminds.com/jung.html

Your Temperament

There are 16 possible types based on the *4-Letter Code* combinations. These 16 can be meaningfully grouped into four temperaments:

- SJ (Sensing/Judging)—Guardians
- SP (Sensing/Perceiving)—Experiencers
- NF (iNtuitive/Feeling)—Givers
- NT (iNtuitive/Thinking)—Thinkers

Based on your own *4-Letter Personality Type Code*, determine which of the four temperaments represents you best. Record your temperament in the *My Temperament* box below. Add the main descriptor for your temperament: *Guardian, Experiencer, Giver*, or *Thinker*. Then read about your own temperament, as well as the other three. The benefits of reading about all four temperaments are:
1) To determine if another temperament may better describe you than the one indicated according to your results;
2) To understand others whose temperaments differ from yours.

My Temperament

My Descriptor: _____

Guardian (SJ), _Artisan_ (SP), _Giver_ (NJ), or _Thinker_ (NT)

SJ	SP	NF	NT
ESTJ	ESTP	ENFP	ENTP
ISTJ	ISTP	INFP	INTP
ESFJ	ESFP	ENFJ	ENTJ
ISFJ	ISFP	INFJ	INTJ

Guardian (SJ): Service & Duty Keeper

All four types that contain S and J (Sensing and Judging) are known as "guardians" or "traditionalists" (ESTJ, ISTJ, ESFJ and ISFJ). This group comprises 46% of the American population. Their compulsion is _TO BE USEFUL._

If you are a _Guardian_, you are drawn to base your perceptions on what your five senses tell you–facts, data, and previous experience. You value law and order, security, rules, and conformity, and are driven by a strong motivation to serve society's needs.

As a _Guardian_ you have a need to belong, to serve, and to do the right thing, seeking stability, orderliness, cooperation, consistency, and reliability. You are practical, organized, thorough, and systematic, and take great pride in doing something right the first time and every time. You can be counted on to get the job done.

The four types who share the _Guardian_ (SJ) temperament are:

- **Inspector** (ISTJ): Has an abiding sense of responsibility for doing what needs to be done in the here-and-now. Exhibits excellent organizing abilities and command of the facts.
- **Protector** (ISFJ): Takes practical action to help others. Brings an aura of quiet warmth, caring, and dependability to all they do.
- **Supervisor** (ESTJ): Needs to analyze and bring into logical order the outer world of events, people, and things.
- **Provider** (ESFJ): Expresses active and intense caring about people. Takes action naturally to help others, to organize the world around them, and to get things done.

> If you are a *Guardian*, which specific type descriptor is yours according to your 4-Letter Personality Type Code: *Inspector, Protector, Supervisor,* or *Provider*?
>
> MY DESCRIPTOR: _____

Artisan/Experiencer (SP): Teacher of Freedom & Joy

All four of the types that contain S and P (Sensing and Perceiving) share the "artisan" or "experiencer" temperament (ISTP, ISFP, ESTP or ESFP). This group comprises about 27% of the American population. Their compulsion is *TO ACT FREELY.*

If you are an *Artisan/Experiencer*, you are among the most adventurous of the four temperaments, living for action, impulse, and the present moment. Your focus is on the immediate situation, and you have the ability to assess what needs to be done and move into action.

You value freedom and spontaneity, and are risk-taking, adaptable, easy going, and practical. You like moving from one challenge to the next. Because you can see clearly what is happening, you are agile at seizing opportunities. You are excellent at recognizing practical problems and approaching them with flexibility, courage, and resourcefulness, and are not afraid to take risks or improvise as needed.

Four types share the *Artisan/Experiencer* (SP) temperament:

- **Crafter** (ISTP): Driven to understand how things and phenomena work in the real world in order to make the best and most effective use of these realities. Logical, realistic, and a natural troubleshooter.
- **Composer** (ISFP): Exhibits a deep-felt caring for living things, combined with a quietly playful, sometimes adventurous, approach to life. Expresses warmth and concern in very practical ways, preferring action to words.
- **Promoter** (ESTP): Has an acute sense of how objects, events, and people in the world work. Excited by continuous involvement in new hands-on activities and the pursuit of real-life challenges.
- **Performer** (ESFP): Seeks excitement through continuous involvement in new activities and relationships. Has deep concern for people, showing this caring through warm and

119

pragmatic gestures of helping. Prefers to experience and accept life rather than to judge or organize it.

> If you are an *Artisan/Experiencer*, what is your specific descriptor according to your 4-Letter Personality Type Code: *Crafter, Composer, Promoter,* or *Performer?*
>
> MY DESCRIPTOR: _____

Giver (NF): Bearer of Truth & Meaning

All four of the types that contain N and F (iNtuitive and Feeling) are known as "givers" or "idealists" (INFJ, INFP, ENFP, ENFJ). This group comprises about 16% of the American population. Their compulsion is *to "BE."*

If you are a *Giver*, you are highly concerned about personal growth and understanding, both for yourself and for others. You are on a perpetual search for the meaning of life, placing a very high value on authenticity and integrity in people and relationships, and focusing on human potential.

You are an excellent communicator, and can be an effective catalyst for positive change. Knowing instinctively how to bring out the best in others, you understand how to motivate others to do their highest level of work. You are excellent at resolving conflicts and helping people work together more effectively.

The four types who share the *Giver* (NF) temperament are:

- **Counselor** (INFJ): Dominated by the inner world of possibilities, ideas, and symbols. Has a deep interest in creative expression as well as issues of spirituality and human development.
- **Healer**: (INFP): Captured by a deep-felt caring and idealism about people. A skilled communicator who is naturally drawn to ideas that embody a concern for human potential.
- **Champion** (ENFP): Thrives on what is possible and new—ideas, people, activities. Deeply concerned about people.
- **Teacher** (ENFJ): Takes action naturally and conscientiously to care for others, organize the world around them, and get things done. Enjoys helping others develop their potential.

> If you are a *Giver*, what specific descriptor is yours accord-
> ing to your 4-Letter Personality Type Code: *Counselor,
> Healer, Champion,* or *Teacher?*
>
> MY DESCRIPTOR: _____

Thinker (NT): Provider of Logic & Understanding

All four of the types that contain N and T (INtuitive and Thinking) are
known as "thinkers" or "conceptualizers" (INTJ, INTP, ENTP, ENTJ).
This group comprises approximately 10% of the American population.
Their compulsion is *TO IMPROVE*.

If you are a Thinker, you are among the most independent of the
four temperaments, driven by an urge to acquire knowledge and to set
very high standards for yourself and others. You are naturally curious,
and usually see many sides of an argument or issue.

As a Thinker, you are excellent at seeing possibilities, understanding complexities, and designing solutions to real or hypothetical
problems. You enjoy using your abilities to analyze possibilities
logically in order to solve problems. With your vision, you can be a
great innovator. You enjoy being challenged, and excel at strategizing,
planning, and building systems to accomplish your goals.

The four types who share the *Thinker* (NT) temperament are:

- **Mastermind** (INTJ): Attends to the inner world of possibilities and thoughts—ideas are the substance of life. Driven to
  understand and to know. Works intensely to transform visions
  into realities.
- **Architect** (INTP): Needs to make sense of the world, naturally questioning and critiquing ideas and events in a quest for
  understanding. Logical and analytical. Enjoys opportunities to
  be creative.
- **Inventor** (ENTP): Compelled by the outer world of possibilities. Energetic and enthusiastic. Seeks patterns and meaning in
  the world, having a deep need to analyze, to understand, and to
  know the nature of things.
- **Field Marshal** (ENTJ): Driven to analyze and bring into logical order the outer world of events, people, and things. Prefers

a world that is structured and organized. A natural leader who builds conceptual models as plans for strategic action.

> If you are a *Thinker*, what specific descriptor is yours according to your 4-Letter Personality Type Code: *Mastermind, Architect, Inventor, or Field Marshal*?
>
> MY DESCRIPTOR: _____

Why Does Type and Temperament Matter?

In your past life, when it is probable that much was defined by your career, your employer, your clients, your family demands, you, like many others, may have set yourself aside as you progressed, adapting to the requirements and needs that drove your work and life.

Now that you are entering a time when, as we have discussed, YOU are the definer, all of this changes. To the degree that you know yourself at a deeper level, and give yourself full permission to BE yourself as a condition of your retirement work and career, your work and life ahead will be highly fulfilling, even remarkable.

Now that you know yourself, your type and temperament, your needs and compulsions, your natural abilities and instinctive ways of operating, you have achieved the all-essential first step.

But *knowing* is not all that is important now. The other part of the equation is *acting*. Now that *you* are the definer, it is time to expect more. Determine that your work from this point forward will be work that fully expresses and fulfills you, in all your uniqueness.

SNAPSHOT

Sherry started out as a secondary art teacher, but her heart wasn't in it. She loved the work of a graphic artist, and wanted so much to start her own business. After a few years, her husband convinced her to take the leap to strike out on her own.

As fate would have it, the entire world of graphic design was shifting from an analog to a digital platform. Sherry enrolled in a computer-based graphic design program at her local community college. The rest is history. Sherry developed a web site, advertised locally, and gradually gained a base of clientele.

But that's not the best part of this story. In the meantime, Sherry became interested in restoring antique cars. This endeavor captured her need for challenge and problem solving. Over time, she found herself spending more time finding cars to restore, and less time working as a graphic artist.

At first Sherry outsourced the mechanical aspects of her car restoration projects. But she gradually became adept at performing the aesthetic aspects herself.

Twelve years ago, Sherry retired from graphic arts and turned over her business to her two children. She now spends her time on her passion. So far she has restored seven cars. Her goal is to leave one vehicle to each of her grandchildren. The family teases her whenever a new grandchild is born, asking what she is going to do if her grandchildren begin to outnumber her restored autos. But, so far, Sherry is ahead of schedule!

And So...

What fun you have had analyzing who you actually are versus who you thought you were, or should be. What surprises did you uncover about yourself? Perhaps you were a bit caught off guard because your actual psychological profiles did not always align with your conventional, comfortable vision of who you thought you were based on what you have done in your life so far.

Maybe your type and temperament descriptions resonated with what you have suspected about yourself for a while. Or perhaps you are confused now because your results indicate that you seem to have undergone a shift in values or personality. So which version of *you* are you really?

Now is *not* the time to abandon ship, to "throw out the baby with the bath," nor to plunge into a deep chasm of denial. Just let the data and facts speak to you for a while. Even better, share your newly discovered persona with a close friend or your partner.

Open up your heart, mind and psyche to the possibility that perhaps, just *perhaps*, these descriptions accurately reveal your authentic self, even if this is a re-discovery, or new discovery. Or possibly this self-portrait is still an incomplete picture of who you really are.

Certainly there is more to be added to your self-portrait. In particular, what about the four essential ingredients of your *Interests, Values, Skills, and Traits?*

These four, when combined with your *Type* and *Temperament*, will complete the profile of your *Reinvented Self*. So we will set out to explore and add these remaining four elements in the next chapter.

CHAPTER 7
Step #4: Rediscover Your WORK

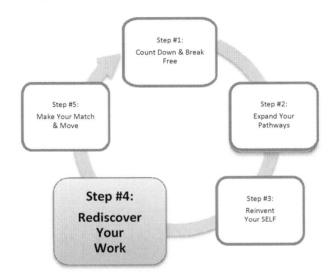

Long before my sister and I understood classical music and opera, my dear Aunt Hannah, who was bent on serving us a healthy dose of "culture" at an early age, dragged us, reluctant though we were, to a series of classical concerts at our local community center. After a few unsuccessful attempts, and several less than pleasant "incidents," she decided that perhaps we were too young or too hopelessly bourgeois to ever have an appreciation for these finer pursuits.

But, never one to abandon her determination to "culturize" us, she decided to try her luck taking us to a Broadway show—"Auntie Mame." This captivating musical comedy was my first encounter with live theatre, and I was hooked. From then on, I became an ardent fan of all facets of live theatre. This passion has remained with me to this day.

Likewise, my best friend's dad was a classical violinist. She was raised in a home where it was taken for granted that she and her brother would learn, and become proficient at mastering, a musical instrument. She became an expert clarinet player, regularly recruited as a member of various local musical groups. But more, she developed a love and appreciation of all types of classical music—an interest that has become one of the centerpieces of her cultural life.

My friend and I represent examples of *nurture*'s influence over the interests, talents, and passions to which we are introduced early in life and that continue to develop throughout our adulthood. These interests enrich our lives and provide hours of enjoyment. And now they may come to bear on our work rediscovery process.

As we move ahead to *Step #4: Rediscover Your Work*, you will be asked to carry forward the "what you are like" dimension of your SELF from *Step #3*, then reexamine and integrate four other dimensions: your interests, values, skills and traits. Whether through nature or nurture, these additional dimensions play a critical role towards forming an authentic, rich, multidimensional picture of your full and essential SELF as they guide your progress towards your rediscovered work and life after retirement.

What *Engages* You? Your Interests

Although you may have had some surprises when you reexplored your personality type and temperament and reinvented your SELF, certainly you already know what your interests are. Or do you?

Interests are key to contentment and fulfillment in work as well as life. Time spent in pursuit of your interests is engaging, sometimes to the point where you enter what positive psychologists call "flow," losing all track of time because you are so engrossed.

It is important to understand, particularly at this point in your personal renewal process, that your *interests* to date have been heavily influenced by your history. These interests may or may not have been fully generated by your own unique SELF.

"How so?" you ask. Good question.

Your parents were your initial window to the discovery of your *interests*. Based on their limited or extensive financial resources, educational and cultural backgrounds, geographical location, and time commitments, your parents offered you what they considered to be desirable and worthwhile activities. As a child, you tested these activities, willingly or unwillingly, and formed your own responses to them.

Once you were exposed to an activity that captured you, the degree to which it became an *interest* for you depended heavily on whether your efforts in that direction were reinforced, positively or negatively, or even ignored.

Positive reinforcement in the form of praise, accomplished goals, improved self-concept, and sometimes monetary reward, established a particular activity as an interest. Negative reinforcement, including punishment, negative remarks, denial of opportunities, and damage to self-concept, led to a dampening of interest, or even an aversion, to an activity. If your parents ignored your efforts, this had an even more powerful stifling effect than that of negative reinforcement.

Reinforcement, both positive and negative, had a cumulative effect over time, determining which of your explored activities turned into sustained *interests*. Other role models—people whose success you admired and wanted to emulate—were another powerful source of influence as you fashioned your life *interests*. Thus, through a combination of influences—exploration, reinforcement, attention, and modeling—your interests formed and became a part of you.

All of this tells you something important about your SELF and your interests, as you have come to know them. Since you needed *both* the exposure, and also the positive reinforcement and attention to your efforts in order that an activity you experienced became one of your *interests*, this means you may not have discovered some of your potential interests YET. Possibly these undiscovered interests could become some of your most profound interests.

So, although your interests may seem fixed and stable at this point in your life, you may find that they will expand in important ways if you open yourself to exploring and discovering additional ones. Depending on your own history, you may have potential interests that you have not yet identified—interests that could be among your most passionate pursuits once you discover them.

To identify and measure your interests, and the predominant categories in which they fit, begin by asking yourself what you genuinely like to do. According to Dr. John Holland, there are six principal categories of interests:

- **Realistic Interests: the DOERS**
  Doers prefer practical, hands-on, physical activities, with tangible results, and generally have athletic or mechanical abilities. They enjoy working with objects, machines, tools, animals or plants—building, fixing, repairing, caring and cultivating.
- **Investigative Interests: the THINKERS**
  Thinkers prefer to solve abstract problems in science-related or engineering subjects. Curious about the physical world including why and how it works, they enjoy intellectual challenge and original or unconventional ideas. They are engaged by work that involves observing, learning, investigating, analyzing, evaluating, and solving problems.
- **Artistic Interests: the CREATORS**
  Creators prefer unstructured situations that offer them opportunities for self-expression of ideas and concepts through different artistic media such as art, music, theater, film, dance, multimedia, or writing. They have artistic, innovative, or intuitional abilities, and enjoy using their imagination and creativity.
- **Social Interests: the HELPERS**
  Helpers prefer work that engages them in direct service that helps people —advising, counseling, coaching, mentoring, teaching, or guiding group discussions. Skilled with words, they are drawn to humanistic or social causes, and like to work with people—to inform, enlighten, help, train, develop, or cure them.
- **Enterprising Interests: the PERSUADERS**
  Persuaders prefer business situations where they engage in persuasion, selling, or otherwise having influence on others. They are enthusiastic, energetic, assertive, self-confident, and like working with people, and are drawn to management, leadership or marketing roles.
- **Conventional Interests: the ORGANIZERS**
  Organizers become highly engaged when working in a structured business situation involving data analysis, finance, planning and organizational tasks. They value efficiency and order, and have an exceptional ability to carry out projects in detail and follow through on instructions.

SNAPSHOT

Jerry was a self-educated, self-made man—someone who had followed the traditional vocational path of so many in his generation. After serving a 4-year term in the Navy, he attended a post high school vocational training school, where he learned the trade of tool making—fabricating parts using machine tools. With his inquisitive mind, mathematical acumen, and knack for problem-solving, he soon found himself *designing* the high-end, complex parts and tools needed for the wire and cable industry, not just fabricating them.

Jerry's talent for *troubleshooting* broadened his work even further. He moved into solving problems with the equipment that produced the parts and tools. Thus he advanced over the years, from fabricating parts, to designing them, to troubleshooting the equipment that produced them.

The demand for his skills and services gradually grew to the point where he was able to retire early, in his late 50's. So what work did he choose to do next? He went back to the beginning of it all—when he was the DOER—the hands-on task of producing parts—and spent the remainder of his life earning a comfortable supplemental income doing what he loved most, fabricating parts on a contract basis.

Self-Assess Your Interests

In order to determine your own current and expanded interests, take some time now to complete either the *Interest Self-Assessment* on the pages that follow and/or the online assessment on the site provided below in the section entitled *"Assess Your Interests Online."*

Use the descriptions above, and the check sheet that follows below, to assess yourself. The purpose of this exercise is to "mine" your past for interests that have emerged so far, and then to envision any further interests you may want to add in the future. These interest categories are the keys to what does or does not, will or will not, engage you.

Self-Assessment Instructions: For each item in the following six tables, check those that describe you *now* in terms of what you *are* *like*, as well as what you *can do* and what you *like to do*. Then expand your lists, going back to tag anything that you may want to explore in the *future*, but may have not yet experienced.

Use a different color pen for these future items so that you will be able to tell them apart from your past and present ones. Some of your most compelling interests may be ones you added as you expanded your interests list. After checking off items, total up each category. Be sure to include in your totals the items that you add when you expand your list.

When you have a total for each category of interest, identify the *three* categories that scored the highest. These combine to create the most accurate picture of your interests.

Interests Self-Assessment

REALISTIC (R)					
Are You...		**Can You...**		**Do You Like To...**	
☐	Practical	☐	Fix electrical things	☐	Tinker with mechanics
☐	Athletic	☐	Solve mechanical problems	☐	Work outdoors
☐	Straight forward	☐	Pitch a tent	☐	Be physically active
☐	Mechanically inclined	☐	Play a sport	☐	Use your hands
☐	A nature lover	☐	Read a blueprint	☐	Build things
☐	Good with tools and machinery	☐	Work on cars	☐	Repair things
		R Total =			
INVESTIGATIVE (I)					
Are You...		**Can You...**		**Do You Like To...**	
☐	Inquisitive	☐	Think abstractly	☐	Explore ideas
☐	Analytical	☐	Solve math problems	☐	Use computers
☐	Scientific	☐	Understand physical theories	☐	Work independently

	Are You...		Can You...		Do You Like To...
☐	Observant	☐	Do complex calculations	☐	Perform lab experiments
☐	Precise	☐	Work on cars	☐	Read scientific or technical magazines
☐	Curious	☐	Analyze data	☐	Do puzzles
			I Total =		

ARTISTIC (A)

	Are You...		Can You...		Do You Like To...
☐	Creative	☐	Sketch, draw, paint	☐	Attend concerts, theaters, art exhibits
☐	Intuitive	☐	Sing ,play a musical instrument	☐	Read fiction, plays, poetry
☐	Imaginative	☐	Write stories, plays, poetry,	☐	Work on crafts
☐	Innovative	☐	Design fashions or interiors	☐	Take photographs
☐	An individualist	☐	Compose music	☐	Express yourself creatively
☐	Original	☐	Act, dance	☐	Design gardens or landscaping
			A Total =		

SOCIAL (S)

	Are You...		Can You...		Do You Like To...
☐	Friendly	☐	Teach/train others	☐	Work in groups
☐	Helpful	☐	Express yourself clearly	☐	Help people with problems
☐	Idealistic	☐	Lead a group discussion	☐	Participate in meetings
☐	Insightful	☐	Mediate disputes	☐	Do volunteer service
☐	Outgoing	☐	Plan and supervise an activity	☐	Work with young people
☐	Understanding	☐	Cooperate well with others	☐	Play team sports
			S Total =		

ENTERPRISING (E)		
Are You...	**Can You...**	**Do You Like To...**
☐ Self-confident	☐ Initiate projects	☐ Make decisions affecting others
☐ Assertive	☐ Convince people to do things your way	☐ Be elected to office
☐ Sociable	☐ Sell things	☐ Win a leadership or sales award
☐ Persuasive	☐ Give talks or speeches	☐ Start your own political campaign
☐ Enthusiastic	☐ Organize activities and events	☐ Meet influential people
☐ Energetic	☐ Lead a group	☐ Promote ideas
E Total =		

CONVENTIONAL (C)		
Are You...	**Can You...**	**Do You Like To...**
☐ Well groomed	☐ Work well within a system	☐ Follow clearly defined procedures
☐ Accurate	☐ Do a lot of paper work in a short time	☐ Work with data
☐ Numerically inclined	☐ Keep accurate records	☐ Work with numbers
☐ Methodical	☐ Use a computer efficiently	☐ Type or take shorthand
☐ Conscientious	☐ Write effective business letters	☐ Be responsible for details
☐ Efficient	☐ Assure quality and accuracy	☐ Organize
C Total =		

Assess Your Interests Online

To confirm your self-assessment results, complete the free assessment on the Career Zone site at: *http://www.cacareerzone.org/ip/*. For each of 180 items, you will be asked to click on **L** if you think you

132

would LIKE to do the activity, **D** if you think you would DISLIKE the activity and **?** If you are not sure.

As you select your response to each item, include both your current and your expanded interests. Mark as "Like" both those tasks that have interested you in the past, and also those that you think may possibly interest you in the future.

When you have completed the online assessment, you will receive immediate results, showing your top three categories of interests. Compare these results to your self-assessment.

Now on the *My Interests Diagram* below, highlight the boxes for each of your three top-scoring categories. Then use the first letter of each of your top three to record your *3-Letter Interest Code*.

My Interests Diagram

Realistic:
Doers

Conventional:
Organizers

Investigative:
Thinkers

3-Letter Interest
Code

____ ____ ____

Enterprising:
Persuaders

Artistic: Crea-
tors

Social:
Helpers

What Your Interest Results Tell You

What were the results of your *Interests Assessment*, and what do those results reveal about your SELF and your WORK?

Your *3-Letter Interest Code* provides essential clarification to ensure that you will be able to choose work that engages and satisfies you. Consider each of your three categories separately, then in combination. If one part of your interest code is *R (Realistic)*, you need to work with your hands, making, fixing, assembling or building things, using and operating equipment, tools or machines. If a part of your code is *I (Investigative)*, your work needs to challenge your mind in order to keep you interested. You like to discover and research ideas... To observe, investigate and experiment... To ask questions and solve problems.

If a part of your code is *A (Artistic)*, it is essential that your work enables you to express yourself through creating and designing things. You like to use words, art, music or drama to communicate and perform. Suppose a part of your code is *S (Social)*. Your work needs to support the well-being and welfare of others, through teaching or training them, informing or helping them, healing or curing them.

Is one part of your code *E (Enterprising)*? If so, your work needs to include influencing and encouraging others. You have a need to work with and to lead people. If *C (Conventional)* is part of your code, you are most engaged when working outdoors or when carrying out work that depends on you for the organizing, planning and follow through.

Consider, too, what each opposite indicates. For example, if you are an *Artistic (A)*, but your work is routine, requiring that you replicate work designed by others, you will not be engaged because you will have nothing to create. If you are a *Social (S)* who operates equipment, tools or machines to complete tasks or produce products, you will not be engaged because you are not working with people.

If you are an *Investigative (I)* who teaches or trains group after group of people, repeating the same concepts over and over, you will not be engaged unless you are being mentally challenged. In each of these cases you will *not* be fully engaged because the work does not capture your interests at a very fundamental level.

What Has *Meaning* for You?—Your Values

Many things are meaningful, in theory. But for each of us, the legacy we choose to leave varies according to what is most uniquely meaningful to *us*. And what is most meaningful to *us* is based on our *values*.

The word *"values"* is a broad term that means different things to different people. Most values are qualities that are universally recognized to be worth pursuing in life. But here we are talking about what you, *yourself*, value *most*—what are the values to which you particularly want to dedicate your energies and skills, talents and time, during your lifetime? What is it that you uniquely care about leaving better than you found it in this world? What will be your legacy?

In order to determine your own values, particularly as they apply to the work you do, take some time now to complete the self-assessment below. Then visit the website provided in the *"Assess Your Values Online"* section that follows to complete a free online assessment.

Self Assess Your Values

Self-Assessment Instructions: For the statements that follow, circle a number 1 to 5 to indicate how important each item is to you. Many items may seem to be of value in general. But the key question is which are of highest value to *you* personally?

1 = Unimportant
2 = Of Little Importance
3 = Moderately Important
4 = Important
5 = Very Important

If an entire grouping does not apply to you *now*, even if it did apply to you in the past, mark it as NA (Not Applicable), and move on.

When you have completed this exercise, total up the numbers for each grouping.

Values Self–Assessment	

CREATIVITY: Work that permits me to invent new things, design new products, or develop new ideas.
     I value the opportunity to create something new.
        5 4 3 2 1
 I value being able to contribute new ideas.
        5 4 3 2 1
	TOTAL

135

	TOTAL
MANAGEMENT: Work that permits me to plan and lay out work for others. I value the opportunity to use leadership abilities. 5 4 3 2 1 I value being able to plan and organize the work of others. 5 4 3 2 1	
ACHIEVEMENT: Work that gives me a feeling of accomplishment doing a job well. I value the feeling of doing a good day's work. 5 4 3 2 1 I value knowing by results that I have done a good job. 5 4 3 2 1	**TOTAL**
WAY OF LIFE: Work that permits me to live the life I choose and be the type of person I wish to be. I value the opportunity to be the kind of person I would like to be. 5 4 3 2 1 I value being able to lead the kind of life I most enjoy. 5 4 3 2 1	**TOTAL**
ASSOCIATES: Work that brings me into contact with fellow workers I like. I value being able to feel like one of the gang. 5 4 3 2 1 I value having good connections with fellow workers. 5 4 3 2 1	**TOTAL**

AESTHETIC: Work that permits me to contribute beauty to the world.
 	
I value the opportunity to make use of my artistic ability.
 	
     5 4 3 2 1
 	
I value being able to add beauty to the world.
 	
     5 4 3 2 1
	TOTAL

INDEPENDENCE: Work that permits me to work my own way, as fast or slow as I wish.
 	
I value being able to have freedom in my area.
 	
     5 4 3 2 1
 	
I value the opportunity to make my own decisions.
 	
     5 4 3 2 1
	TOTAL

VARIETY: Work that provides me an opportunity to do different types of tasks.
 	
I value not being required to do the same thing all the time.
 	
     5 4 3 2 1
 	
I value the opportunity to work at a variety of tasks.
 	
     5 4 3 2 1
	TOTAL

ALTRUISM: Work that enables me to contribute to the welfare of others.
 	
I value having opportunities to help others.
 	
     5 4 3 2 1
 	
I value adding to the well-being of other people.
 	
     5 4 3 2 1
	TOTAL

INTELLECTUAL STIMULATION: Work that provides opportunity for independent thinking and to learn how and why things work.	**TOTAL**
I value being challenged to solve problems. 5 4 3 2 1 I value being required to remain mentally alert. 5 4 3 2 1	

SCORE TOTALS: Add together the numbers for each category.
1–4   Of Little Importance
5–7   Important
8–10   Very Important

List your *top five* in the *My Values Diagram* below. Also list any additional categories where your total was in the "Very Important" range (8 to 10).

Assess Your Values Online

If you would prefer to take a version of this assessment that is self-scoring, or to confirm your results from the self-assessment, use the free assessment at:

http://people.usd.edu/~bwjames/tut/time/workinv.html

Note that the online assessment includes some additional value categories beyond those in the self-assessment. For each of the 45 items in the online assessment, click the box and choose your one best response. When you have finished, click the "*Calculate*" button at the bottom of the screen.

You will be given a personalized report based on your responses. Print your entire report and keep it on file by following these instructions:

1. Select the entire table.
2. Click Ctrl-C to copy it.

3. Open a blank WORD document and position the cursor at the beginning.
4. Click Ctrl-V to paste your results into the document.
5. Save and print the file.

Record your *top five* value categories in the *My Top 5 Values Diagram* below. Also record any other categories where your scores totaled in the "Very Important" range (8 to 10).

My Top Five Values Diagram

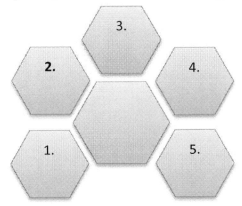

What Can You *Do*? Your Skills and Traits

Think about the marketable skills you developed during your Stage II career. If you refer back to your many résumés, you will find that, over the course of 30 to 40 years or more, you have gradually accumulated both a formal body of knowledge required for your career, and also a bank of practical skills that served as complements.

Take the time now to make a preliminary list of the skills you already have to offer. Make it a long list, including not only those skills you have used in your work most recently, but also those you used at some point in the past, even if you have not used them lately. Include skills you used when you were in school or as a community member or volunteer, as well as those you used as part of your employment. Note your people skills, as well as your mental and physical skills.

If an item you list is actually a personal *trait* rather than a skill, note it on the *Traits List* in the section that follows. People often confuse *skills* with *traits*. If an item is something you can *do*, list it as a *skill*. If it is a positive personal *characteristic*, list it as a *trait*. For example, you may have *skill* at "building," and the *trait* of being "resourceful" when you are building.

Consider your current skills within each of the ten categories below. Check all you are able to do. Add skills in each category, as applicable.

Skills Inventory

Using Your Hands					
☐	Assembling	☐	Building	☐	Operating machinery
☐	Fixing	☐	Repairing	☐	Refurbishing
☐		☐		☐	
Using Words					
☐	Writing	☐	Speaking	☐	Training
☐	Reading	☐	Editing	☐	Ghostwriting
☐		☐		☐	
Using Numbers					
☐	Calculating	☐	Computing	☐	Analyzing
☐	Managing money	☐	Taking inventory	☐	Keeping financial records
☐		☐		☐	
Using Intuition					
☐	Sizing up a person	☐	Sizing up a situation	☐	Acting on gut reactions
☐	Showing foresight	☐	Having insight	☐	Sensing what lies ahead
☐		☐		☐	

Using Analytical Thinking					
☐	Researching	☐	Classifying	☐	Organizing
☐	Gathering information	☐	Problem-solving	☐	Diagnosing
☐		☐		☐	

Using Creativity					
☐	Inventing	☐	Creating	☐	Designing
☐	Developing	☐	Improvising	☐	Adapting
☐		☐		☐	

Using Helpfulness					
☐	Listening	☐	Counseling	☐	Understanding
☐	Building trust	☐	Developing rapport	☐	Guiding
☐		☐		☐	

Using Artistic Abilities					
☐	Acting	☐	Singing/dancing	☐	Painting
☐	Fashioning	☐	Composing music	☐	Playing a musical instrument
☐		☐		☐	

Using Leadership					
☐	Organizing	☐	Directing	☐	Making decisions
☐	Negotiating	☐	Persuading	☐	Promoting
☐		☐		☐	

Using Follow-Through					
☐	Classifying	☐	Recording data	☐	Filing & retrieving

☐	Carrying out plans	☐	Following instructions	☐	Attending to details
☐		☐		☐	

Now think beyond what you currently can do to what you might want to add. Are there skills that you have not developed YET, but have always wanted to acquire? Or are there skills you developed in the past but set aside and now would like to rekindle or expand? Return to your *Skills Inventory* using a different color pen, and add these other skills to your list. The skills you add when you expand your list may be the ones that will excite you most in your work ahead.

Skills Sort: What Can I Do That I Want to Do?

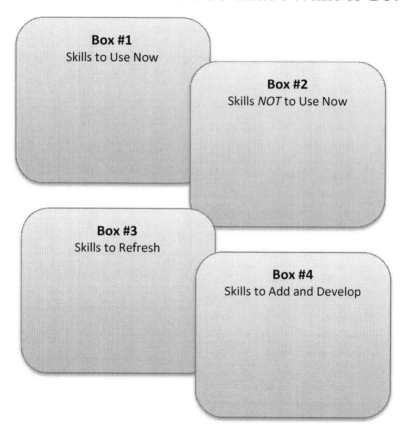

Look through your lists of skills, current and future. You will want to carry some forward, while leaving others behind. Just because you *CAN* do something does not necessarily mean you *WANT* to do it now. Sort each skill you checked into one of the *Four Boxes* below: 1)skills to use, 2) skills NOT to use, 3) skills to refresh, or 4) skills to add.

After you have sorted your skills, then focus on those skills you have placed into Box #1, Box #3 or Box #4. Select your *Top 5 Skills of Choice*. These will be your actionable skills—the skills to be carried forward into your action plan for your next phase.

My Top Five Skills of Choice

Assuming your Box #3 skills will need to be refreshed, and your Box #4 skills will need to be developed anew, part of your action plan should include opportunities for you to learn and practice these skills in order that you are able to use them all at a high level of competency.

Now Focus on Your Traits

Starting with any items you listed above as *Skills* that actually were personal *traits*—positive personal *characteristics*—compile a list of your strongest.

1. Check off ten or more of your strongest traits.

2. Start with these samples, and add others that describe you.

3. Then select your Top Three Positive Personal Traits.

My Positive Personal Traits					
☐	Accurate	☐	Adaptable	☐	Confident
☐	Cooperative	☐	Creative	☐	Diligent
☐	Dynamic	☐	Empowering	☐	Energetic
☐	Flexible	☐	Independent	☐	Innovative
☐	Outgoing	☐	Perceptive	☐	Persevering
☐	Persistent	☐	Professional	☐	Punctual
☐	Resourceful	☐	Self-motivated	☐	Versatile
☐		☐		☐	

My Top 3 Traits

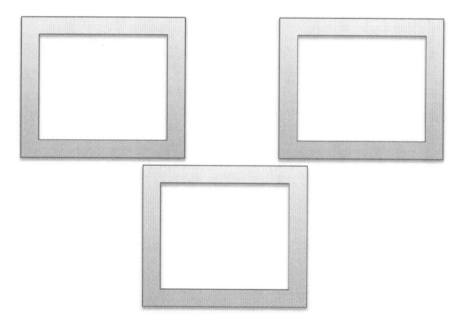

Now Pull It All Together—The Sum of Your Parts

Your task now is to synthesize these dimensions of your SELF to create a full profile. Taken as a whole, these elements create a picture of your full and unique SELF. The work or pursuits you choose from this point forward will be fulfilling to you to the degree that they express the combined essence of YOU.

- What you are *like*

- What *engages* you

- What has *meaning* for you

- What you can *do*

- Your main positive *traits*

My Personal Summary

What Are You LIKE? Your Type & Temperament

In the figure below, write: 1) your *4-Letter Personality Type Code & Descriptor*, 2) your *2-Letter Temperament Code & Descriptor* (Guardian, Artisan, Giver, Thinker), 3) your *Compulsion*.

My Type & Temperament

MY TYPE: __ __ __ __

_____

MY TEMPERAMENT: __ __

_____

MY COMPULSION: _____

What ENGAGES You? Your Interests

In the figure below, write: 1) your *3-Letter Interest Code*, 2) the names and descriptors for your primary interest categories.

My Interests

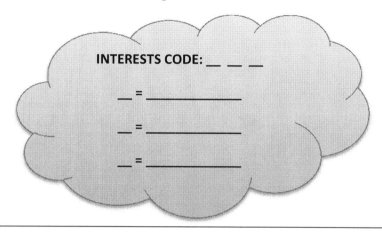

INTERESTS CODE: __ __ __

__ = _____

__ = _____

__ = _____

What Has MEANING for You? Your Values

In the figure below, note your *Top Five Values*. Add any others that are in the "Very Important" category for you.

My Top Five Values

1._____

2._____

3._____

4._____

5._____

What Can You DO? Your Bank of Skills

In the figure below, write your *Top Five Skills of Choice.*

My Top Five Skills of Choice

1. _____
2. _____
3. _____
4. _____
5. _____

What Are Your Positive Personal TRAITS?

In the figure below, write your *Top Three Positive Personal Traits.*

My Top Three Positive Traits

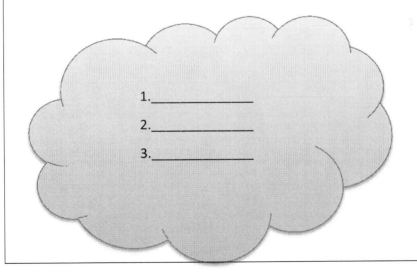

1. _____
2. _____
3. _____

Your SELF Statement

Now it is time to bring all of these elements of your SELF together into a single *SELF Statement*. This statement will become your guide for the chapters ahead, and for your future life.

Keep this statement close by to guide the actions you take next in *Step #5: Make Your Match & Move.*

My SELF Statement

In the blanks below, fill in the blanks in this order:

1. Your Type
2. Your Temperament
3. Your Compulsion
4. Your Interests (3 categories)
5. Your Values (top 5)
6. Your Skills (top 5)
7. Your Positive Personal Traits (top 3)

See the sample *Self Statement* below as a model.

Sample Self Statement

I am a Mastermind, a Thinker with a compulsion to Improve. I am engaged by pursuits that are Investigative, Creative and Enterprising.

For a pursuit to have meaning for me, it needs to satisfy my values of: Creativity, Intellectual Stimulation, Achievement, Way of Life, and Variety.

I am skilled at: Researching, Systematizing, Designing, Writing, and Speaking. My positive personal traits are that I am: Insightful, Communicative and Empowering.

SELF Statement

I am a _____(1)_____, a/an _____(2)_____
with a compulsion to _____(3)_____

I am engaged by pursuits that are
_____(4)_____, _____, and

_____

For a pursuit to have meaning for me, it needs
to satisfy my values of: _____(5)_____,
_____, _____, _____, and

_____

I am skilled at: _____(6)_____, _____,
_____, _____, and _____

My positive personal traits are that I am:
_____(7)_____, _____, _____

And So...

Where does all this leave you, and what needs to happen next? You now have looked at your SELF and have attempted to see yourself more clearly in terms of what you may be uniquely and even passionately ready and able to do next. And you have formulated a profile that combines what you are *like* with your own particular *interests, values, skills* and *traits.*

All this time that you have invested to take a new look at your SELF and your WORK will repay you repeatedly with the gift of the rest of your life well spent. Your recent introspective work now positions you to move happily into your next phase, armed with purpose, focus, and valuable self-knowledge.

The self-exploration, self-reinvention and rediscovery you have undertaken so far have been challenging. Moving to the final step in the *5-Step Process* will add another layer of complexity, as you hold in the balance all that you have determined so far, and then look at how and where all of it will best fit.

Your next all-essential task is to align your reinvented SELF and your rediscovered WORK with actual possibilities for your retirement career. Read on to work through the next critical *Step #5* of the process toward your own best new retirement—*Make Your Match & Move.*

CHAPTER 8
Step #5: Make Your Match & Move

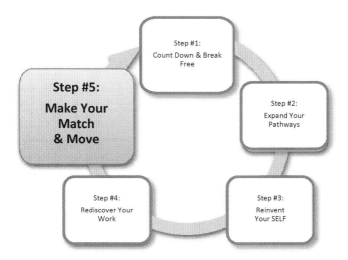

As delightful as it has been to think about potential pathways for your retirement, and then to reinvent your SELF and your WORK, the time eventually does come to take action. Many things are possible. With various barriers now removed, the questions are "What do you want to do now?" and "Who needs what you have to offer?" Then it will be time to make a match and make your move.

To quote Pogo, you are "surrounded by insurmountable opportunity." And from this mound of possibilities, it will be your task to pick a direction, then announce it to the world, and set off into your new life work—or into a new form of your old one. So which of the many things you *could* do, do you *want* to do next?

Up to this point we have focused on the "big picture" and on self-reflection. The active process of weeding out, narrowing down, and then taking action, will be the focus of this chapter, beginning with these six actions:

1. Define your "I Woulds" and "I Would Nots."
2. Create your Expanded List of Job Titles—your "I Coulds."
3. Write your own *Job Description*.
4. Develop your *Break Free Résumé*.
5. Create your new *Business Card*.
6. Announce your new work title to your *Intentional Network*.

The five chapters to follow later in Section III will define, clarify, and guide you through each of five major retirement work options:

1. Work in Cyberspace
2. Work "Out There"
3. Hire Yourself or Partner Up
4. Work for "Us"
5. Work for Free, but *Your* Way

Action #1: Define Your *Terms of Engagement*

The first step is to define what future work *would* or *would not* engage and excite you. Think in general terms. I *would* like to create and learn. I *would* like my work to be intellectually stimulating and to have variety. I *would not* like my work to be repetitive or routine.

You already have uncovered the major clues you need to arrive at your own *Terms of Engagement* by looking back at your *SELF Statement* from Chapter 7. *Would* you want to work with people? If so, what people? The public? Children? Seniors? Or NOT? *Would* your work be with animals—or plants—or nature? *Would* you want to do creative work? Investigative work? Organizational work? *Would* you want to be in charge of people? *Would* you want to work independently?

There is no need to limit yourself to what you have done in your career so far, or even to what you already are good at doing. For now focus on what you are *enthusiastic* about doing, with your type and temperament, your interests and values, and your favorite skills and traits. Consider the *expanded* version of your SELF—including what you would like to learn as well as what you already know. Last, but certainly not least, base your choices on what you *value*, as well as on what you have to offer.

My Terms of Engagement: I Would's & I Would Not's	
INSTRUCTIONS: Review and consider your *SELF Statement*, and any other thoughts you have. What do you see clearly now about what you *would* and what you *would not* want to do next?	
I WOULD's	**I WOULD NOT's**

Action #2: Identify, Then EXPAND, Your I Could's

With your I would's and I would not's firmly in mind, shift your focus to what specifically you *could* do next. One or two thoughts may immediately come to mind. But why stop there? As part of shifting gears to your retirement work, make it a point to expand your horizons to include new skills and abilities, or to reengage skills you set aside in the past, for one reason or another. Then repackage yourself in this "new and improved" version.

Use action verbs when you speak about yourself, not categorical nouns. For example, say, "I *could* write," not "I am a writer." I *could* build garden benches," not "I am a woodworker."

The point is to focus on *actions* in which you will engage, not on the "box" into which you will squeeze yourself. What *could* you actually *do* next? "I *could* care for shut-ins," or "I *could* create stained glass," or even "I *could* pilot a water taxi" or "I *could* lead culinary tours through France."

Learn the Job Titles for What You *Could* Do

In the past, when you accepted each of your jobs, you knew what the *name* of the job was—the job title. You also had a job description that told you what tasks and duties you would carry out—what you would actually be *doing* on a daily, weekly and monthly basis. You were directed by the "wizard" behind the curtain.

Now that you are in self-defining mode, you ARE the wizard. YOU are the one who will create your own job titles. Later you will be the one to write your own job descriptions for these job titles.

This all may sound daunting. Or it may be intriguing. Either way, these tasks certainly will involve some challenges, given the combination of major changes in your personal and professional life, as well as in the nature of work and the workplace.

But the time you devote to exploring the job titles for the work you *could* do will be time well spent. To consider a future of doing a particular type of work, you will need to know what those jobs are actually called.

For example, *could* you be a Photogrammetrist? And if you were one, what would you actually *do*? Would this be a type of work that would engage and excite you? Before you can answer these questions, you first need to know what a "Photogrammetrist" is.

Good News—You Have the Resources to Find Out

Thanks to the Internet, you have the resources you need to research any and all job title questions quickly. Treat this process like a treasure hunt and expect to find gold.

As a start, learn to use *The Occupational Outlook Handbook* website at *http://www.bls.gov/ooh/*, published by the U.S. Department of Labor's *Bureau of Labor Statistics*, and described as "the Nation's premier source for career information." This site lists over *5000* job titles, indexed A to Z, with a link to a webpage that provides detailed information for each job title, including:

- the purpose of the work;
- what you would be doing if you did this work;
- what the work environment would be like;
- how you would prepare yourself to do this work;
- what the work pays;
- the 2010-2020 employment outlook for this work.

Bookmark the *bls.gov* website now so that you can return to it again and again throughout your search.

Get Ready to Surprise Yourself

This is where all of your efforts so far will begin to pay off. Working backwards from your SELF Statement, begin to consider sample job titles and whether you *could* do the work each job entails. These four sample questions will help get you started.

1. *Are you excellent at gathering information and data, then providing accurate written answers to questions?* You may be a natural as a...

Correspondence clerk

As a correspondence clerk you would review and respond to inquiries from the public, other businesses, or other departments in order to give accurate answers to questions and requests. You would gather information and data, then write letters or emails in reply to requests for merchandise, damage claims, credit and other information, delinquent accounts, incorrect billings, or unsatisfactory services.

2. *Are you patient, positive, and proficient in reading, writing, and spoken English?* You may find fulfillment and earn an income as an...

ABE teacher (Adult Basic Education)

As an ABE teacher you would:

- Evaluate students' strengths and weaknesses and work individually with each student to overcome weaknesses;
- Plan and teach lessons to help students meet their goals, such as mastering spoken and written English or earning their GED;
- Monitor students' progress toward their goals;
- Emphasize skills that will help students find jobs;
- Help students develop effective study skills.

3. *Do you know how to do something others may want to learn for fun or self-improvement... music, foreign languages, sketching, wood carving, Web searching, public speaking?* You may enjoy working as a...

Self-enrichment teacher

Self-enrichment teachers instruct in a variety of subjects that students take for fun or self-improvement, such as music, cooking, art and foreign languages. These classes are entirely voluntary, and generally do not lead to a degree or certification, but provide participants with personal enjoyment and professional growth.

Some self-enrichment teachers offer instruction in computer programming, computer software use, public speaking, and other subjects that help workers gain marketable skills in order to make themselves more attractive to prospective employers.

Employment for self-enrichment teachers is expected to grow by 21% from 2010 to 2020. This growth rate is faster than the average growth for education, training and library occupations (15%), and also more than the projected total growth for all occupations (14%). Growth in demand is expected to continue as increasing numbers of adults and children seek new hobbies, pastimes, and skills.

4. *Do you love working with shrubs and trees and are you artful at shaping them and improving their appearance and health?* Maybe you have a future as an...

Arborist

Arborists, cut away dead or excess branches from trees or shrubs to clear roads, sidewalks and pathways, striving to improve the appearance and health of trees and plants. Some arborists specialize in diagnosing and treating tree diseases. Others specialize in pruning, trimming, and shaping ornamental trees and shrubs.

Think Beyond What You Can Do Already

As you explore the treasure trove of job titles on the *bls.gov* website, give yourself permission to be curious, daring, and maybe even a bit impractical. Be open to surprises. Think beyond what you already can do. Remember, you are not limited to skills that you currently possess. With so many readily available resources, online and at local colleges, you are within reach of learning whatever you need to be able to do, starting now.

Shift your thinking from "I don't know how to do that," to "I don't know how to do that YET." If there is something you need to learn to do, add it to your list of courses or lessons or workshops or programs or certifications you plan to pursue as you update yourself and prepare for what comes next. Augmenting your arsenal of skills and talents is a necessary part of the redefining process. And accomplishing this self-expansion will be exhilarating—even fun.

Could you be any of the following? Check all that may be worth looking into, and take the time to learn more about what they do.

- Aesthetician
- Animal Care Worker
- Recreation Worker
- Greens Keeper
- Arson Investigator
- Asset Property Manager
- Association Planner
- Audio-Visual Production Specialist
- Autism Tutor
- Meeting, Convention and Event Planner
- Archivist
- Museum Technician

To return to an earlier question, what skills would you need to add to your current arsenal to become a Photogrammetrist?

Photogrammetrist

As a Photogrammetrist you would use aerial photographs, satellite images, and light-imaging detection and ranging technology (LIDAR) to build 3-D models of the Earth's surface and features for purposes of creating maps. Also, you would collect and analyze spatial data such as latitude, longitude, elevation, and distance, and develop base maps.

Now What About You?

Take time now to complete your own personal *Expanded List of Job Titles*. Have fun with this activity. Engage your curiosity. Resist the temptation to be limited by any engrained ideas you may have.

My Expanded List of 10 Job Titles

INSTRUCTIONS: Your task is to use the *Bureau of Labor Statistics* website at *http://www.bls.gov/ooh/* to discover your choice of 10 job titles that sound interesting, and that you possibly could do if you were determined to do so.

Include on your list even those job titles for which you would need to do some additional preparation. Do not be overly concerned at this point about practicalities. Later you will have a chance to winnow down your list.

For each of these 10 job titles, scan the information on the *bls.gov* website, and copy/paste the key points into a WORD document, including:
- job purpose and duties,
- potential earnings,
- 10-year employment outlook.

You will return to use this critical information later to develop job descriptions for three of these job titles. Save and print your WORD file, then note your *Expanded List of Job Titles* below.

1.		2.	
3.		4.	
5.		6.	
7.		8.	
9.		10.	

Action #3: Write Your Own Job Description

Your next task is to write job descriptions for three of the job titles you included on your *Expanded List of 10 Job Titles*. So...where to begin? As a model, here is a brief job description for the job title: *Fitness Trainer*.

The details for this came from the Bureau of Labor Statistics website: (*bls.gov*). Locate and bookmark this site. We will be using it throughout this and future chapters.

Model Job Description: Fitness Trainer

PURPOSE: Fitness trainers are passionate about health, wellness and exercise, and use their skills to help motivate others to reach their fitness and weight goals. The purpose of this job is to work with people from many different backgrounds and skill levels, from professional athletes to elderly people, helping them to improve their health through exercise and nutrition.

MAJOR DUTIES AND RESPONSIBILITIES:
- Demonstrate various exercises and routines.
- Watch clients complete exercises and demonstrate correct techniques to minimize injury and improve fitness.
- Design alternative exercises during workouts or classes for different levels of fitness and skill.
- Monitor clients' progress and adapt programs as needed.
- Explain and enforce safety rules and regulations on sports, recreational activities, and the use of exercise equipment.
- Give clients information or resources about nutrition, weight control, and lifestyle issues.

QUALIFICATIONS:
- *Certifications*: CPR Certification required. Also recommended is ACE Certification (from the *American Council on Exercise*: *http://www.acefitness.org/*).
- *Customer-Service & Motivational Skills:* Known ability to motivate and encourage clients while remaining friendly.
- *Listening Skills:* Ability to listen carefully to clients to determine their fitness levels and desired fitness goals.

- *Personal Physical Fitness:* Ability to serve as role model by being physically fit personally, as well as able to participate in classes and demonstrate exercises to clients.
- *Problem-solving Skills:* Ability to evaluate each client's level of fitness and create an appropriate fitness plan to meet his or her individual needs, while maintaining safety.
- *Speaking and Communication Skills:* Ability to explain exercises to clients, as well as to motivate them verbally.

Now What About You?

Look back at your *Expanded List of 10 Titles* now, and select the top three for which you will create job descriptions. Use the material you collected earlier as a basis for each of your three job descriptions.

To supplement the material you already have gathered, do Google searches using each job title, along with other search terms such as "job description" and "certification." For example, for *Fitness Trainer*, two highly useful Google searches are: "*Fitness Trainer Job Description*" and "*Fitness Trainer Certification.*"

This activity may seem like work, but it will pay off significantly by expanding your list of "I coulds" and possibly leading you in a new and surprising direction.

My Top Three Job Descriptions

INSTRUCTIONS: Your task is to use material from the *Bureau of Labor Statistics* (*www.bls.gov*) site to write a brief job description for each of the *Top Three Jobs* you select from your *Expanded List of 10 Job Titles*.

After you develop these full job descriptions in WORD, record for each of them below:

1. the job title,
2. a brief summary of what you would do in that job,
3. a note about what you would need to learn before being ready to do that job, and
4. the pros and cons of considering this work for your next career.

Job Title #1: _____

What I Would Do:

What I Would Need to Learn:

Pros and Cons:

Job Title #2: _____

What I Would Do:

What I Would Need to Learn:

Pros and Cons:

Job Title #3: _____

What I Would Do:

What I Would Need to Learn:

Pros and Cons:

Action #4: Build Your *"Breakfree" Résumé*

The next action in the process of matching up your "re-invented" self is to repurpose your *Breakfree Résumé* as part of a major paradigm shift in terms of how and where you present yourself. "Build it and they will come." But *what* will you build? And *where* will you fit once you have built it?

Developing a new résumé for yourself may sound difficult. Résumés have a tendency to become "cast in stone." After all, you already have a résumé—one that you have used successfully and repeatedly over the course of many years. And it has always served you well. True. But that was then. And this is now.

Yes, I know that your standard résumé looks so nice—formatted and perfected, even impressive. And that you have extra copies of it, beautifully printed on ivory parchment paper. And that it represents your highest levels of experience—the domains of your greatest victories and accomplishments—the level of authority and responsibility you achieved through your many years of effort and diligence.

All true. But there's just one problem. The résumé you already HAVE is no longer the résumé that you NEED. Where it once was a vehicle carrying you forward, it now is an obstacle, blocking your way. By all means, keep a copy of your current résumé for old times' sake. Then get to work developing your *Break-free Résumé*.

This all new résumé has a different purpose. It will be the guide and the measure that ensures that you have a clear concept of who you are going to "be" and what you are going to "do" moving forward.

Who is this "new you" you will describe at that next cocktail party or alumni gathering or neighborhood picnic? When you open your mouth to say "I was a _____, and now I am a _____," what words will you use to fill in those blanks?

Write Three "Fantasy" Break-free Résumés

Your task goes beyond writing a single résumé. While you are at it, write *three*—one for each of the three job descriptions you developed for Action #3. Since these are "fantasy" résumés, and so will be refined and moderated later, include your *future* skills and experiences as well as your past ones.

Customize each résumé to one of the three job descriptions, noting those skills, strengths and experiences (current and future) that would make you an excellent candidate and hiring choice for that particular type of job.

To develop these three résumés quickly and effectively, start out with one of the Functional Résumé templates available for free as part of MS WORD. With these templates to provide the format, all you will need to do is to add the *words*.

162

For an excellent selection of résumé templates to download for free, go to:

> *http://office.microsoft.com/en-us/templates/*

Click on "WORD," then on "Résumés." Take a moment now to consult this site and pick the template you will use.

Where Will You Get the Words?

So where will you get these words to add to your three résumés? If your response is "I'll just make up the words," then pause and think again. Invented words will make you sound inexperienced and uninformed. There is no need to take the risk of using the wrong words when you have such ready access to the right ones.

Begin by reviewing what you learned on the *Bureau of Labor Statistics* site *(www.bls.gov/ooh/)*, combined with your additional Google searches. If there are any words or terms you do not understand YET, look them up, then master their meanings.

Once you remove the mystery, and acquire an understanding of any tasks and terms that at first may seem foreign to you, you will find that many of these tasks will be transformed from seemingly out of reach into activities you know you already can do. Others will be translated into tasks you could readily learn to do with some additional study and training. Equally important, some of these tasks may be ones that you would enjoy doing—that you would find engaging and fulfilling—once you actually know what they *are*.

Now locate related model résumés for each of your three top job descriptions. A key resource for model résumés is the *Job Bank USA* website at:

> http://www.jobbankusa.com/resumes/free_samples/
> resume_samples_index.html
> [NOTE: Scroll down past the ad links to see the full list.]

For additional résumé samples to fit your three job descriptions, do Google searches that combine the job title and the word "résumé." As an example, for the "Fitness Trainer" job title, try a Google search for "Fitness Trainer Résumé."

Take the time now to locate useful samples for each of the three résumés you will be developing. Print out any relevant samples and use them to stimulate your thinking.

Now, making sure that you use the appropriate lingo, and using these model résumés to guide you, begin to "translate" between your own skills, experiences, capabilities and talents (past, present and future), and the tasks and requirements for each of these job titles.

This translation process will require some thought and will have a puzzle-like quality to it. Have you sold insurance or real estate or shoes? If so, then you know how to "describe, differentiate and market products," and you are skilled at "anticipating, hearing and responding to customer needs." With a few added skills, you could even "manage and update an online store that promotes and sells products to a niche market."

Have you made presentations at conferences, or taught in a classroom, or written training materials, instructions, or reports? If so, you clearly could translate your skills into developing "webinars" or training videos or even interactive online training, using a Wacom and Skype.

Throughout this translation process, enlist your ability to think divergently. You are by no means limited here by what you *were*. Include your *all*, the *expanded* version of your SELF, including all those skills and abilities you have renourished, and even those that you have or are planning to add.

Focus on Function, Not History

For your *Break-free Résumés,* use the *Functional Résumé* format you downloaded earlier from the résumé template site. The *Functional Résumé* format is a better choice for you now than the *Chronological Résumé* format. A *Functional Résumé* format focuses on what you have done and can do, rather than on the sequence and duties of your past jobs. It focuses on *you,* not on your past employers and job descriptions.

Even more importantly, using this résumé format, you will be able to highlight your relevant skills, such as problem solving, communication, or motivating people, that translate to the job titles and descriptions you may hope to pursue next.

To create a *Functional Résumé*, start by taking a sheet of paper and brainstorming everything relevant you have ever proven yourself able to do, at work or elsewhere. Include work you have done for yourself or for your family or friends, for school or during a training class or tutorial, and as a volunteer. Think of everything. What can you do? Who have you helped? What have you studied or read about in depth? It may work best to have a friend or partner help you with this brainstorming process.

Once you have brainstormed and noted everything you can think of, then think again, this time more divergently. Have you done online research? Have you pulled that research together into a clear written format? Or used it to create an action plan or budget? Or to produce a PowerPoint presentation?

Have you provided customer service and worked through "client" problems with either external or internal clients, family or friends? Have you engaged in finding solutions or resolutions to ensure repeat business? Have you offered counseling or advice? Or planned a new project with new clients or colleagues? Or with fellow members of the PTA? Have you answered questions, or provided guidance about how to perform a task...or how to perform it better?

What uses have you made of technology? Have you tracked and managed expenses using Excel? Posted communications using social media? Created, cropped, edited and uploaded photos or videos to Facebook? Have you maintained an active e-mail correspondence? Planned and scheduled a project or event? Researched and set up a trip using online resources?

Don't be shy. Own your capabilities—all of them!

Generate Bullets, Lots of Them

When you have generated a page filled with your brainstorm of everything you have proven yourself able to do, your next task is to turn these capabilities and accomplishments into bullet points. Focus on the activities and skills that directly address the essence of the particular job or work description for which each of your new résumés will be used. Choose *action* words for each bullet point.

Since these are your "fantasy" résumés, allow yourself to go wild. For now the task is to invent—to craft—to think beyond your life and work so far. Later you will have a chance to refine your résumés and tone them down, if need be, before you actually submit them.

Sample Bullet Points for "Fitness Trainer" Résumé

- Provided one-on-one guidance to clients, helping them to achieve their fitness goals.

- Measured and assessed blood pressures, heart recovery rates, and body fat ratios.

- Designed and advised on dietary programs.

- Provided personal training sessions to private clients in their home or work settings.

- Maintained gym equipment and ensured its safety.

- Explained to clients the results they could expect from particular exercise regimes.

Think broadly. If you have not actually performed some of these functions YET as part of your past work, have you performed other functions that are related? Or have you carried out these types of tasks outside of work, for your family or friends? Or for yourself?

After you have noted and acknowledged everything you have already done, look back at your models from the résumé site to identify the types of skills and tasks that are not on your bullet list *yet*.

Considering these missing but essential items, are there any that you could accomplish? How soon could you do this? How could you study or do research to fill any gaps, or otherwise develop these needed additional skills? What outside resources could you call upon to become qualified?

Brainstorm how you could develop these skills "immediately or sooner." Then add them to your bullet list as though you have already done them. In other words, get to work immediately to make these statements true!

For example, as a future *Fitness Trainer*, you may wish you had more expertise about nutrition and weight management, or about how to incorporate results-oriented exercise techniques, or how, specifically, to work with older adults.

You can achieve all these learning goals by taking advantage of relevant continuing education classes such as those offered by *The American Council on Exercise* (*http://www.acefitness.org*). You could start adding to your knowledge and skill base today.

Your goal here is to list as many *powerful* bullets as you can, including skills you plan to add. Emphasize those accomplishments that are most relevant to the current position.

This will provide substantive evidence, current and future, to prove that you are capable of doing this particular type of work. And it will generate for you a critical learning list so you can get started immediately filling in any gaps.

Sort Your Bullet Points into Categories

Next sort and organize these bullet points into broad categories, using two or three subsection headings. Organization. Supervision. Writing. Customer Relations. Design. Troubleshooting. Management. Quality Control.

As you are creating categories, this may stimulate you to recall additional bullet points that will round out each category. Good. Add more points as you think of them. Include points from all venues of activity in which you have accomplished tasks and projects. If you saved money, increased effectiveness, wrote a winning proposal, solved a problem, added customers or improved relations with existing ones, integrated technology, trained staff, presented a workshop, created an instruction manual... this is the time to say so.

And make sure to include at least one category that pertains to the work you want to do next. If you discover that an essential category that pertains to the work you would like to do in your retirement is missing, add it now. Then generate bullet points to *show* what you have done in that category.

Now Add Your Work History & Education

Once you have generated your bullets, and sorted them into subsections, add to your résumé a list of your past jobs, in reverse chronological order. Then add your education background, training and credentials, again in reverse order.

But keep this section brief. Have mercy on potential employers. They will not want to read more than two pages, at most.

Be Your Own Matchmaker as You Write

As you write your *Break-free Résumé*, think like a matchmaker. Your résumé is NOT your autobiography. In the past, you may have had the idea that your résumé is all about *you*. But for a résumé to be effective now, the focus needs to be more about THEM—those employers or clients who will benefit from your efforts.

Present yourself in the very best light to attract a good job "match." Make this new résumé as vital and communicative as if you were applying to *The Dating Game*.

Throughout this process, practice the five "Be"s:

- Be the one who knows;
- Be the one who can;
- Be the one who will;
- Be the one they need;
- Be all that you are—the *full you*.

Put yourself into the mindset of those people who *need* you to work for them—to assist them—to guide them—to create for them. Your résumé needs to answer for them the question: "How well would this person match up with what I need to have done?"

Creating an excellent résumé is hard work. You may be tempted to rush through it to get it *over with*. DON'T! Think of it this way. *Your Break-free Résumé* will, hopefully, make you money, now and far into the future. Whatever time you spend will be time well spent.

WOW FACTOR

If you spend three hours to develop a 400 word Break-free Résumé that gains you $40,000 a year in work, over the course of 10 years this will add up to $400,000.

That is the equivalent to being paid over $133,000 an hour, or $1000 per word! You will NEVER earn more per hour or per word than you will writing an excellent résumé.

After you complete the first of your *Break-free Résumés,* keep your momentum going and develop your other two, each targeted to a specific job description. As a "career changer," it is absolutely essential that you have more than one résumé to use as needed—one for each area you may engage in next.

There will be commonalities among your three résumés, so the second and third will likely come together much more quickly than the first.

Completing your three résumés is an accomplishment in itself, but also an ongoing process. Every time you add additional work experience, or study and learn something new, update your résumés with additional bullet points, or even insert a whole new category of bullets. Your résumés are as much dynamic "works in progress" as you are!

It's Fine to Seek and Enlist Help

If you find the task of writing your own résumé to be overly stressful, consider enlisting your partner or a friend to help. An added, unexpected perk to soliciting input—he/she may reveal to you surprising strengths, skills and talents you took for granted, underestimated, or about which you were completely unaware. And it will probably be only a matter of time before you find yourself returning the favor.

Another option is to engage a résumé service, preferably one that is Boomer-friendly, with experience creating *Break Free Résumés. Super Writing Services (www.SuperWritingServices.com)* is one such service. This service will assign you your own "Personal Writer" who will assist you as much or as little as you want or need—with brainstorming, bullets, words, format and variations. Or your personal writer will write the whole thing, if you prefer, consulting you for specifics.

Final Versions of Your *Break Free Résumés*

With your three "fantasy" résumés in hand, now it is time to refine, print, and distribute them. Even now, try to retain some of the sense of freedom you felt when developing your fantasy résumés.

Your new résumés hopefully will be VERY different from the one that brought you (and kept you) where you are today. As you finalize your *Break Free Résumés,* follow these do's and don'ts.

DO...

- Choose a professional template that is uncluttered and understated, so that form will not distract from function and content.
- Write a brief summary paragraph of 3-5 specific qualifications that strongly match you to your hoped-for job title. Place this at the top of your résumé where you once would have included an "objective."
- Include relevant contact information to enable potential clients and/or employers to reach you, such as phone number and e-mail address.
- Use headings and subheadings, bullets, and overall formatting, to present a clean, modern, readable, document.
- Focus on your skills, accomplishments and results that directly address the job description of interest.
- Give specific examples of how your experience can positively make a difference in the job title of interest.
- Follow the adage—"less is more."
- Use politically correct and current professional terminology, as well as flawless grammar and spelling.
- Be ready to upload a digital version of your résumé online, either as a WORD or a PDF file. As well as making your résumé more immediately available, this will provide evidence of your technical savvy. [NOTE: If you don't know how to do this, have someone teach you ASAP.]

DO NOT...

- Give in to the temptation to just recycle a revised version of your standard résumé from the past.
- List personal interests, activities, hobbies, unless they are directly applicable to a specific position.
- Use slang, abbreviations or colloquial, trendy, or cliché language.
- Include irrelevant personal information.
- Use an ornate or distracting template, multiple fancy fonts, or elaborate paper.

- Underestimate the absolute importance of correct spelling and grammar.

Action #5: Create Your New Promotionals

Next, create your new business card. Then create your choice of additional promotionals—brochures, postcard notifications, flyers, websites, video segments. The idea here is to get prepared to announce yourself when you embark on your retirement career.

Creating a card can be one of the fun parts of this entire process. Use VistaPrint (*http://www.vistaprint.com*) to speed this along. Under the "Business Cards" category, select either "Premium" or "Personal," then select a template. This will enable you to design your own unique and professional looking product, quickly and painlessly.

Once you have designed your business card, preview it carefully. Check that all information is accurate, and that the card presents you in the exact way that you wish. Double check to make sure that ALL grammar and spelling are 100% perfect. What you DO NOT need is 1000 copies of a business card with spelling errors!

Then click "Pay" and place your order. Your new cards will be at your doorstep within a week, at which point you can begin distributing them. Developing your new business card is one essential action that you will be able to check off your list almost instantly.

Developing your promotionals is equally doable using VistaPrint. Select the type of item you wish to design—brochure, flyer, postcard, car magnet—then choose a template. Fill in the blanks. Preview and approve. Check out. And your materials will be on their way.

If you design a postcard announcement, VistaPrint even will mail out your postcards for you to a targeted mailing list you have selected according to the demographics, household make-up, income, and location most appropriate to your market. You will receive a copy of all the addresses on the customized mailing list for reuse at a later date. Keep this list, and plan a series of "campaigns" through which you will present yourself and what you have to offer and reach those who are most likely to be interested.

Also, explore Google Adwords (*adwords.google.com*) as an option for advertising yourself and your services, and helping you connect with those who are looking for you. This form of advertising can be controlled by assigning a budget, limiting the geography where your ads will be shown, and otherwise tailoring your ad campaigns to suit your needs and designs. Unlike print, TV or radio advertising, with Google Adwords you pay ONLY if an interested potential client clicks on your ad to find out more.

Action #6: Announce Your New SELF and Job Title

Have business cards, will travel... So who needs to know about your new career and what you have to offer? And where will you go to find these potential clients? Start with three major frontiers:

1. Your current and expanded *Virtual Network*

2. Your current and expanded *Physical Network*

3. Your new and emerging *Invited Network*

New Worlds: Your *Virtual Network*

For starters, if you have not already done so, it is time to for you to become a member of LinkedIn. LinkedIn is the place to network professionally with those you know, as well as with "those they know." Go to *http://www.linkedin.com* and register. Then post your professional profile, including a current résumé, and begin to connect with old and new colleagues. This site is the "Facebook for Professionals."

And speaking of Facebook... Remember to "Update your Status" on Facebook as you venture out into your new retirement career. Also revise your profile. And if you create a website to promote your new enterprise, send a note to your Facebook friends asking them to visit your site and "Like it."

Additional websites you might find helpful in marketing your newly created self and skills will be discussed at length in Chapter 9. For now, focus on establishing and communicating with your own *Intentional Online Network*.

Old Worlds: Your *Physical Network*

What other networking options can provide you with powerful, effective ways to market your new creative abilities and skills? Do not underestimate the many traditional opportunities available to "get the news out" about your new career path.

Join as many local, civic and social groups as your time and energy allow. Advertise in free brochures and community newsletters. Post your business card, descriptive brochure or flyer on public bulletin boards in markets, colleges, and other business establishments. Offer to teach a community or adult education course. Sign up to be a guest presenter or speaker on your local cable channel or for the many clubs and civic organizations within your community.

And don't be shy about notifying members of your immediate and extended family about your new career direction. Undoubtedly, they will "know somebody who knows somebody" who can help you launch your new career path energetically and effectively.

Your Invited Network

Next, think of the *network* of professional colleagues and other associates you acquired along the way, but with whom you since may have lost touch. Reflect back on every job or position you held throughout Stage II. You will easily be able to construct a significant scaffolding of people connections, some of whom will be worth the effort to relocate and reestablish as colleagues and associates. And, thanks to current technologies (Facebook, LinkedIn, Plaxo, Twitter, Blogs, Google search, YouTube) it is easier than ever to reconnect with this network and even see what they have been up to!

Now What About You?

Start your *Intentional Network List* now, and add to it as you start moving ahead into your engaging and fulfilling "new" retirement. Reflect back on your Stage II employment, but also think beyond employment to all those others with whom you have associated— classmates with whom you collaborated on significant projects, fellow community or school or church or organization members with whom you shared creative, organizational or leadership tasks.

Consider which of your past contacts may continue to hold positive promise for you. Remember any projects you worked on with them, especially those where you enjoyed working together and where the two of you seemed to complement each other well. As you rethink the individuals on your list, think beyond the confines of the actual work, school, or organization in which you knew them. Break them out of their "boxes"! They represent more than what you knew them to be "back then." They are more multidimensional, more multi-talented, and certainly more connected now.

Imagine the multifaceted web of experiences and contacts they, too, have woven over the past 25+ years. And if they are fellow Boomers, they probably are now engaged in a "reinvention" process similar to your own, and you may well find ways you can be of mutual benefit to each other.

Compile your "A List" of connections, including those from your deeper past. These will be the people with whom you will plan to stay connected or to reconnect—your *Intentional Network*." Using current technologies like Google, Facebook, and LinkedIn, begin now to track down and reconnect with former contacts with whom you have lost touch over the years. When you relocate this, your network of choice, learn where they are now, what they are doing, what they would like to be doing, and even what they may consider doing in partnership with you. Which of these could become potential contacts, partners, mentors, collaborators, or even clients? To assist you as you begin to consider and expand your own *Intentional Network*, review the completed sample provided below to serve as a model.

Model Intentional Network List

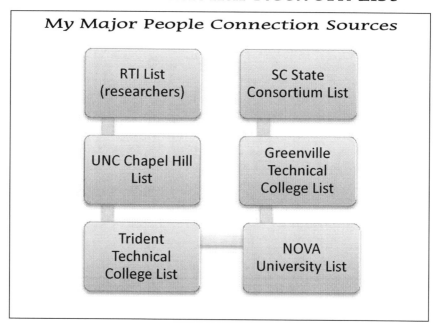

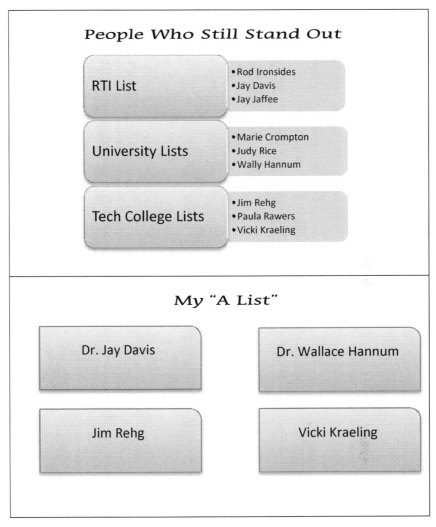

Using this sample as a model, take the time now to consider, cull, reconnect with and reengage your own *Intentional Network*. Follow these steps to complete this process:

1. Compile your scaffolding of people connection sources (work, school, community, family, extended family, friends).

2. List the people who still stand out in memory from each of these sources.

3. From this list, select those who may continue to hold positive promise for inclusion in your "Intentional Network"—your "A List."

4. Make notes as you reconnect.

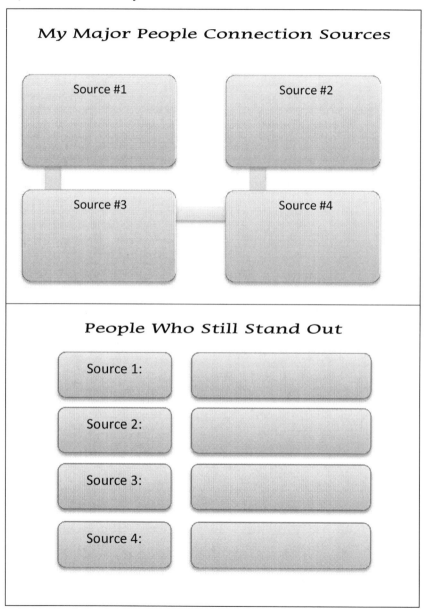

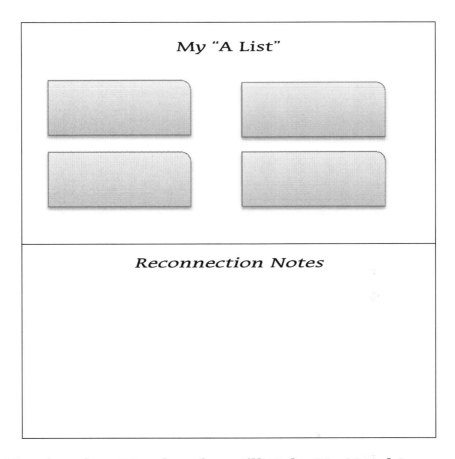

Matchmaker, Matchmaker, *I'll* Make My Match!

So what will it be? What out of all the possibilities will you do next? Look back at what you have discovered so far, and get ready to select your first match—one that fits you, engages you, excites you, and makes full use of your value.

To choose your first match, follow this process:

1. Read ahead into the next five chapters to explore five specific sets of options:

   - Option 1: Work in Cyberspace (Chapter 9)
   - Option 2: Work "Out There" (Chapter 10)
   - Option 3: Hire Yourself or Partner Up (Chapter 11)
   - Option 4: Work for "Us" (Chapter 12)
   - Option 5: Work for Free, but Your Way (Chapter 13)

2. Bring back from each of these options three specific actionable ideas and record them here. Even if you initially think one (or more) of these five options are not ones you would even consider, read about them anyway for any ideas that may be of use to you elsewhere.

3. When you have compiled your collection of options, narrow it down to the one that is your first choice, or combination of choices. Then set out to act on it fully. Later you may decide to consider additional quests.

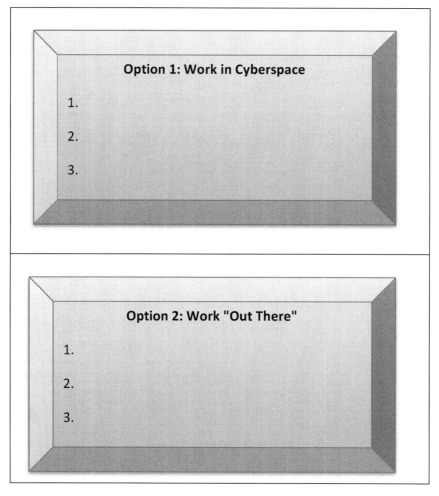

Option 1: Work in Cyberspace

1.

2.

3.

Option 2: Work "Out There"

1.

2.

3.

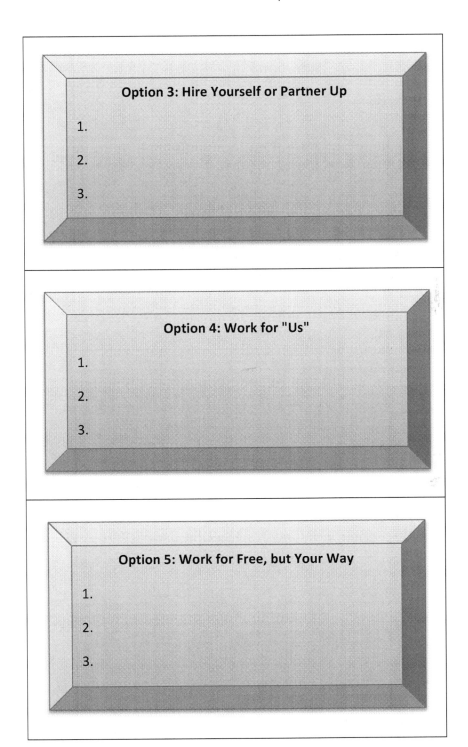

Option 3: Hire Yourself or Partner Up

1.

2.

3.

Option 4: Work for "Us"

1.

2.

3.

Option 5: Work for Free, but Your Way

1.

2.

3.

Your retirement can be, and probably will be, a work in progress. The direction you choose now may take you directly into a happy and engaging retirement life. Or you may need to return later to shift directions once again.

And So...

Yes, let's reiterate all the clichés..."Now is where the rubber meets the road'... "It's time to walk the talk"... "Put your money where your mouth is"... "Tether your nose to the grindstone"...

The bottom line—now is the time for you to act. But note the internal and external tools and resources you now have at your disposal to accomplish your tasks. And think about the sense of satisfaction and accomplishment you'll experience when you print out those three living proof résumés of the newly invented you.

Actually, your new adventure is just beginning. There is great fun in store as you re-discover all those virtual and physical network members, some of whom are destined to become members of your intentional and invited network.

Whether you realize it or not, you are on the cusp of weaving a fascinating web of past contacts, discovering where former colleagues are, how they arrived at that place, what they are doing now, their current "mojo.". Reconnecting with these past professional and personal 'significant others'—this endeavor alone will provide you with a labyrinth of surprises and realizations you could never have anticipated.

But first, there's work to be done! The résumés, the business cards, the marketing materials and strategies, the lists of networks! And the reading ahead into the Five New Retirement Options to bring back ideas before you select your first match.

Let the work begin!

SECTION III: FIVE "NEW RETIREMENT" OPTIONS

Option #1:
Work in Cyberspace

Option #2:
Work "Out There"

Option #3:
Work for Yourself
or Partner up

Option #4:
Work for "Us"

Option #5:
Work for Free,
but YOUR Way

CHAPTER 9:
Option #1: Work in Cyber Space

Where, oh, where have all the jobs gone? One answer: *online*. According to many sources, there has been a *structural change* in traditional employment, as more businesses have adopted online and "contingent" hiring as a core business strategy.

Businesses have developed innovative workforce models that blend full-time and part-time, local and online, permanent and contracted workers. The ability of businesses to gain instant access to qualified talent with in-demand skills, regardless of location, is a global trend that is starting to change the way businesses and people work.

Knowledge workers are building independent careers by working online, for one or multiple clients, from their home office, from public spaces, or from a co-located office (at home and on site combined).

WOW FACTOR

The online contract work segment is growing at twice the rate of the standard workforce. For one agency, monthly demand for online workers has surpassed supply by over 30%, leaving thousands of contract jobs unfilled.

Just as online shopping has transformed our patterns, habits and expectations as consumers, online employment has profoundly changed the landscape of employment and work. Savio Rosati, CEO of *ELance* (a major online hiring platform) summarizes these changes: "Fueled by technology, work is no longer confined to the 9-to-5 office environment."

Job Shortages or Worker Shortages?

While global economies have continued to struggle with job creation, online work has thrived, up more than 100% between 2010 and 2011. In 2012, the market for online contingent work doubled again, as increasing numbers of businesses across the globe hired and managed workers online.

According to the *Online Employment Situation Summary* issued by oDesk, the world's largest and fastest-growing online workplace (*www.oDesk.com*), more than 90% of US firms now use contract talent on a regular basis, and are spending $120 billion on this type of expertise each year. More than 350,000 businesses now use oDesk to find contractors, posting over 770,000 jobs in 75 job categories in the first half of 2012 alone.

Even during these recent years that have been marked by widespread concerns about unemployment, the *demand* for online employees has *exceeded* the supply. A reasonable conclusion is that the *quantity* of total jobs is sufficient, but that many of these jobs now have moved online.

For example, oDesk alone posted almost 400,000 jobs in the first quarter of 2012, but had fewer than 275,000 applicants, leaving over 125,000 jobs unfilled.

WOW FACTOR

Over 80% of small businesses surveyed by ELance (an online job matching platform) indicated that they plan to hire up to 50% of their workers as online contractors.

Job *Gains* Overseas

In addition to providing the connections that make possible plentiful online work opportunities in the US, online employment platforms also have broken down global barriers, and opened up opportunities for working abroad. In 2011, US-based contract workers exported their services to more than 140 countries.

This work trend is the opposite of the trend that has persisted over the past four decades, where American jobs were *lost* to workers overseas. Now, increasingly, Americans are *gaining* jobs from overseas, while working from home—online.

Training for the Online Workforce

In order to train the next generation of highly-skilled online workers, *oDesk* launched the industry's first international university program In November of 2011, enlisting colleges and universities around the world in the project. The new *oDesk University Program* includes seminars and an extended apprentice program through which students learn the essential skills to build a career online—skills that are key to success in today's global economy.

Many other sources of training for the online workforce are readily available—again, online. Locating courses, seminars, tutorials and materials to learn needed skills is barely more than a web search away, with many opportunities immediately accessible via webinar, online video, download or same-day shipment.

The Win-Win of Online Contract-Based Work

The extensive gains in market share by online contract-based employment agencies results, at least in part, from the win-win advantage these agencies offer both their business clients and their contract employees. The *oDesk* guarantee enumerates some of these mutual advantages, promising that…

As a contractor, you have a right to:

- Be paid for every hour worked—on time, every time;

- Work where you want, when you want;

- Set an hourly rate based on your skills, experience, and reputation;

- Have access to the tools you need to build your business online.

As a client, you have a right to:

- Benefit from a "results-only work environment";

- Audit and pay only for hours actually worked;

- Find the right person for the job, no matter where he/she lives;

- Build an online workforce, on demand, and on your own terms;

- Manage and pay a global team with ease.

The emerging workplace is one where the work is brought to the worker instead of the worker being brought to the work. Businesses gain from this the results they need, when they need them. Workers gain the considerable benefit of being able to work where and when they choose.

Gary Swart, CEO of *oDesk,* summarizes the transformation of the workplace, and the shift in expectations as follows:

> *"The Internet has catalyzed job creation across the board by eliminating geographic barriers—and not just in industries that deal with new technologies. Even in age-old professions such as legal work and writing, the Internet has brought growth to countless industries by creating opportunities that didn't exist before, that are unrestricted by geography. And the growth is staggering: from 2009 to 2012, hours worked on oDesk have grown 8 times.*
>
> *Everyone's talking about the rise of "telecommuting" and "virtual work" —all of which refer to leveraging the Internet to bring work to the worker, rather than the worker to the work. Today, it's about enabling the best minds to work together, regardless of where they happen to be. Technology makes this possible. And we predict increasing connectivity and Internet savvy is going to continue to fuel this employment revolution, with one in three workers hired to work online by 2020. Now that is what I call an employment revolution."*

Cost savings is one of the prominent benefits companies realize when hiring workers through outsourcing. These corporations and organizations also appreciate the greater flexibility derived by outsourcing tasks, as well as the ability to quickly scale their capacity to meet shifting demands.

Envisioning the Virtual Work World

To envision the virtual workplace, make a virtual visit to *oDesk.com* on a typical Thursday at 2:00 PM. You will find almost 7,000 workers connected to the oDesk work platform from all over the world. Even if you "stop by" on the following Saturday at 2:00 PM, you will find 4,000 workers at work online.

Or visit *ELance.com*, another of the major freelancer sites. Take time to explore worldwide trends and hiring patterns using the graphic of the world, with the multi-colored bar above it.

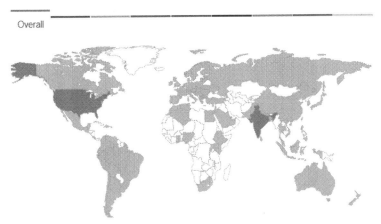

Each of the various colors on the bar represents a category of jobs. Hover your mouse over a color to see what category it represents. Select a category to explore, and you will see what countries around the world have contractors who work through *ELance* in that category.

Or hover your mouse over a specific country to learn how many contractors work for *ELance* from there. Below the interactive world map graphic are revealing charts and graphs that show totals for job postings and job earnings for that category in the past two years.

Try to imagine the actual composition of any particular work team, composed of workers from around the world. If you work online, you will become part of this vast collection of talent and effort.

SNAPSHOT

oDesk Contractor: Portsmouth, Rhode Island (Jun 2012)

"I have an online profile with the company where I am able to apply for the jobs that are posted on the site. I applied for 13 jobs over a three day period, and received two responses that resulted in my being hired for two-long term assignments.

One of the two employers that hired me had 24 applicants, and interviewed me and one other applicant. The other employer only had six applicants, as the position was highly specialized.

Why Work Online in Retirement?

Think about it. Online opportunities are *growing at twice the rate* of the standard workforce, and non-traditional contract workers are predicted to make up *more than 1/3 of the US workforce by 2020.* What better place could you consider for your own retirement work?

There are many possibilities for working online, with openings and possibilities that include, but are not limited to:

- ☐ Web Development
- ☐ Software Development
- ☐ Networking & Information Systems
- ☐ Writing & Translation
- ☐ Administrative Support
- ☐ Design & Multimedia
- ☐ Desktop Publishing
- ☐ Research
- ☐ Teaching
- ☐ Customer Service
- ☐ Sales & Marketing
- ☐ Business Services

Pause now to check off any of these online work areas that may be a potential match for you.

Three Major Advantages of Working Online

Whatever hesitations and trepidations you may have about working online, consider these advantages:

- Freedom of location
- Broader options for employment
- Fewer expenses, resulting in more take-home pay

Freedom of Location

Undoubtedly, accepting employment in the brick-and-mortar workplace confines your movements. Not so with online work that generally can be done from any location you choose—the mountains, the beach, or a condo on the coast of France, with a view of the Mediterranean.

The only essential need is to have access to a Wi-Fi hot spot. And in today's cyber world, access is ubiquitous. Today, in addition to the local library and coffee shop, many restaurants, and even fast-food establishments, offer free Wi-Fi, as do most major hotels and vacation rentals. Based on personal experience, I can even report that it is possible for you to work online via satellite from the middle of the Atlantic Ocean while cruising transatlantic to Europe.

Would you consider working online in order to free yourself? Have laptop, will travel! The new reality is that conducting business online now may be as simple as waking up in the morning wherever you happen to be at the moment, donning your shorts, T-shirt and flip flops, and heading out for breakfast at the nearest café.

If you are designing a retirement that combines several pathways—like perhaps work plus travel or work plus leisure or work plus study (possibly with the one providing funding for the other)—online work could be the answer to your question "How can I have my cake and eat it too?"

Broader Options for Employment

Another major reason for working online is to expand your options beyond your own geographical area. Locating work in your surrounding geographic area can be very limiting. You may even find that in order to expand your options to find a job "out there," you will be forced to factor in a move. These opportunity-versus-location constraints increase exponentially if you are married, and need to consider two sets of location and relocation needs in order that both partners have the opportunity to work at engaging jobs.

You may think that if you decide to work during retirement, you will be forced to make difficult choices and compromises, based on how far you are willing or able to drive to work every day. Even if you aspire to starting your own business, you may feel confined to offering something in your own town that hopefully will generate enough local traffic and commerce to become profitable.

If your options are limited near home, working online may be the answer that will expand your potential "workplace." By shortening your commute to a walk up the stairs or down the hall, you will widen your customer base to encompass the entire world! Talk about significantly increasing your target market!

When you work online, you can work where you want to work and live where you want to live. Yes, you *can* have the best of both worlds. If you wish, you can even live in multiple places over the course of the year, following "snow bird" or other migratory patterns. You could summer in Colorado and winter in Key West—while still working on the same projects, for the same employer and/or clients, year round.

Fewer Expenses Means More Take-Home Pay

Working online also results in more money in your pocket, and less money lost to expenses. While flexibility is appealing, increased profits can prove to be even more enticing.

According to the reported results of an online workers' survey, nearly 50% of online workers said they actually made more money working from home than if they had continued to commute to a traditional job. Of those who reported that they made more money working from home, 25% said they made *significantly* more money.

Looking purely at the math, and factoring in driving time, commute distance, dress codes, lunch and break expenses, and parking, a *$20/hour* in-town job can quickly shrink down to the equivalent of a *$12/hour* job working online from home.

Looking at the obverse—a *$20/hour* online job can translate to the take-home pay of a *$33/hour* job in town, while earning *$25/hour* online will put as much money in your pocket as earning *$42/hour* "out there."

How to Work Online in Retirement

Working online from home may sound ideal. But exactly where do you find your next job, client or commission? Where in the worldwide web do you GO to find the employers or customers who will want to pay you to do what you do best?

That is, without a doubt, the most common question raised by those who are thinking about hanging up those car keys, or cashing in those subway tokens, for a morning walk into the den. The Web is big. REALLY big! Finding a place to start when you do decide that, yes, you want to work online, can initially seem overwhelming. But there are ways to tame what may at first seem to be a vast and new frontier, fraught with unknowns.

So how *will* you and your potential employers find each other in the vastness of Cyberspace?" And when you do find each other, how will *they* know that *you* are the very one they need to hire? What evidence will *show* them that you will produce for them at the quality level that is essential to their reputation, while fostering the life and growth of their business?

Although the enormous size and anonymity of the Web may indeed seem intimidating to you at the outset, you actually will be able to make its vastness work *for* you, not *against* you.

Translate Your "To Do"s from "Out There" to Online

Start by thinking about how you searched for and found jobs in the past "out there" in the brick-and-mortar work world. Then plan how you will replicate what you did then, but this time do it "virtually."

Out there you would:

- Knock on doors
- Provide résumés that show your value to potential employers
- Look for tasks that need to be done and offer to do them
- Scan the classified ads
- Register with job placement agencies
- Network with business people who might "know someone who knows someone" with a potential need or opening

Online, the "doors" that you knock on will be websites. So, as with the agencies you would approach in town, you will need to keep track of the web addresses you visit online. Start a notebook, or even an Address Book, to record all your important addresses in one place, as you would if you were looking for work "out there."

In order to *provide résumés and show your value* to potential employers, you now will post those résumés online, electronically. And now, since your résumé can be easily adapted, you would do well to customize it, as well as the cover letter that accompanies it, so that it fits, hand-in-glove, the specific job you are addressing. Since these communications will be the only "face" potential employers will see, every word of every communication you send will need to be 100% perfect. If you are not confident in your own ability to express yourself in writing, enlist an editor to work with you to achieve the perfection required to make a good impression.

The equivalent of *looking for work that needs to be done and then offering to do it*, will be consulting online job boards, signing up with freelance sites, and doing web searches.

To *scan the classified ads* and *register with agencies*, you will be doing much the same as you would in the brick-and-mortar world, except that you will be doing these things online. The same is true for *networking with business people who may know someone who knows someone* to discover potential openings. Again you will be doing this online. Only now every contact you know, regardless of where they live, may potentially have a valuable lead for you.

These and other job-search activities will open up many possibilities beyond your local geographical area. Once you have made the translations from "out there" to online, create an action list for yourself, including, at a minimum, a virtual form of everything you would be doing if you were looking for work the old way. Then just get started, beginning with the links and resources provided later in this chapter.

This might be the time to think ahead and establish a user-friendly file that includes categories to record whatever data you might find useful in the future. Such a file or spreadsheet might include:

- Date

- Website name

- Web address

- Description of actions taken

- Response date

- Contact: Name, e-mail, phone

Consider the Three Ways to Work Online

As you get down to the business of finding online work, begin by considering these three primary ways to work and earn money online:

- **Employment:** *Find contract work through an agency;*

- **Self-Employment:** *Find your own clients and offer your services;*
- **Your Own Business:** *Set up an online business.*

You also may think in terms of combining two, or even all three, of these three primary ways to work online. If you elect to seek employment doing contract work online, you also may want to set up a business through which you do that contract work (think tax benefits). If you offer your services through self-employment, attempting to gain clients through your own enterprises, you also may seek out contracts that have already been posted through the online employment brokers. If you open a business online, you may combine the online element with a local off-line component.

Think "Work," Not "Job"

Consider some of the types of services that are always needed and are typical for online work. Each agency or employment service site has such a *Needed Services List*. These lists can be valuable as you make your plans.

For example, ClickNWork *(http://www.clicknwork.com)* is one outsourcing agency that enables experienced online professionals to deliver business services to companies worldwide. The job categories on the ClickNWork *"Always Needed Services List"* include:

- **Analysts/consultants**—with skills specific to an industry or trade.

- **Information professionals/specialists**—with strong track records and proficiency at a range of information sources (e.g., Factiva, Lexis Nexus, Profound).

- **Writers/editors**—experienced at high quality business, technical, marketing, or personal writing.

- **Web searchers**—proficient at quickly locating information on the web in answer to specific business questions.

- **Data entry specialists**—skilled at rapid and accurate data entry and reporting.

- **Shoppers, Trend spotters, Social observers**—adept at seeing trends, drawing parallels and generating valuable commercial insight.

- **Telephone interviewers**—skilled at conducting interviews to surface opinions, needs and/or preferences.

- **Photographers**—skilled at photographing buildings, real estate, stores, and products.

- **Translators**—able to translate accurately between languages commonly used for business.

Here's a sample of an actual online job listing seeking to hire a telecommuting contract worker.

Sample Job Post for Content Writer with Fitness Background

Work at home: TeleCommute. 20-40 hours per week.

We are looking for a candidate to write content for an online company selling nutritional supplements. This candidate should:

- Have a working knowledge of fitness and supplement practices.
- Be able to produce high quality content & maintain social network sites.
- Creativity is a MUST.

Job Requirements: The candidate will create content for new products and post blogs, Twitter and Facebook updates to help increase product awareness and boost page rankings. A broad knowledge of general fitness, popular supplements and their ingredients are needed, as well as the ability to transfer this understanding into quality online content.

Six Types of Places to Look for Online Work

So where do you start? Finding contract work online is something of a treasure hunt. Depending upon what you have to offer, your task will be to locate potential clients and or employers who need you, and then to demonstrate to them that you are the one they need. They are looking for you. You are looking for them. And the meeting ground for both of you is the Web.

So where exactly in the vastness of cyberspace do you "go" to seek out and find each other, then check each other out, and ultimately form a match? There are six common hunting grounds where the millions of online employment matches are made. Plan to explore all six types. Remember to record the URL addresses for sites you plan to use, in each of these categories:

1. Online Outsourcing, Employment and Staffing Services sites

2. Online options through the major sites for jobs "out there"

3. Online job boards

4. Online classifieds

5. Newsletters and newsgroups

6. Freelance networks

Work Source #1: Online Outsourcing, Employment & Staffing Services

There are many online agencies that focus on hiring online workers. These agencies fall into three main types:

- Online Outsourcing Services

- Online Employment Agencies

- Virtual Staffing Services

We will consider each of these types of agencies here, with examples and URLs for you to pursue.

Online Outsourcing Services

Outsourcing is the business practice of contracting out services that previously would have been performed by internal employees of an organization. The most common reasons why companies decide to outsource work include: cost savings; the ability to focus internal staff on its core business; access to a broader range of knowledge, talent and experience; and increased profits.

Online outsourcing service agencies recruit a network of workers with a variety of capabilities, and make optimum matches between these workers and a range of business and corporate accounts, based on the specific project work needed.

Then, on a project-by-project basis, the agency identifies from its network a list of people capable of completing each client request, accurately and reliably. These project assignments may be permanent, temporary, full-time, part-time or *ad hoc*.

Start with these eight Outsourcing Services. Add additional Outsourcing Services to this list by searching Google or another search engine using the search term: "outsourcing services."

Outsourcing Services	
oDesk *www.oDesk.com/*	**ClickNWork** *clicknwork.com/*
Prime Outsource *Prime-Outsource.com*	**VIP Desk** *VIPDesk.com*
AccounTemps *AccounTemps.com*	**Balance Your Books** *BalanceYourBooks.com*
ABGlobal Translations *abglobal.net/joining.htm*	**OutSource Your Books** *osyb.com*

Select three or more of these Outsourcing Services to explore now. Make hand-written (or copy/paste) notes about:

- categories of work assignments,
- requirements,
- the application/registration process.

Add these three resources to your notebook of URL addresses, plus any others you may want to use regularly. If you register for any of these services, record your login information in your notebook as well.

The importance of keeping accurate, correct notes during this process cannot be overestimated.

An Example: Working for an Outsourcing Service

As an example of what your experience would be working for an outsourcing service, we will explore here the specifics of *ClickNWork*, an outsourcing company that "partners with companies to see what work their online workforce can complete for them remotely."

ClickNWork recruits a network of workers with a variety of capabilities. Companies post project requests with *ClickNWork* for tasks that can be done remotely, such as:

- research
- report preparation
- data entry
- writing
- analysis
- customer service

Then, on a project-by-project basis, *ClickNWork* identifies from its network people capable of completing each specific client request. Assignments may be permanent, temporary, full-time, part-time or *ad hoc*. Sometimes clients require that people be in a particular country or time zone. Otherwise contractors complete the project work from a location of their choice. To become part of the *ClickNWork* network and be assigned project work, you first must pass rigorous tests and submit references as part of your background check. And all applicants must have a reliable broadband-connected PC and speak excellent English.

Experienced *ClickNWork* managers quality check all assigned work. If an individual fails to meet the high quality standards, they are quickly replaced on that project. This competitive approach to project work ensures that companies will get their work done and delivered at a high quality level, and on schedule.

Some assigned contractors work by accessing the client's server through a secure remote connection, and thus are able to complete the work project without data ever leaving the client's server. Some clients provide laptops to individuals to give them access to internal systems and to integrate them more seamlessly into the work of the company. Here is a sample posting for contract work.

Sample Online Contract Work

Customer Service Rep

Location: Virtual (Anywhere)

Shift availability: Must be flexible to work at least 8 hours between the hours of 7:00AM to 2:00AM, as schedules will be based on performance and tenure. Shifts may not include weekend days off.

Purpose: To represent American Support and their clients by ensuring cable entertainment satisfaction through excellent customer service, offering courteous problem solving, quality information and other services in response to customer needs.

Major Duties and Responsibilities:

1. Sign in and out for scheduled shifts at appointed times.

2. Access customer information and convey necessary information to customers.

3. Answer customer questions (basic information such as prices, programming, installation of services, billing).

4. Communicate effectively, both verbally and in writing.

5. Resolve basic customer problems/complaints promptly and refer complex issues and concerned customers to the appropriate lead representative or supervisor.

6. Acquire and maintain current up-to-date cable product knowledge and provide it using appropriate persuasive communication skills.

7. Determine service outages (using Knowledge Base and other systems).

8. Contact customers concerning scheduled service calls. Handle basic dispatch duties in the absence of dispatch personnel.

Online Employment Agencies

Online employment agencies, also called virtual employment agencies, undertake the hiring process for corporate and business clients in order to guarantee quality of work, and to match expert workers with serious employers. These agencies remove some of the risk for employers who have actual work that must be accomplished, and deadlines that are essential to success.

To increase employer confidence, these agencies provide money-back guarantees, and carry out expert hiring practices on behalf of their clients, selecting the right workers that are so crucial to the success of client projects. If the employee will have access to company trade secrets, the agency arranges for non-disclosure agreements. Also, the agency serves as a payment go between, creating escrow accounts that are released to virtual workers upon successful delivery of the work. Thus employees are guaranteed being paid, and employers are guaranteed receiving high quality work in a timely manner.

In order to make such assurances and guarantees, these virtual employment agencies practice expert hiring techniques. They verify certifications, obtain performance ratings for potential workers, and participate actively in mediation and arbitration, when necessary.

Although these agencies generally do offer employers the option of hiring international workers from emerging economies, they also disclose the pros and cons of employing these types of workers. At the top of the list of cons are: legal issues, where the protection of intellectual property may not be enforceable; time zone issues; and the English proficiency of non-native speakers, with the resultant potential for communications breakdowns.

Explore these eight Online Employment Agencies. Again, add additional agencies to this list by searching Google or another search engine using the search terms: "online employment agencies" or "virtual employment agencies."

Online Employment Agencies	
AssistU	**Electric Quill**
AssistU.com	*Electric-Quill.com*

CyberSecretaries	Executary
YouDictate.com	*Executary.com*
DeskTopStaff	**HireAbility**
DeskTopStaff.com	*HireAbility.com*
Hire Me Now	**V Worker**
hiremenow.com	*vworker.com*

Select three or more of these Online Employment Agencies to explore more completely and make notes about categories of work assignments, work requirements, and the application or registration process. Don't forget to add to your URL address notebook those agencies you will revisit.

Virtual Staffing Services

Virtual Staffing Services assist small businesses in meeting their staffing requirements by using a virtual workforce. This relieves smaller businesses of major expenses such as renting office space, providing necessary computer equipment, and paying staff when no work is available.

Virtual Staffing Services allow companies to acquire the services of professional staff, then manage them virtually. Advantages of virtual staffing, from the viewpoint of an employer, include:

- No additional infrastructure is required in your office;
- Your own personal presence in the office is not necessary;
- Quick and efficient startups of new projects are possible;
- Access to a large, skilled and viable work force yields higher-performance workers;
- You are enabled to focus on your core business;
- A virtual workforce can provide great support to your existing team, when needed;
- You have no long-term payroll commitments;
- Costs are reduced;
- Quality of results is increased;
- Turn around is quicker;
- Your business can offer 24/7 service by hiring across time zones.

Now explore these eight *Virtual Staffing Services*. Add additional staffing services sites to this list by searching Google or another search engine using the search term: "Virtual Staffing Services."

Virtual Staffing Services	
Global Staffing *GlobalStaffing.com*	**Staffing Services** *StaffingServices.net*
ProfessionalSupportServices *ProfessionalSupportService.com*	**V Staff** *VStaff.com*
BV Staffing *bvstaffing.com/*	**Virtual Office Temps** *VirtualAssistantJobs.com*
Virtual Corp *www.Virtual-Corp.net*	**VirtualStaffing** *VirtualStaffing.com*

Select three or more of these Virtual Staffing Services to explore and make notes. Be sure to make additions to your URL notebook for follow-up.

If you are not already familiar with an agency you find through a web search, then "buyer beware." The website *www.scam.com* is a good resource for determining whether an agency is offering legitimate employment options or is selling employment "opportunities."

Unfortunately the word "opportunity" sometimes translates to the word "SCAM" when it is applied to working online from home. Avoid any "offer" that will make you "rich quick," or that otherwise sounds too good to be true. If it sounds *too* good, it probably *is not* true.

Work Source #2: Telecommuting Posts on Job Sites

In addition to conducting searches on Google and other search engines, you can find another important source of online work leads buried within job search sites for work "out there." Some of these sites do include jobs that can be done via telecommuting. Explore these six sites first...

Major Job Search Sites	
Monster *www.monster.com*	**Career Builder** *www.CareerBuilder.com*
Jobs *www.jobs.com*	**Outsource 2000** *www.Outsource2000.com*
Flex Jobs *www.FlexJobs.com*	**Workaholics for Hire** *www.Workaholics4Hire.com*

From within each of these job sites, search using terms such as:

- "telecommute"
- "work from home"
- "remote"

When exploring the *FlexJobs.com* site, use the "New Jobs" drop-down menu to narrow your search to "Only Telecommuting Jobs." Another technique when you are searching from within a job site is to try a search without specifying a location. Some telecommuting jobs can be performed from any location, while other employers prefer a local candidate even for online telecommuting positions.

As an example, a search on *CareerBuilder.com*, using the search term "telecommute," yielded 306 job options at the time of this printing. Employers included: United Health Group, TEK Systems, Dell Computers, and Carlson Wagonlit Travel (a global company specializing in business travel management, offering services in more than 150 countries).

Job categories included:

- Information Technology (142 jobs)
- Insurance (93 jobs)
- Management (52 jobs)
- Health care (40 jobs)
- Customer Service (38 jobs)
- Sales (31 jobs)
- Engineering (30 jobs)
- Finance (28 jobs)

- Marketing (19 jobs)
- Admin/Clerical (16 jobs)

Work Source #3: Online Job Boards

For many individuals who work online, trawling the online job boards is one of the most common methods of looking for project work. Even those who plan to open their own business, or to be self-employed, use these job boards to assist them with "cash flow" until they have attracted enough clients of their own. Online workers have found that job boards are an effective source of employment.

Looking through the online job boards works well as you build a cadre of clients who use you regularly. When you have gained more regular, repeat customers, you may become less dependent on this method. But no matter how successful you become, it is always wise to return to these locations to see if you can discover a few new clients.

Some job board sites are run as auctions, where a potential employer places a job on the board, and a potential contract employee (that would be you) bids against others to get hired. This sounds great in theory. But an unfortunate byproduct of this type of board is that its competitive nature can actually drive down pay rates for the work.

Check out these websites for starters, listed, then described below. Once you have become familiar with what each of these sites has to offer, select three to visit in depth.

Online Job Boards	
Genuine Jobs *http://www.genuinejobs.com/*	**JuJu Job Search Engine** *http://www.job-search-engine.com/*
Yahoo Hotjobs *http://hotjobs.yahoo.com/*	**Job Line** *http://jobline.net/*
Quintessential Careers *http://www.quintcareers.com/*	**Home Job Stop** *www.HomeJobStop.com*
Guru.com *http://www.guru.com/*	**Homeworkers** *www.Homeworkers.org*
Employment 911 *http://www.employment911.com*	**2 Work at Home** *www.2Work-at-Home.com*

Genuine Jobs: *http://www.genuinejobs.com/*
Sign up as a free member to gain access to their work from home and freelance job listings. You will receive an email whenever new jobs are added to the Members Only database.

Yahoo Hotjobs: *http://hotjobs.yahoo.com/*
Search for telecommuting jobs in your area. Refine the search by job category for better results.

Quintessential Careers: *http://www.quintcareers.com/*
Use the search feature. This site also offers free expert career and job-hunting advice (through articles, tools, tips, and tutorials), as well as links to many of the best job sites.

Guru.com: *http://www.guru.com/*
Jobs and more jobs to bid on, including jobs in:

- Technology: websites, E-commerce, programming, databases;
- Creative arts: graphic design, writing, illustration, photography, fashion and interior design;
- Business: administrative support, marketing and communications, sales, legal, finance and accounting.

Employment 911: *http://www.employment911.com*
Use the onsite tool to search over three million jobs posted on hundreds of job listings and employment sites. The site also offers expert résumé writing services and many other features.

JuJu Job Search Engine: *http://www.job-search-engine.com/*
An extensive search engine for jobs by job title, company, location or keyword. Search job titles for work that can be done online, like Virtual Assistant or Web Writer. The site allows you to sign up for e-mail alerts.

Job Line: *http://jobline.net/*
Use the search tool to check many nationwide and international job boards. Check the Information pages for Job Seekers.

Home Job Stop: *www.HomeJobStop.com*
One the few job boards on the Internet that successfully maintains a support-based structure that is completely free of commercial

advertising. All content is manually verified and approved before appearing in the Job Bank.

Homeworkers: *www.Homeworkers.org*
There are no fees associated in using the Homeworkers jobs database. To assure that job listings be as "fresh" as possible, the site archives job listings older than 3 months.

2 Work at Home: *www.2Work-at-Home.com*
2Work-At-Home.com has been providing free work at home job listings and support since 1999. Listings are from a variety of other job sites, focusing on those jobs that can be performed remotely, from home.

Sample Job Board Post

Virtual Assistant To Fine Artist

Company: iHARTphotography@gmail.com

Address: 637 St Marks Ave, Brooklyn, NY

May Work Remotely

Position: Part-Time, Paid

Hours: 60 Hours/Month Long Term

BONUS: 15% COMMISSION FOR BOOSTING SALES

For this position you MUST be self-directed and committed to meeting deadlines as well as showing initiative.

Major Duties and Responsibilities
- Web Search, Information Sourcing/Collection,
- Content Writing/Creation,
- Data Entry and Order Processing,
- Customer Support,
- Sending Emails, Uploading Content/Videos,
- Miscellaneous tasks including, but not limited to, Personal Assistant work.

Work Source #4: Online Classified Ads

Another excellent place to look for online work is in the *online classified ads*. The most heavily used of *online classified ads* resource is Craigslist (*CraigsList.com*). Many of the work-at-home leads listed on other websites actually have been taken from *CraigsList*.

Each geographic area has its own *CraigsList*, where every type of classified ad is posted, including job openings, organized into 32 categories. Employment categories range from "Art/Media/Design" to "Accounting & Finance" to "Writing & Editing" to "Web & Info Design" to "Skilled Trades & Crafts."

To locate work that you could do remotely:

1. Do a Google search to locate the *CraigsList* for your own area.
2. Scan the categories under the word JOBS and select those that may appeal to you.
3. Click on the word JOBS to reach a search screen that allows you to screen for only those jobs that can be done by telecommuting.
4. Check the box labeled "telecommute," then click on *Search*.
5. If your search yields too many results, back up and screen by category of jobs.

Start with your own city, but don't stop there. Since the work you are looking for can be done remotely, you are not by any means limited to your own "neighborhood." So feel free to check out *CraigsList* for other cities to find additional telecommuting job options.

This is one of the most difficult mental leaps to make when you first step out of the boundaries of your own local area and enter the world-wide work world. Your mind will need to grow accustomed to new ways of thinking when all those former preconceived notions are removed.

As an example, in addition to checking out my own local Charlotte *CraigsList*, I also searched for telecommuting work in San Antonio, Charleston and Seattle. As it turned out, there were more options in San Antonio (1000 postings) than in Charlotte (904 postings). But there also were some interesting possibilities in Seattle (525 postings) and Charleston (374 postings). Here are two sample telecommuting listings, one from Charlotte and the other from Charleston.

Script Writers needed (Charlotte)

Script writers needed for youth news and sports shows. Please include contact phone numbers.

Location: Charlotte

Compensation: Negotiable

Telecommuting Is OK

RN Telephone Triage: Work from Home

Carenet Healthcare Services is currently seeking highly motivated, caring, compassionate, committed and talented Registered Nurses to join Carenet's Clinical Team. If you have greater than average flexibility, you'll thrive as a *Care Advisor* for Carenet.

Carenet provides 24/7 telephone *Demand Management* services that include Nurse Triage, Medical Decision Support, Medical Device Monitoring Services, Member Engagement Initiatives and Healthcare Support programs.

Job Requirements:

- Unrestricted RN license with the ability to become licensed in additional States as required.

- Recent 3 years clinical experience in areas of Med/Surg, Pediatrics or Emergency Nursing desired.

- Minimum of an Associate's degree from a two-year college or technical school or Diploma Nursing Program

- Strong critical thinking skills and desire to provide outstanding customer service

- Ability to work as part of a team

- Effective communication skills to interact with members, patients and physicians, both oral and written communications

- Proficient computer skills with the ability to use multiple programs simultaneously

In addition to *CraigsList,* other "help wanted" classified ads sites include:

- Jobs.Oodle: *Jobs.Oodle.com*
- Help Wanted Site: *HelpWantedSite.com*
- Jobvertise: *Jobvertise.com*

Also, some newspapers include Online Employment sections in their online editions. For links that connect to over a thousand online editions of newspapers that post online employment, follow the link to the *Job Factory* site at *http://www.jobfactory.com/onnews.htm* and click on the state of your choice.

As an example, here's a list of several newspapers in Colorado that include *Online Employment* sections in their online editions:

Online Employment Listed in Newspapers	
Aspen, Colorado	**ASPEN DAILY NEWS** *AspenDailyNews.com*
Boulder, Colorado	**DAILY CAMERA** *BoulderNews.com*
Denver, Colorado	**DENVER POST** *DenverPost.com*
Durango, Colorado	**DURANGO HERALD** *DurangoHerald.com*
Steamboat, Colorado	**STEAMBOAT PILOT** *STMBT-Pilot.com*

Make a note on your *To Do List* to monitor these sites regularly. Job listings change on a daily, even an hourly, basis. Bookmark your "finds" as you go. Record URLs in your notebook, and keep notes on all actions that you take so that you can efficiently return to sites of particular interest. Return several times weekly to view updates.

Online Work Source #5: Newsletters & Newsgroups

There are many helpful work online websites that will send you recent job advertisements regularly. Join their mailing lists, and subscribe to their newsletters, for free on their websites.

Some examples are:

- Bassador Company: *Bassador.com*
- Home Job Stop: *HomeJobStop.com*

E-mail Alerts are also available from many job and career websites including:

- Career Builder: *CareerBuilder.com*
- Help Wanted Site: *HelpWantedSite.com*
- I Hire Accounting: *IHireAccounting.com*

Work Source #6: Freelance Networks

Working as a freelancer means that you are self employed and that you charge by the hour, day, or project. Typically, on a freelance network site, an employer posts a project to be completed, and freelancers from within the network express interest in completing the project, usually through a bidding process, with the lowest bid usually winning.

Freelance networks allow freelancers to look for work within their own field, or even to break into a new career market, through access to hundreds, even thousands, of potential income opportunities.

WOW FACTOR

ELance had over 78,000 new jobs posted within the past 30 days at the time of this printing, with over 2 million registered contractors. Total earnings for freelance services delivered to date were $654 million, starting at $20 million in 2006 and showing steady and significant increases each year.

Check out some of the freelancer networks and select those you may want to join if you are interested in working as a freelancer, perhaps in combination with a more long-term online job, or if you aspire to expand your work experience into new areas.

ELance.com is one major freelancer site, with job opportunities in a range of categories, including:

- IT & Programming

- Design & Multimedia
- Writing & Translation
- Sales & Marketing
- Administrative Support
- Engineering & Manufacturing
- Finance & Management
- Legal

As an indication of the magnitude of these work opportunities, at the time of this printing, in the category of *Writing & Translation* alone:

- The US, with 192,570 contractors, averaging $23/hour;
- The UK had 18,547 contractors, averaging $22/hour;
- Canada had 14,112, and an average hourly rate of $24;
- Australia had 6,503, averaging $30/hour;
- Spain had 2,969, averaging $17/hour;
- France had 2,257, averaging $13/hour;
- Sweden had 1,529, averaging $17/hour.

Contractor Earnings

$654,037,124
Lifetime Earnings (in USD)

Freelancers.net is another freelancer network that has been matching freelancers seeking work with clients needing their services since 1999. *Freelancers.net* is focused on the United Kingdom, but lists many jobs from across the globe that regularly use freelancers from outside Great Britain. Listing yourself on *freelancers.net* is free, both for freelancers and potential employers.

Other freelancer networks include:

- Freelancer: *http://www.freelancer.com/*
- VWorker: *http://www.vworker.com/*
- All Freelance Directory: *http://www.allfreelance.com/*

There is a downside to freelancer networks. As more freelancers register, the competition increases, leading people to offer to work for less money. Also, be aware that some freelancer sites do charge monthly fees.

Three Tips for Finding Online Work

Stay Organized While Searching

Throughout the search process, keep URLs and Login information organized in a small notebook. Also, take excellent notes. Create bookmarks as you go for sites that you plan to return to regularly. Organize these sites into folders, using the Favorites option.

Keep an updated log of sites where you post your résumé and portfolio or apply for a job, leaving space to record the results when you hear back. Use index cards or an online calendar to keep track of what you are sending to whom, when, and with what results.

Request Feedback

When you receive a response, request additional feedback on any application for which you are not selected. Sometimes even small changes to your résumé or cover letter could make all the difference. Adding one piece of equipment to your home office, or finding a way to create a quieter work environment, or taking one class, or adding one certification could be the key that changes a "no" to a "yes" response. Find out what you need to be doing better or differently, then do it.

Knowing how to improve your game and become more marketable is a valuable skill in itself as you go through the job hunting process. The more you invest in yourself through ongoing learning, the more valuable you become to potential employers.

Know How Much Search and Action Is Enough

How much job search activity is enough to locate the optimum online work for you? Use the same "job search math" as you would if you were looking for a job "out there." The magic number cited by job hunting experts is **100**.

Roughly stated, assume that it will require 100 genuine actions on your part to yield 10 responses, that will turn into 5 serious possibilities, that will result in the one job that is perfect for you.

What constitutes an action? Blanketing a hundred employers with a generic résumé that does not specifically show how you match their needs... This does *not* count as an action. E-mailing everyone in your e-mail address book that you are "looking for a job"... This does not qualify either. These typical patterns are known *not* to work.

What *does* count are actions where you actively attend to the matchmaking process. Since you are the one who knows best why you would be great at doing a particular job, it is your task to take the lead in making your own matches. Some actions that *do* count towards your goal of 100 include:

- Applying for a specific job, following the application guidelines and requirements;
- Sending a customized cover letter and résumé to a contract employer seeking additional expertise and talent;
- Presenting yourself and your portfolio to someone who needs what you are able to do;
- Listing yourself with an online agency and responding to a specific work posting.

To determine how many actions to take each week, think of how many weeks you have available to locate work, then do the math. If you take one action a week, for example, how long will it take you to complete 100 actions? That would be 52 actions a year. So to get to 100 would take you almost **two years**!

$$\frac{100\ actions}{52\ actions/year} = 2 \text{ years}$$

What if you follow the typical pattern of applying for one job, then waiting three weeks (or more) to learn if you've landed it? Following that strategy, how long will your job search require? If you do the math, you will discover that at that rate you would accomplish only 17 actions per year. So getting to 100 would take you about **six years**.

$$\frac{100\ actions}{17\ actions/year} = 6 \text{ years}$$

Too long? Then work the numbers in the other direction. Five genuine actions a week would bring you to 100, and the culmination of the process, within **20 weeks**.

$$\frac{100\ actions}{5\ actions/week} = 20 \text{ weeks}$$

Even better, 20 actions a week would bring you to the culmination within **five weeks**. Sound better?

$$\frac{100\ actions}{20\ actions/week} = 5 \text{ weeks}$$

Of course, these numbers are guidelines only, not absolutes. The specifics may vary somewhat, depending on a number of factors. But the concept holds. Decreased activity increases the duration of the job search timeline. Increased activity decreases that duration. The key is to plan enough activity to meet your goals within the timeframe you have in mind.

So go for 100! Job hunting is an action sport. 100 yards to a football field. 100 actions to get your ideal job. Play ball!

Now What About You?

So many possibilities for working online... And so many types of interesting work you could be doing, while preserving part of your time for other retirement pursuits.

Select three specific actionable ideas for working in cyberspace to add to what you will consider later when you "make your match and move." Record your three top choices here for now, then copy them to the composite of possibilities you began creating in Chapter 8.

Of course, if you wish, feel free to note more than three…

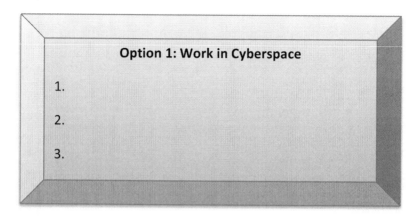

Option 1: Work in Cyberspace

1.

2.

3.

And So…

You now know something about working online in retirement. This may be the ideal plan for you as you set out on your own particular combination of pathways, expressing your own unique self and talents in ways that engage you and make full use of what you have to offer.

But, wait, there's more.

In the next chapter, we will look at some of the many, many options for working "out there," wherever "there" is, in ways that are engaging and new… or that at the very least are new to *you*.

Again, prepare to think outside the box… or at least to think outside YOUR box. For starters, have you ever considered a career as Santa Claus?

Read on to learn about retirement work "out there." There are many, many more options beyond becoming the stereotypical Wal-Mart greeter. And there are important ways to choose among these options in ways that optimally suit your reinvented SELF.

CHAPTER 10:
Option #2: Work "Out There"

Well now you are confused. Why would you consider working "out there" when retiring just recently freed you from all that? If you wanted to stay "out there," working at a job, why were you counting the days until your retirement? After a lifetime of work, culminating in the eventual "promised land" of retirement, isn't work "out there" exactly what you DON'T want to do?

Yes and no. Yes, it is probably true that you do *not* want to work as much you did before—too many hours, too much time away from home, too much all-out effort. And, yes, you may *not* want to work at the same type of job you held during your lifetime career—too much compromise, too much being defined by the job and not by your unique self, too much feeling drained and exhausted by the end of the day. Also, you may wish for more balance and more freedom in your life after 30 or 40 years of too much stress and too many constraints.

What's "New" About Working "Out There"?

In order for you to consider working "out there" again, you likely will want, to some degree, to keep control of *the where, the what and the when*. You will want your work to fit in with your life, and not the other way around as it was before. And you will want assurance that your life will continue to "belong" to you, not to your employer. Remember, this is YOUR time. Work YOUR way.

Now that you are "retired," the essence of what will be new and different about working "out there," if you do decide to do it, is mainly a change in your mindset about who is in charge of what. Then it was *them*, now it is *you*!

When you entered your career three or four decades ago as a young and upcoming worker, you may have been willing and content to find a job and to let that job define you—what you did, when you did it, and how it meshed with your personal life. But now you are apt to be more demanding. *You* expect to be the one to determine for yourself who you are, what you will do, when you will do it, and how it will fit in with the rest of your life. Most importantly, you will want any work that you take on next to match and to engage your reinvented, or reawakened, SELF.

Another important difference—now at least part of your income needs are already being met through some combination of retirement benefits, Social Security, and retirement savings. And you are paying less income tax. You may have additional significant financial advantages, such as a home that is fully paid for, children who are fully launched and financially independent, and possibly a simpler lifestyle.

The sum of these changes in your financial reality is that if you do work "out there" again, you will be less driven by how much income your choice of work generates. Where once you may have set aside as impractical career options that you thought would not earn you a full living, now that you have a somewhat adequate retirement income, those previous options are back on the table.

Furthermore, now any new income will supplement, and not replace, the retirement benefits and Social Security to which you are entitled as a result of your lifetime of hard work. So it is highly likely that if you do consider working "out there" again, you will want that work to be on a part-time basis.

SNAPSHOT

Kathleen studied nursing after her children were grown, and rose to the level of supervisor of the oncology unit at the hospital where she worked. Among her many accomplishments, she designed and implemented an innovative patient care model that assigned a regular team of doctors and nurses to remain with an individual patient throughout their treatment period.

In a late career change, Kathleen went back to school to study medical ethics. She then became the Director of Medical Ethics

---

at a major university medical school, a job that she found highly fulfilling.

When her husband was incapacitated from a stroke, Kathleen retired from the University to be able to stay home with him. After he passed away, she found that she was still interested in working *some* of the time but not *all* of the time, so she considered what she wanted to do next.

Although she did decide to respond to the University's fervent plea that she return to work, she made it clear that she would do this only on the condition that she set her own schedule in a way that would not impact either her University retirement income or her Social Security.

She now works two or three days a week, except for the months of October and May, which she keeps free to pursue her own interests. She also takes off major blocks of time during the Christmas and Easter holiday seasons.

In addition to her work, Kathleen's list of retirement priorities includes continuing as a Guardian Ad Litem and also spending blocks of quality time with her children and grandchildren. She travels to London each year, taking up residence in the same flat, where she devotes herself to reading, exploring the city she loves, and creating lovely miniature watercolors.

Do Employers Want You?

The short answer to the question "Do employers want you?" is "Certainly yes!" Whatever factors led to your retirement you're your previous work, they likely had nothing to do with your capabilities.

Even if you did not anticipate or actively seek your retirement, in many cases you were still highly valuable to your employer. But you also were very expensive. Many of us have had our lives changed because of an employer's budget decisions.

Or maybe you instigated your retirement yourself, for one reason or another. Even so, you may be willing to continue to work, only not at that job, with that level of stress, and that level of time and energy commitment.

Retiring from one job can open the way for another. And there are many employers "out there" who do want you and need what you have to offer.

What Do You Have to Offer an Employer?

Before setting out to navigate the job jungle "out there," consider what in particular you have to offer *due to* your age and status. In an article entitled "Part-Time Jobs for Seniors Continuing Work After Retirement," *EmploymentSpot.com* cites experience, wisdom and commitment as three major elements you have to offer the job market.

Your years of professional experience are invaluable, and can only be gained with time, thus setting you apart from younger job seekers and recent college graduates. In addition to professional experience, you are seasoned in the ways of the world. From decision-making to people skills, your wisdom is a huge asset to companies.

And as a senior employee, you are more likely to feel a sense of commitment and loyalty to the company. Because of this, employers know that you are less likely to jump from one job to another in hopes of advancing your career. Instead, you will want to make the most of the job that you have.

WOW FACTOR
By 2017, over 28 million Baby Boomers 55+ will be employed out of a total of 77 million. That is more than 1 out of every 3 of us.

Four Views of Working "Out There"

To navigate this new world of defining, then finding, your "intentional" work, consider the possibilities "out there" from four viewpoints:

1. **Work that is Available to Us**: What jobs are out there for 55+ workers?
2. **Work that Appeals to Us:** What kinds of work do 55+ workers most want to do?
3. **Work that Engages Us**: What kinds of jobs best fit us, based on which of the four temperaments we fall into—Guardian (SJ), Artisan (SP), Giver (NF), Thinker (NT)—to ensure that our new work engages our authentic selves?

4. **Work that Balances with Our Lives**: What work complements the rest of our retirement lives, without confining us, or exhausting us, or otherwise consuming us?

We will discuss each of these further, with an eye to what actions to take to ensure that if you do seek out and sign on to work "out there," the outcome will be one that fully suits you and enhances your life.

View #1: Work that is Available to Us

Times have changed in terms of what work is available to us after we retire. Data from the *Bureau of Labor Statistics* and the *Census Bureau* estimates that most of the job growth between now and 2018 will be in the "social sector," adding 7 million new jobs. Many of these jobs (about 5.9 million) will be particularly well suited for older workers.

Some types of work are particularly likely to be performed by "mature" workers. Work areas where *20% or more* positions will be held by workers who are 55+ include a range of jobs, from *Tour/Travel Guide* to *Archivist/Curator* to *Social/Community Service Manager* to *Animal Trainer* or even *Private Investigator*. A fuller list of those work areas where 20% or more jobs will be held by mature workers is shown in the table below, again based on data from the *Bureau of Labor Statistics* and the *Census Bureau*.

As you look through this list, highlight any you would consider if you were qualified, or could become qualified, and if you could find a good placement that fits in with your other retirement priorities.

Over 20% of Jobs Held By 55+ Workers	
Promotional worker 44%	Entertainment worker 23%
Instructional coordinator 32%	Cost estimator 23%
Clergy 32%	Transportation inspector 23%
Brokerage clerk 30%	Animal trainer 23%

Religious activities director 28%	Personal assistant 23%
Tour/travel guide 27%	Veterinarian 22%
Management analyst 27%	Writer 22%
Postsecondary teacher 27%	Engineer 22%
Construction inspector 26%	Usher/lobby attendant 21%
Locksmith/safe repairer 25%	Pharmacist 21%
Archivist, curator 25%	Ambulance driver/EMT 21%
Correspondence clerk 25%	Environmental scientist 20%
Social service manager 24%	Private investigator 20%

Job Growth Projections for 55+

Looking at a complete list of job areas that will grow substantially in the next five years, then combining them into 40 job groupings, reveals hundreds of thousands of job openings, in dozens of interesting areas of work, including many where substantial numbers of those jobs are predicted to go to seniors.

The largest numbers of jobs for 55+, factoring in the associated growth in the job market for these areas between now and 2017, and the proportion of those jobs that will be filled by seniors, range from community service, computers or social work, each with around 160,000 jobs for seniors, to medical or instructional jobs, each with over 600,000 jobs for seniors.

Top 15 Job Groups for Seniors	
AREA	JOBS FOR SENIORS
1. Medical	636,145

2. Instructional	617,454
3. Financial	501,060
4. Health	475,878
5. Children	399,714
6. Information	355,465
7. Customer Service	326,846
8. Personal Assistance	280,293
9. Religious	230,525
10. Management	214,341
11. Landscaping	211,378
12. Sales	211,168
13. Community Service	162,424
14. Computers	158,685
15. Social Work	155,786

The table below shows all 40 groupings of high growth areas of work, with projections of how many people aged 55+ will be employed in each by 2017.

Look through these groupings and highlight any that may appeal to, challenge, and interest you. Include those you would consider only if the work could be done on a part-time basis.

High Growth Job Groupings for Seniors			
Grouping	**Sample Job Titles**	**Growth by 2017**	**55+ Employed**
Animal Service	Animal Trainer Veterinarian Assistant	23-36%	33,064
Archiving	Archivist, Curator Museum technician	22%	17,022
Business	Operations Specialist	21%	22,813
Children	Childcare, Preschool & Kindergarten teacher	18-24%	399,714

Groupings	Sample Job Titles	Growth by 2017	55+ Employed
Communications	Correspondence Media	18%	19,420
Community service	Community specialist Community manager	25-28%	162,424
Computers	Software engineer Systems analyst	29-38%	158,685
Counseling	Counselor	21%	156,327
Customer service	Counter clerks Service reps	23-25%	326,846
Data systems	Network Systems Data communications	53%	33,432
Design	Architect	18%	47,347
Diagnostics	Technologist Technician	17%	41,114
Engineering	All types	18%	112,363
Entertainment	Ushers Lobby attendant	18-24%	54,031
Estimation	Cost estimator	19%	30,595
Financial	Accountant Auditor	18-41%	501,060
Food	Preparing Serving	18%	62,494
Gaming	Supervisor Manager	19%	32,657
Health	EMT Practitioner Physical therapist	18-28%	475,878
Information	Receptionist Information clerk	17%	355,465

Groupings	Sample Job Titles	Growth by 2017	55+ Employed
Inspection	Building Transportation	18-19%	39,727
Instructional	Training Coordinator Adjunct	18-23%	617,454
Investigation	Private investigator	17%	21,280
Landscaping	Supervisor/Manager Greenskeeper	18%	211,378
Legal	Paralegal Legal assistant	22%	43,601
Management	Analyst. Consultant	22%	214,341
Medical	Pharmacist Nurse	23%	636,145
Personal Assistance	Personal aide Homecare aide	51%	280,293
Planning	Meeting planner Convention planner	20%	9,188
Promotion	Model Demonstrator	18%	41,337
Recreation	Recreation worker Fitness worker	19%	47,173
Religious	Clergy Religious activities Religious education	19-21%	230,525
Repairs	Locksmith Safe repairs Other repairs	23%	7,832
Research	Computer research Information research	24%	36,938
Sales	Advertising sales Service sales Product sales	21-28%	211,168

Groupings	Sample Job Titles	Growth by 2017	55+ Employed
Science	Environmental Geoscience	24%	25,658
Social Work	Social worker	22%	155,786
Surveying	Cartographer Photogrammetrist	24%	8,800
Travel	Tours Travel guides	20%	12,798
Writing	Technical writer, Web content, Ghostwriter	20%	13,809

View #2: Work That Appeals to Us

Another way to look at working "out there" from a new viewpoint, is to consider what fields interest and appeal to us. Interestingly, many of the fields that are of particular interest to us are in the social domain—a domain that promises some of the highest growth and personal satisfaction over the years ahead.

In fact, the list of job areas experiencing the most growth is remarkably parallel to the top fields of interest to 55+ workers. For example, 31% of workers 55+ are interested in working in the instructional area, a domain that is predicted to grow by 18%-23% by 2014, with over 600,000 jobs for older workers.

As another example—almost one third (32%) of workers 55+ are interested in working with children, a work area that promises 18%-24% growth by 2014, with almost 400,000 jobs for older workers. So, too, in the fields of healthcare, spiritual/religious work, and working with older people. Senior workers have high proportions of interest in these areas. These interests are matched by projections of strong employment growth, and high numbers of jobs that will go to this group.

Study the chart below showing top fields of interest for 55+ workers, and highlight those areas that may be of particular interest to you.

Top Fields of Interest for 55+ Workers	
MOST DESIRED FIELDS	PERCENT INTERESTED
Advocacy	36%
Work with children/youth	32%
Conservation	31%
Instruction	31%
Community safety	24%
Local or global poverty alleviation	24%
Spiritual/religious work	23%
Work with older people	17%
Health care: hospital, hospice	17%

View #3: Work That Engages Us

A third way to view work "out there" is to consider the best fit according to each of the four temperaments we focused on in Chapter 7. Take a moment now to recall and review what you determined your own temperament to be. Use this as your "window" to consider the areas of work available "out there" that may be a good match for you.

- SJ: Guardian
- SP: Artisan/Experiencer
- NF: Giver
- NT: Thinker

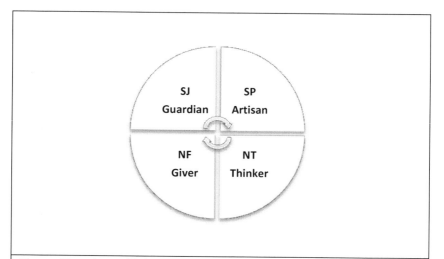

Guardian/Traditionalist: SJ (Sensing/Judging)

Keeper of Service and Duty.
Compulsion: to be useful.
[Inspector. Protector. Supervisor. Provider.]

Artisan/Experiencer: SP (Sensing/Perceiving)

Teacher of Freedom and Joy.
Compulsion: to act freely.
[Crafter. Composer. Promoter. Performer.]

Idealist/Giver: NF (iNtuitive/Feeling)

Bearer of Truth and Meaning.
Compulsion: to "BE."
[Counselor. Healer. Champion. Teacher.]

Thinker: NT (iNtuitive/Thinking)

Provider of Logic and Understanding.
Compulsion: to improve.
[Mastermind. Architect. Inventor. Field Marshal.]

Although you may expect that the best fit for your reinvented SELF will be work in your own temperament category, look also at the work areas for the other three temperaments. Determine if there are other areas that may sound interesting to you as well as your own.

Retirement Work for Guardians (SJ)

If you are a *Guardian*—a "keeper of service and duty," compelled to be useful—below are four possible types of new work that you may consider. Picture yourself in each of them, and highlight any that look interesting. Fuller information about each of these types of work follows the graphic.

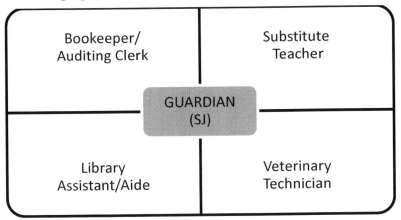

Guardian Job #1: Bookkeeper/Auditing Clerk

As a *Bookkeeper* for a small business, you would handle all financial recordkeeping. Also, you might purchase supplies, process payroll, establish and maintain inventory database systems, track accounts receivable and accounts payable, maintain checking and savings accounts, produce financial reports, follow up on delinquent accounts, oversee audits and reviews, and create quarterly and year end reports.

The hours: Vary by business. Frequently limited to one week mid-month and one at the end of the month, for invoicing or bill-paying functions.

Median pay range: $10.23 to $24.25/hour.

Qualifications: *Certified Public Accountant* (CPA) certification is best. Relevant experience or formal training in accounting/auditing services is a plus. Also: data entry skills, attention to details, working knowledge of financial software such as

QuickBooks and Excel, and a calculator.

Guardian Job #2: Substitute Teacher

As a *Substitute Teacher*, you would assume classes midstream, sometimes working from a lesson plan and at other times called upon to improvise. Depending on your background, you may be tapped to teach a range of subjects in grade levels from Kindergarten through Grade 12. If you work with special needs children, you may be more in demand.

Flexibility is essential. School districts typically keep an active roster of substitutes on call who are willing to step into a classroom with little advance notice.

The hours: Ranging from flexible half-days to several weeks of full days. Assignments may become available on a fairly regular basis, but it is your prerogative to refuse a request.

Median pay range: Each school district sets its own pay scale. According to the *National Substitute Teachers Alliance,* the current pay rate for substitutes averages around $105/day.

Qualifications: Most substitute teaching jobs require a bachelor's degree. The *National Education Association*'s (NEA) provides a *State-By-State Summary* of requirements at: *www.nea.org/home/14813.htm.* To learn the full requirements for your state, consult the *National Substitute Teachers'* (NSTA) site at *www.nstasubs.org/DOE.html*.

Guardian Job #3: Librarian Assistant/Aide

As a *Librarian's Assistant* you would field questions, shelve books, help patrons check out materials, track overdue titles and send notices, as well as process and keep an eye out for lost and damaged items. Most libraries now also include computer workstations, so you may have additional duties of assisting people with conducting online searches to obtain the materials and information they need.

The hours: Schedules vary widely. Large libraries, or those on university campuses, tend to stay open 24 hours a day, while small, local libraries offer more limited daytime and evening hours.

Median pay range: Smaller libraries may rely on volunteers. College, large city, and specialty niche libraries range from $7.69 to $17.82 per hour.

Qualifications: Experience working in libraries is desirable, as is an undergraduate or master's degree. Larger libraries favor research skills using databases and other tools. Other needed skills include: word processing, data entry and online searching, ability to keep accurate records, and an understanding of library operations.

Guardian Job #4: Veterinary Technician

As a *Veterinary Technician*, you would work alongside primarily small animal vets. Your duties might include: preparing pets for surgery, performing lab tests, administering medication and vaccines, emergency nursing care, collecting blood and samples, and the more mundane tasks of recording pet histories and checking their weights. Employment of veterinary technicians is expected to grow 14% by 2020.

Median pay: $10.60 an hour.

Qualifications: A two-year associate's degree in veterinary technology is desirable. In 2011, there were 191 veterinary technology programs accredited by the *American Veterinary Medical Association*. Although each state regulates *Veterinary Technicians* differently, most require you to take the *Veterinary Technician National Examination* for credentialing purposes. Clear and calm communication skills are essential.

Retirement Work for Artisans (SP)

If you are an Artisan—a "teacher of freedom and joy," compelled to act freely—one of the work areas below may be potentially engaging for you. Picture yourself in each of them, and highlight any that you would consider.

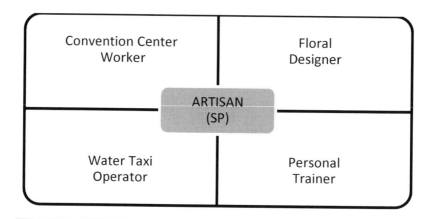

Artisan Job #1: Convention Center Worker

Convention centers in major cities can be wellsprings for a range of part-time jobs with varying skill requirements. Each week, convention venues play host to various industry events, from home to car to boat shows, as well as to concerts and sports competitions.

As a *Convention Center Worker*, you would help with the various tasks of setting up, running, and dismantling conventions. Some part-time jobs include: nurse, parking lot attendant, registration desk attendant, set-up worker, usher, information booth or vendor booth attendant. Many of these jobs require little to no physical labor.

The hours: Work schedules are irregular and no minimum number of hours is guaranteed. Work is typically available on all days of the year, including holidays. Evening and night hours may be required, depending on the job.

Median pay range: Typically $10 to $20 an hour.

Qualifications: People skills are essential. Working knowledge of the event industry —including trade shows, conventions, consumer shows, concerts, athletic events and meetings —is a plus for some positions. Pre-employment drug screening and background checks are common.

Job hunting sources: Visit _Convention.net_, or event management companies such as _SMGWorld.com_ (a firm that manages convention centers, exhibition halls and trade centers, arenas, stadiums, performing arts centers, theaters and specific-use venues such as equestrian centers).

Artisan Job #2: Floral Designer

As a _Floral Designer_ you would use your artistry to cut and arrange live, dried, or silk flowers and greenery into decorative displays. You would help customers select flowers, containers, ribbons, and other accessories, adjusting to their budget, and considering the sentiment or style of the occasion.

Other duties may include: growing flowers; ordering flowers from wholesalers; ensuring adequate supplies to meet customer needs; determining arrangement types, occasions, dates, times, and locations; answering phones and taking orders.

The hours: Hours vary. Most (46%) floral designers work for florists that are open during normal business hours. Another 11% work for grocery stores, where the hours are generally longer.

Part-time or seasonal opportunities abound, particularly around holidays such as Christmas, Valentine's Day, and Mother's Day.

Median pay: $11.35 per hour.

Qualifications: Artistic ability and knowledge of design are crucial. Also important are customer service, communication and organizational skills.

Artisan Job #3: Water Taxi Operator

As a _Water Taxi Operator_, you would operate a small, motor driven private boat, generally carrying 6 to 20 passengers, providing tours of harbors, canals or rivers, and possibly also offering commentary on the environs. Employment of motorboat operators is projected to grow 15% from 2010 to 2020, about as fast as the average for all occupations, driven by the growth in tourism and recreational activities.

The hours: Hours can be daylight as well as evening, and generally include weekends. Many water taxi operators service vacation destinations, and have seasonal schedules.

Median pay: Average pay across all water transportation occupations is $22.81 an hour.

Qualifications: Most water transportation jobs require the *Transportation Worker Identification Credential* (TWIC) from the *US Department of Homeland Security*. Most mariners also must have a *Merchant Marine Credential* (MMC). Boat pilots are licensed by the state in which they work; requirements vary.

Other essential qualities include: customer service skills, hand-eye coordination, mechanical ability, and visual acuity.

Artisan Job #4: Personal Trainer

As a *Personal Trainer*, you will demonstrate exercise techniques, adjust machine settings, help clients gauge their physical fitness level and set reasonable goals, and design course plans for your clients' workouts. You also will need grounding in nutrition and diet issues that go hand-in-hand with a fit physique. Most trainers work at health and fitness club facilities. Some offer one-on-one training at clients' homes.

Senior living communities, wellness centers, civic associations, and nonprofits like the *Arthritis Foundation* (*www.arthritis.org*) are often on the lookout for individual or small group trainers.

The hours: Flexible. Mornings, evenings, weekends, according to clients' needs.

Median pay range: $17 to $30 an hour. In larger cities, hourly rates can be $60 to $100 or more. Most health clubs collect payment for sessions, then pay a percentage to you.

Qualifications: Certification is not required by law, but most fitness clubs prefer it. Several national groups offer credentials, including the *American Council on Exercise (ACE)*, the *International Sports Sciences Association* and the *National Strength and Conditioning Association*.

Also, you must be certified in *Cardiopulmonary Resuscitation* (CPR). People skills are essential, as well as a physique that shows that you practice what you preach.

Retirement Work for Givers (NF)

If you are a Giver—a "bearer of truth and meaning," with a compulsion to "BE"—the four work areas below may be some possibilities for you. Picture yourself in each of them. Highlight and make notes about any that you might consider.

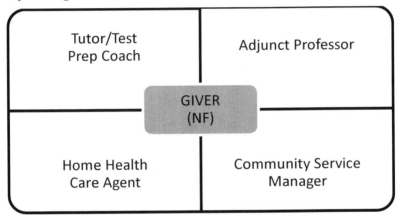

Giver Job #1: Tutor/Test Preparation Coach

As a *Tutor/Test Preparation Coach,* you will work one-on-one with individual students, tutoring them in their areas of need—core curriculum subjects such as world history, physics, science, math, English, and world language, or test prep review—at the student's home or a local library.

Public and private schools often pass along tutor referrals to parents, so inform the guidance counselors at schools know you are available. You can also post on community bulletin boards, or even create your own website to market your business.

Online tutoring and test prep jobs, arranged through a tutoring website such as *Tutor.com* or *SmarThinking.com* enable you to work with students inside a secure online "classroom." Teaching and coaching are done using a combination of instant messaging for dialog, interactive whiteboard to draw and work problems, and email attachments to send work back and forth.

The hours: Online sessions may be as short as 25 minutes, but most in-person tutoring sessions range from one to three hours per session, with one to three session per week.

Most tutoring takes place during the school year, although some parents continue tutoring for their children throughout the summer. Fall and spring are the prime times for test prep tutoring for college-bound students scheduled to take the SAT and ACT aptitude tests. Prep for a range of other standardized tests, such as the GDE, GRE, LSAT and others, are in demand year-round.

Median pay range: $10.27 to $24.21 an hour.

Qualifications: A college degree, background in education and experience working with students is generally preferred. Subject matter expertise, communication skills and an ability to help others succeed, are also essential.

Giver Job #2: Adjunct Professor

As an ***Adjunct Professor,*** you will teach in a University or a 2-year community or technical college classroom, on a class-by-class basis, in your area of expertise. Your students will range from recent high school graduates to career-transitioning adults who are adding new skills or updating old ones.

The *Bureau of Labor Statistics* anticipates that over 523,000 more adjunct teaching jobs will be created in the next few years. Because adjunct professors are paid considerably lower salaries than permanent faculty, and receive no benefits, many colleges are recruiting more adjuncts on a contractual basis in favor of hiring full-time faculty.

WOW FACTOR
Adjunct and "contingent" faculty now make up more than half of all faculty positions in the United States.

Go online to obtain a copy of current course listings from the college where you would like to teach. Also check to discover what courses may be missing from the course schedule in your field of expertise. Most colleges now offer online courses, which may be another option for you if you have technology savvy, and would be at ease teaching classes via computer.

The hours: Vary widely, depending on the number of courses you teach. Summer courses are common. Night and weekend classes are standard. Expect one to three hours of classroom time per week per class, plus preparation and grading time.

Median pay range: Pay rates vary according to the course taught, ranging from $2,500 to $5,000 per course, depending on the number of credit hours, your degree level and teaching experience, and the department for which you will be teaching.

Qualifications: Master's degree in your discipline is preferred.

Giver Job #3: Home Health Care Agent

As a *Home-Care Agent*, you will help elderly, ill or disabled people with everyday activities, ranging from bathing and getting dressed, to running errands. Other duties may include: light housekeeping, companionship, grocery shopping, meal preparation and monitoring medications.

WOW FACTOR
Employment of home health care aides is expected to grow by 70% from 2010 to 2020, much faster than the average for all occupations.

The Hours: In-home care jobs can average three to four hours a day, two to three days a week, per client, according to his/her needs. These jobs are often booked through a home-care agency. If you opt for a part-time position in an assisted living facility or hospice, hours will be according to an assigned schedule.

Median pay range: Median pay is $9.70 an hour, ranging from $7.36 to $12.45, depending on experience and certification.

Qualifications: Some employers may require a Certified Nurse

Assistant (CNA) certification. CPR training is preferred. Good bedside manner is a must. Some positions require transferring or lifting patients as well as many hours spent on your feet.

Giver Job #4: Community Service Manager

As a *Community Service Manager*, you would coordinate and supervise social service programs and community organizations, directing and leading the staff who provide social services to the public through organizations dedicated to a particular population—such as children, homeless people, or veterans—or that focus on helping people with particular challenges—such as hunger or joblessness. Duties may include:

- Confer with members of the community to determine what types of programs and services are needed.
- Design and oversee programs to meet the needs of the target audience or community.
- Create methods to gather and analyze data in order to evaluate program impact and effectiveness.
- Report findings to administrators or funders.
- Identify areas that need improvement.
- Develop and manage program and organization budgets.
- Raise funds for programs though the agency's budget process or fundraising campaigns.

WOW FACTOR
Employment of Community Service Managers is expected to grow by 27% from 2010 to 2020, faster than the average for all occupations.

The growth of an aging population accounts for the increased needs for Community Service Managers. Other growth factors include the fact that more people with addictions are seeking treatment, and drug offenders are increasingly being sent to treatment programs rather than to jail.

The hours: In larger agencies, *Social and Community Service Managers* typically work full time. Smaller organizations may have part-time positions. Job sharing may be an option.

Median pay: $27.86 an hour.

Qualifications: A bachelor's degree in social work, urban studies, public administration, or a related field is the minimum requirement, with a master's preferred. For those whose highest education level is a bachelor's degree, work experience is generally required as well. Also important are analytical, communications, leadership, managerial, and people skills.

Retirement Work for Thinkers (NT)

If you are a Thinker—a "provider of logic and understanding," with a compulsion to improve—the four areas below may interest you. Picture yourself in each of them, and highlight any that may be a possibility.

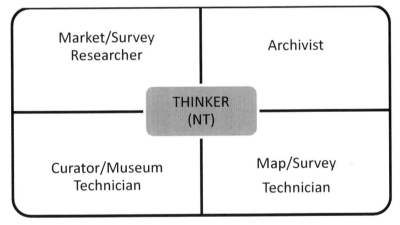

Thinker Job #1: Market/Survey Researcher

As a *Market/Survey Researcher*, you will participate in research tasks, ranging from conducting surveys—by phone, online, mail or door-to-door—to analyzing and reporting results.

Market Research projects vary—evaluating potential sales of a product or service, gathering statistical data on competitors, measuring the effectiveness of a program or service. Potential employers include consumer products firms, university research centers, financial services organizations, government agencies, health care institutions and advertising firms.

Survey Researchers work in research firms, polling organizations, nonprofits, government agencies, colleges and universities.

WOW FACTOR
Employment of Market Research Analysts is expected to grow 41% from 2010 to 2020, much faster than the average for all occupations.

Employment growth of *Market Researchers* will be driven by an increased use of data and market research across all industries in order to understand the needs and wants of customers and measure the effectiveness of marketing and business strategies. *Survey Research* is expected to grow 24%, also faster than the average.

For information about careers and salaries in market and survey research, contact the *Council of American Survey Research Organizations* (*casro.org*) and the *Marketing Research Association* (*mra-net.org*).

The hours: Flexible, project-based, full time or short assignments.

Median pay: $17.33 an hour for Survey Research; $29.10 an hour for Market Research.

Qualifications: Both *Market Researchers* and *Survey Researchers* need a combination of research and people skills. A bachelor's degree is the baseline, with a background in liberal arts and social science, including economics, psychology and sociology. Employers generally prefer candidates who have previous work experience using statistics, analyzing data, or conducting interviews or surveys.

Quantitative skills are important, so courses in mathematics, statistics, sampling theory and survey design, and computer science are helpful. Curiosity and being a stickler for details are positives, since this kind of work relies on precision.

Thinker Job #2: Archivist

As an *Archivist* you will appraise, edit, and maintain permanent records and historically valuable documents, perform research on archival material, and preserve and assess documents and records for their importance, potential value, or historical significance. Also you may coordinate and offer educational and public outreach programs, such as tours, workshops, lectures, and classes relevant to your collections.

Some *Archivists* specialize in an area of history, such as colonial history, in order to more accurately determine which records should become part of the archive. Other archivists specialize in a particular format of records, such as manuscripts, electronic records, websites, photographs, maps, motion pictures, or sound recordings.

Employment of *Archivists* is projected to grow 12% from 2010 to 2020, based on needs for greater organization of, and access to, increasing volumes of electronic records and information.

Duties may include:

- Preserve and maintain documents and objects; safeguard records by copying to film, videotape, disk, or computer formats.

- Authenticate and appraise historical documents and materials

- Organize and classify archival records for ease of access; create and maintain accessible computer archives and databases.

- Direct workers who arrange, exhibit, and maintain collections.

- Provide reference services and help for users; administer policy guidelines concerning public access to materials.

- Locate new materials and direct their acquisition and display.

The hours: Part-time or full-time.

Median pay: $21.73 an hour.

Qualifications: Although archivists may enter the profession with a variety of undergraduate degrees, most employers prefer a graduate degree in history, library science, archival science, or records management. Many colleges and universities offer courses or practical training.

Thinker Job #3: Curator/Museum Technician

As a *Curator*, you will oversee collections, such as artwork and historic items, and prepare and restore objects and documents in museum collections and exhibits. Working at the level of *Museum Technician*, you will assist the *Curator* with preparing and caring for museum items. You also will interface with the public, responding to their questions, as well as with outside scholars, helping them to make use of the collections.

Curators and *Museum Technicians* work at museums, zoos, aquariums, botanical gardens, and historical sites. *Curators* in large institutions may travel extensively to evaluate potential additions to the collection, organize exhibits, and conduct research.

The hours: Part-time or full-time.

Median pay: $20.34 an hour

Qualifications: Most museums require curators to have master's degrees in a discipline appropriate to the museum's specialty, or in museum studies. Museum technicians usually need a bachelor's degree related to the museum's specialty, as well as training in museum studies, or previous experience working in museums and designing exhibits.

Other important skills include: *Analytical and critical-thinking skills*—to determine the origin, history, importance and authenticity of the objects with which they work. *Customer-service skills*— to work directly with the public, describing the collections to non-technical visitors. *Organizational skills*— to organize collections logically for display. *Technical skills*— to use chemicals and techniques for preserving documents, paintings, fabrics, and pottery, in order to prevent further deterioration.

Thinker Job #4: Map/Survey Technician

As a *Map Technician*, you will collect and use geographic data to assist surveyors and cartographers in making maps of the earth's surface. As a *Survey Technician* you will make site visits to take measurements of the land, working outside in all types of weather, walking and sometimes climbing hills, with heavy packs of instruments and other equipment.

Map Technicians work primarily indoors on computers. *Survey Technicians* travel as a part of the job, sometimes staying overnight, or even relocating temporarily, to be closer to a survey site.

The hours: Typically full time, possibly with longer hours in summer, when weather and light conditions are most suitable for fieldwork.

Median pay: $18.22 an hour

Qualifications: For *Map Technicians*, postsecondary training is more common. *Survey Technicians* generally need a high school diploma, although some have postsecondary training. An associate's or bachelor's degree in a relevant field, such as geomatics, is beneficial.

Other useful background includes: algebra, geometry, trigonometry, drafting, mechanical drawing, and computer science. Also needed are well-developed skills at decision-making, listening, teamwork, technology and troubleshooting.

View #4: Work that Balances Well with Our Lives

So, you say, "I see so many job opportunities that do sound interesting and could be fun. And I know I have the *experience* and the *wisdom* prized by employers. But ... I'm not so sure about my level of *commitment*! Yes, I *do* want to work. But I *don't* want to work...

...during January, because we live in the north... and I hate the winters... so I need to get away...

... in the summer... because we have a boat... and nothing interferes with our nautical trips...

...early in the morning... it would interfere with my early golf game, because we tee off at 7 AM...

...late at night... I don't drive in the dark... too many intoxicated people on the road...

241

...on or near the Christmas holidays... it's my favorite time with my extended family...

...full-time... I did that for too many years... putting in 10-12 hour days... I'm done with that...

too far from my home... due to the high price of gas, and how much I value my time...

In other words, I want to be in the driver's seat. I want to work when it is convenient for me to work, doing something that is interesting and fun, on a schedule that fits into my new lifestyle. Am I living in Xanadu? Am I totally out of touch with reality? Do I really believe that such ideal opportunities exist for someone 55+?

In fact all of this is, indeed, possible. Starting with the jobs we have already discussed, and adding a few more, here is a smattering of the types of part-time work available to those of us who want to work when we want to work, or who otherwise do not want our next work to interfere with our play.

Jobs with Summers Free

Good plan! You want your summers free—so that you can travel...take care of the grandkids...work in your garden...sail. There are options workwise, especially if you plan to work with your local school system in in some capacity. Some job options include:

- tutor
- teacher's aide
- adult education teacher
- substitute teacher
- athletic coach
- referee
- adjunct professor
- school secretary
- school photographer

Winter-Only Jobs

Winter-only jobs leave you lots of options during the rest of the year. These work out especially well if you have a migration pattern of living in different places based on the season and the weather. If you want to work only in the winter, some options would include:

- ski lodge employee
- seasonal employee in mountainous regions people seek out during the winter months
- holiday decorator
- holiday party organizer
- supplemental gift store staff
- trip or expedition guide to warm destinations closer to, or South of, the equator
- Santa Claus

Summer-Only Jobs

Perhaps you want to work only in the summer. Or maybe you are migrating from one place to another and hope to combine a winter job in one place with a summer job in another. If this work pattern sounds ideal to you, some options could include:

- camp counselor or camp bookkeeper
- lifeguard
- swimming teacher
- child care provider
- art, drama, science or other children's summer program leader
- summer resort employee
- national park employee
- enrichment class teacher
- house or pet sitter
- refreshment stand operator

Spring-Only Jobs

If you are migrating hither and thither throughout the year, following optimal climates, or checking in with your family on the opposite coast, a spring-only job may be ideal for you. Sample jobs include:

- tax preparer
- landscaper
- tour guide
- graduation or wedding photographer
- graduation or wedding caterer
- home or closet organizing specialist

Confined-Duration Jobs

If you do want to work, but only for a defined period of time, and then be done with it, at least for a while, you may prefer a confined-duration job. Some examples of these jobs include:

- grants writer
- convention staff
- usher
- market survey researcher
- census worker
- event organizer

Flexible-Timeframe Jobs

Or maybe you want to work, but only when it suits you. In that case, a flexible-timeframe job may be ideal for you. Sample jobs of this type might include:

- graphic designer
- interior decorator
- handyman
- editor

- personal organizer

SNAPSHOT

Harold and Ann share a love of travel and a spirit of adventure. Soon after they married, they gave up their confining "day jobs," and set off to see and experience the world. Since then, it would be a challenge for them even to say what continent they live on.

Their lifestyle change included selling their home, simplifying their belongings, and moving what they decided to keep into a storage unit. And then they were off, literally, to the four corners of the world. As a financial advisor, with a healthy list of loyal clients, Harold is able to travel at will so long as he can plug in his laptop, connect to the Internet, and check in as needed. Ann has a winter-only job as manager of the gift shop at a ski lodge in Montana, giving this foot-loose pair one fixed location per year—wintering in a Montana ski resort and indulging their love of skiing.

Otherwise, they go where their interests take them. Biking through Provence. Lounging by the side of a lake in upper New York State. Immersing themselves in nature in Costa Rica. Each year they lay out their plan as they wish, and keep their family posted so that everyone will know "Where in the world are Harold and Ann?"

If I Do Want to Work "Out There," Where Do I Start?

So if you decide that you do want to work "out there" again, where *do* you start? The answer to this question may surprise you. Start online!

Begin with the sites and agencies and job boards and classifieds that were described in Chapter 9. Only this time you will not need to limit your searches to telecommuting options.

Spend time looking through *Monster.com* and *CareerBuilder.com*, *Employment 911.com* and *YahooHotjobs.com*, *HelpWantedSite.com* and *CraigsList.com*, and all the others. Set out to complete your 100 actions that will yield your one optimum job. But don't stop there...

More Online Sites for Job Hunting "Out There"

Some additional job hunting sites that are particularly friendly and appropriate to Baby Boomers include: *Work Search* (the AARP job search site), *Workforce 50*, *Senior Job Bank*, *Internet Senior Success Center*, *Now What Jobs*, *Retirement Jobs*, *Future-Jobs-o-Matic*, and *Retire & Consult*. These are described below. Visit them and follow up on leads and registrations, as you see fit. Add them to your URL list and return to them regularly.

Work Search
http://foundation.aarp.org/WorkSearch

WorkSearch is an AARP site that offers help for seniors who want to re-enter the workforce. The *Worksearch Assessment System* on the site allows you to:

1. Do a *job search* by key word, job category, or zip code.

2. Do a *job match* to discover what type of work best suits you.

3. Improve your skills using their free *Tutorials & Demos*.

Workforce50.com
http://www.workforce50.com/

This site allows job searching by job title, keyword, city, state, zip. The *Career & Education* section provides:

*   salary and job growth data for a wide range of opportunities;

*   information on training and education for each career listed;

*   sample list of careers in which site visitors have expressed strong interest.

Internet Senior Success Center
http://www.internetseniorsuccess.com/seniorsites.htm

This site provides links to the top websites for seniors and Baby Boomers…providing access to products and services that might be of value and interest.

NOTE: Ignore the commercial advertisements included on this site that may not be pertinent to finding a job.

NowWhatJobs.net
http://www.nowwhatjobs.net/

Geared to Baby Boomers and active seniors, this site provides job opportunities, timely advice, corporate profiles, and continuing education options. Other highlights of the site include:
- **The Law**: the actual content of applicable laws protecting against age discrimination: *Age Discrimination in Employment Act of 1967*
- **Radio Segments**: Live streams from "Careers From the Kitchen Table" and "The Dr. Anne Marie Evers Show"

Future-Jobs-O-Matic
http://www.marketplace.org/topics/sustainability/future-jobs

This site separates job areas into: 1) Growing, 2) Shrinking, 3) Highest Paid, and 4) Lowest Paid. Site search tools allow you to: Choose Your Field, Narrow It Down, and Choose A Profession

RetirementJobs.com
http://www.retirementjobs.com/

To use this site, you will need to create an account. Once you have joined the site, you will be able to search for jobs by zip code.

Senior Job Bank
http://www.seniorjobbank.com/

The mission of this site is to bring together employers with qualified older job seekers. From this site, you are able to job search by keyword, company, city, state or zip code.

Retire&Consult
http://retireandconsult.com/cm/Home.html

All services and tools on this site are free for job seekers. Using the site links, you will be able to: *Submit Your Résumé, Find Employment,* and *Use The Consultant Center.*

Where Else Do I Look?

In addition to Online Sources, all the more traditional strategies for job hunting also apply to finding your next job "out there." Four powerful approaches to finding work that can be adjusted to fit your own design, include:

Network: Communicate with your network of associates, providing specifics about your plans, including the particular type of work you are interested in pursuing.

Access Community and Local Leads: Keep an eye out for possibilities in publications and postings in your community.

Spot a Need to Fill: Look for what does not exist as well as for what does. What needs to be done that isn't getting done? Who may need help doing what they are doing? Could you fill one of these needs?

Volunteer with a Plan to Transition to Paid Employment: Watch for opportunities to volunteer for projects that could develop into paid employment. This is an excellent way to give yourself a trial run before committing to work long-term.

My Personal Trifecta

My own search for a job after I retired provides a potentially useful model. In sum, my post-retirement jobs came through three sources: *Networking, Community and Local Leads*, and *Online Searching*.

Networking Nets Surprising Results

To paraphrase a line from a song—"Everybody knows somebody sometime." Put another way, never underestimate the potential of networking, and where it will lead. And don't be shy about tapping into the positions and connections of former and current friends and colleagues. After all, remember that, at some point, you, too, will be in a position to return the favor of making connections for them.

After retiring from a demanding career as a public school district-wide administrator, I initially experienced the typical "nowhere to go and nothing to do" syndrome. It seemed as though all my other retired colleagues had a niche of some type. They all seemed settled and content in pursuing one or another meaningful activities—whether for pay or pleasure—or both. I, on the other hand, felt lost at sea, in terms of filling the 12-hour work day void in which I found myself.

All this changed quickly when I began to talk honestly about my sense of being lost, with nothing to do and all day to do it. Two of my former colleagues, who were now supervising teacher interns and student teachers at one or more local universities and colleges, suggested that I call Mr. X at University Y to ascertain whether there were any needs or openings for more supervisors. And, yes, I could use their names as a reference. When I made the call, referencing colleagues, I had mutually worked with several of the same faculty members. I soon found myself scheduled for an interview, and the rest is happy history.

For the past three years I have absolutely relished my part-time work as a university supervisor of teacher interns and student teachers. I am working with talented, dynamic, promising young people, while simultaneously remaining current on national and state initiatives related to my former full time career as an educator.

I made this happen by taking the initiative to network with colleagues. Oh, and yes, I'm earning my monthly allotment of "mad money," too!

Filling the Need Next Door

Each quarter, I look forward to reading through the various booklets, brochures, and flyers that local community organizations publish describing workshops, mini-courses, and learning activities where, for a reasonable fee, adults, both young and old, can explore and learn a technical skill, an academic subject, a sports related activity, an arts and crafts technique. These classes are often offered in the evenings, at times that are convenient to students and workers, for a duration of just a few weeks.

I am always in the market to improve current and to learn emerging technology skills. There's so much to know! How to reign in digital pictures! How to master the social networks such as FaceBook and Twitter. How to develop a "marketable skill," such as QuickBooks or the latest version of MS Office. Strategies for searching the Internet for the latest, greatest job-hunting websites. I fully expected to see a menu of choices and offerings to satisfy my technology needs and interests and was eager to sign myself up!

Wrong! Not so! There was not one single technology offering by either of the two major organizations. How could that be? Was it lack of interest on the part of the public? Unavailability of knowledgeable staff? Were these technology needs being filled by more extensive, credit-earning courses at local 2-year community and 4-year colleges?

One phone call to both community organizations indicated that, for a combination of reasons it was true that, no, these two groups had nothing to offer would-be technophiles, although, yes, there was a clear demand and need for such programming. Carpe diem! I seized the day! If, I said, I were willing to design and present some workshops that I thought might grab the general public's attention, would you include them in your next quarterly offerings?! "Yes!" was the enthusiastic response. "And when can you come in for an interview to discuss further your ideas about what you could offer and when? Oh, and would you please just bring along descriptions of the workshops you think might be marketable and attractive to our community audience so we can get started immediately?"

The end (or should I say, the *beginning*!) of this story—for the past year, six different technology-related mini-courses have appeared in their community brochure, and I have been sharing with others two of my passions—teaching and technology—while augmenting my "mad money" fund!

Online Is Where It's At!

So many of us are "poster people" for the maxim—"Luck is when preparation and opportunity meet." In fact, throughout my career, in mentoring younger professionals, I've often used this adage not only to impress upon them the importance of lifetime learning, but also to congratulate them when they secured that perfect job or career opportunity as a result of their hard work and preparation.

And I'd like to think that I've applied this same belief throughout my life as I pursued multiple degrees to prepare myself for that next potential career challenge. But the corollary to my constant drive to learn more about more is that I'm always looking for opportunities to teach—to share what I know with others—to watch for that priceless "aha" moment, when I know my students "get it"!

In my "search to share," I often spend time surfing the online employment opportunities links on local college websites. In our state, we have regional consortiums that offer supplementary academic and training support to our state's public school districts. Services extend to teacher professional development, consulting, curriculum design and development, and policy writing services.

While surfing one such job board, I spotted an opening for a part-time technology trainer. Lo! And behold! A local nursing home needed someone to teach "basic computer skills" to a group of 100 nurses. And a small public library had received a grant to do the same!

Without missing a beat, I submitted a résumé, made a follow-up phone call, then designed and submitted eight different mini-courses, ranging from web usage and strategies to MSOffice skills to organizing and presenting digital photos.

These workshops were to be offered in 2-3 hour increments, with morning, afternoon, and evening choices, to accommodate the nurses, who work a variety of shifts, as well as the 9-5'ers.

It would be a toss-up to determine who enjoyed these sessions most—who learned the most—the instructor or the participants. And adding to my "mad money" fund was a plus!

One More Question: How DO I Become Santa Claus?

To return to an employment option mentioned at the end of the last chapter... How *do* you get a job as Santa Claus? And if you do land such a job, what will you be doing, exactly?

As Santa Claus, you will sit for hours, smiling in a bulky red Santa suit. Wriggling children of all ages will climb up on your lap to whisper their Christmas wishes into your ear. If you are ready and rested, and armed with breath mints, tissues, hand sanitizer and a kind disposition, this work can be pure magic.

If you are hired by an outside Santa Distributor, a firm that places Santas at the 1000+ enclosed shopping malls around the country, the mall to which you are assigned may be at a distance, requiring you to commute, or to spend 40 or more days camped out in a nearby motel room, equipped with a small refrigerator and a microwave.

The Hours: Contract Santas at shopping malls typically work six weeks, starting at Thanksgiving—10 hours a day, with meal breaks. For other Santa jobs—private parties, events, independent stores—hours vary.

Median Pay Range: From $10 an hour to thousands per season. Contract pay for the 40-day season can range from around $10,000 for a rookie to more than $50,000 for a more experienced player, depending on the mall and location.

Qualifications: It helps if you look the part —older, plump, a white beard and a jovial laugh. Santas can be of any race —depending on the venue —but they must be male, although there are some openings for Mrs. Santas and Santa's helpers, too. Having a natural beard is often a prerequisite. You can dye it if necessary—and tuck in padding to get that jelly belly.

Contact smaller malls, department stores, photo shops and special event party planners directly for openings. Also check Craigslist and local classified ads.

National staffing services typically provide Santa impersonators to the larger malls. Three of the larger staffing services are: *Cherry Hill Photo Enterprises Inc.*, *Worldwide Photography*, and *Noerr Programs Corp.*

You will need to apply to these online agencies and appear for an in-person interview. If they like your look and personality, you will be asked to slip into costume and make-up for them to shoot the head-shots that will be sent to mall reps for selection.

If you are selected, the service will negotiate your contract and send you to *Santa School* for tips on appropriate behavior and dialog, how to draw out the shy children and calm down the overexcited ones, and even tips about make-up. There will be a criminal background check and drug screening. And be sure not to forget your flu shot.

Now What About You?

Select three specific actionable ideas for working "out there." to add to what you will consider later when you "make your match and move." Record your three top choices here for now, then copy them to the composite of possibilities you began creating in Chapter 8.

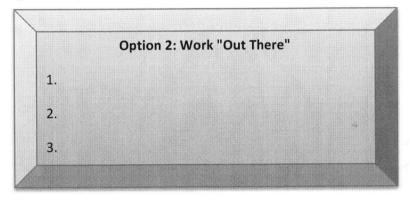

Option 2: Work "Out There"

1.

2.

3.

And So...

You know now what is "new" and appealing to you about working "out there." You know that employers do want you and that there are many interesting job areas available and growing. You know what work appeals to Boomers as a group, and what work is most likely to engage you in particular, according to your temperament. And you know how to balance work with the rest of your life by deliberately selecting jobs that leave you free during your season of choice, or where the duration is confined or the time frame is flexible.

All of these possibilities involve working FOR someone else. And this may be just what you want to do next.

But before you decide to work FOR someone again, read on. In the next chapter we will look at the option of "hiring" yourself or partnering up.

After all, there's no business like YOUR business...

CHAPTER 11:
Option #3: "Hire" Yourself or "Partner Up"

Some things in life are for certain after all. If you do not EVER AGAIN want to work for someone else… Or if you have the notion that no-one will appreciate what you have to offer… Or if you think the economy is such that even if you did manage to find employment, it would not reward you adequately, either in terms of fun or profit, or both… In any of these cases, there is good news.

There is one employer you WILL want to work for, who WILL appreciate what you have to offer, who WILL want to hire you, and who WILL offer you employment that will reward you.

"And who would that employer be?" you ask. That employer would be YOU. YOU could well be your own best possible future employer.

"But what kind of business would I start?" you ask next. In short, plan to start a business that meets a *need*. Needs can come in three main forms, with various combinations thereof:

1. **Needs for Goods:** What goods do people need (or want) to buy.

2. **Needs for Services:** What services do people need (or want) to have provided for them?

3. **Needs for Creativity:** What do people need (or want) to have created for them?

When you have determined which of these types of needs you could meet, either for goods, services or creativity… And once you determine specifically how you would meet them… And after you have thought about the degree to which filling these particular needs would bring you enjoyment and fulfillment… Then you are ready to design a business that meets those needs, making full use of your own unique twist or advantage. Then you would launch, market and promote your business, making connections between what you are offering and the people who may need or want it.

Consider Mark Twain as a role model. What was the need he set out to meet—beyond the obvious one of his audience's need and desire to read his humorous stories? Well, apparently one thing Twain determined that people needed was a replacement for suspenders!

Mark Twain Granted His First Patent

December 19, 1871 *[PRESS RELEASE]*

Samuel L. Clemens received patent #121,992 on December 19, 1871 for an Improvement in Adjustable and Detachable Straps for Garments.

Clemens, better known as Mark Twain, and famous for stories such as *Huckleberry Finn* and *Tom Sawyer*, also was an inventor and received a total of three patents. While living in Hartford, Connecticut, Twain received his first patent for an adjustable strap that could be used to tighten shirts at the waist. This strap attached to the back of a shirt and fastened with buttons to keep it in place and was easy to remove. Twain's invention was not only used for shirts, but for underpants and women's corsets as well. His purpose was to do away with suspenders, which he considered uncomfortable.

In 1873, Twain received a patent for a self-pasting scrapbook that was very popular and sold over 25,000 copies. In 1885 he received a patent for a history trivia game.

If the idea of starting a business that meets a need sounds like too much work, think again. Why would you want or need to do all the work yourself? Instead, consider teaming up. Think about the people you have known in the past who might, like you, be immersed in their own search for a meaningful pursuit for their next phase of life. From this group, consider who might best complement you and your own talents. And who among this group would you enjoy working with?

One of these past friends or associates could become your perfect business partner. Or your life partner may be the one. We will talk more about "partnering up" later in this chapter.

Of course there is always the option of starting a business that creates jobs for others. You could "hire" yourself as the manager, and employ others to carry out all or part of the work, under your guidance. Or you could even hire someone else to function as the acting manager in charge of ongoing operations, and make yourself the "manager in chief."

There are many ways to get the work done, while at the same time limiting the amount of work that you do yourself. These are essential considerations if and when you decide to "hire yourself" and start a business, large or small. Your work does, after all, need to balance with your emerging retirement lifestyle.

Businesses That Meet Needs for Goods

Looking around my own small rural locale for ideas about unmet needs for goods, my first thought is that we need a new source for pie! In past years, the Terrell Country Store, at the main (and only) crossroad in our tiny town, has been our primo pie supplier.

Demand for pie is so great in our town that the Country Store has been able to run a tight ship, pie-wise, over the years. Locals learned early on that they would have little or no hope of purchasing a pie if they just dropped into the store expecting to buy one. Oh no. We knew full well that if we wanted to be "allowed" to purchase the pie of our choice, we had to follow a strict set of "pie rules." Also, of course, we knew that we were going pay a premium for our pies, around $15 each.

The "rules"... All pie orders must be submitted and paid for by Sunday. We then are required to return on the following Wednesday to pick up our pies. These pie deadlines are even more stringent before Thanksgiving and Christmas, when orders must be submitted and prepaid *two weeks* in advance. And, due to the crush of orders needing to be filled during the holidays, cream pie orders are NOT allowed at those times!

Are these pies worth the trouble, not to mention the cost? Absolutely! And, no, a frozen or supermarket substitute will not suffice!

But now a crisis is upon us! The Country Store is going out of business next month. So, with the holidays looming ahead, we already are down to our final round of pie orders. After that—no more pie!

Voila! A golden opportunity for a potential business to meet a pressing need. And this could be a business with *sweet* benefits!

There are hundreds of other ideas for businesses to supply needed (or wanted) goods. We start the list with pie, then add to it, to stimulate your thinking:

- Great pie!

- Specialized parts for classic cars

- Pet treats, toys and holiday costumes (yes, really!)

- Baby and toddler toys and puzzles made from wood, not plastic

- Woven table mats, scarves and garments

- Comfortable walking shoes, especially ones that come in wide

- Yard and patio furniture that lasts

You have your own ideas to add to this list of needs. And if something is on *your* list as a need or a want, it is likely on other people's lists as well.

SNAPSHOT

Rebecca started small when, newly retired, she decided to deal in antiques. Every weekend she'd travel around the state filling her hatchback with items she hoped would earn a hefty return.

Her first purchasing rule—never to buy anything she didn't love enough to use and display in her own home. Soon she found her small cottage overrun with lovely, eclectic pieces. So, her second purchasing rule became—she could not purchase another piece until and unless she first sold an existing one.

Thus was born her eBay business. But, lo and behold, that's not the end of the story. While surfing eBay one day, Becky noticed that some vendors were buying and selling buttons. Yes, buttons! Fast forward to today.

Becky now prowls flea markets searching for antique buttons. She now croons, "I sell and send out a small package and receive a big check in return. It's so much fun, so interesting, and a lot easier than selling antique furniture."

Businesses that Meet Needs for Services

Who needs the services you have to offer? So many choices—so many opportunities—so many roads to Oz!

Let's start by considering some major groups of people who are ripe for services, beginning with:

- children of all ages
- teen through college students
- working adults
- retired people

When you consider the variety, breadth and depth of services that each of these groups uses, demands and needs, just think of all the services you possibly could offer. Again, base your service business concept on your own newly designed lifestyle, taking into account your reinvented and unique SELF—personality, skills, talents, and interests.

Services Children and Their Parents Need

Think about how the society of the family has changed within the last 60 years! When we were young children, working mothers were the exception, not the rule. The" ideal" wife and mother was one who consciously chose to be a stay-at-home mom, dedicating her time and energy to raising her children, tending to household duties and supporting her husband emotionally and domestically. Conventional wisdom dictated that, ideally, children needed to remain home with mom for as long as possible, to be nurtured and raised under her watchful eye, absorbing her moral values within a stable environment. The terms "pre-school" and "pre-K" were nowhere to be found on society's radar screen.

Dad was the sole bread winner. His role was that of CFO—Chief Financial Officer—who earned enough money to tend to the family's material needs, paying a high price by working long hours, and being subjected to the work world's pressures and stresses. His work sometimes required extensive travel that kept him from being a part of family activities and occasions.

Now fast-forward to the 21st century. Mom and Dad both work, often both in demanding professions that require long days, frequent business travel, and a myriad of human, work related pressures. Consequently, many couples today have chosen to have smaller, and often delayed, families.

WOW FACTOR

In 1957, the average number of children per family peaked at 3.7. Currently, the average number of children per family household in the United States is .94—less than ONE. In 1957, children ages 0-17 comprised 35% of the total population. In 2012, this same demographic group makes up only 24% (*www.childstats.gov*).

We all are aware of the many reasons for this decline in the number of children being born in the USA—the costs of raising a child, the priorities that professional couples place on their careers, the trend towards starting a family later in life.

However, while the number of children per household has substantially decreased, for those couples and single parents who do choose to have a family, the importance they place on how they raise their children has become all-consuming.

Average expenditures per year, per child, have risen 40% in the past decade, from around $10,000 to around $14,000 (*The Rising Cost of Raising a Child* by Jessica Dickler, September 2011; CNN Money; *http://money.cnn.com*). Based on findings from the "Cost of a Child" survey, parents spend between $170, 000 and $390,000 to raise each child from birth to age 18, *not* including their college education.

Increasingly demanding dual careers, combined with escalating parental concerns about children's physical safety, material, social and academic needs—all these factors translate into an extensive list of needs for services targeted to children. This, in turn, suggests business opportunities that serve this population.

Parents with children age 0–12 have urgent needs to find:

- a satisfactory sitter
- a suitable nanny

- the ideal day care center
- the best possible pre-school, pre-K, and K programs
- a safe car-pool
- the perfect music, art, dance, athletic program
- an after-school tutoring program
- a reliable after-school care service

If you enjoy working with children, think about each of these categories in terms of your own interests, skills, and talents. Whether you prefer a primary or secondary role, as the one who is in direct contact with children, or as the manager who keeps the enterprise afloat, you have an almost limitless number of opportunities to work meeting one of the above needs, or any number of others.

SNAPSHOT

What an enviable family life Carrie and Bill currently have! Mom, a part-time registered nurse, and dad, a realtor in town, have four lively and lovely children—a 9-year-old son from Carrie's former marriage, a precocious 3-year old brother, and two adorable one-year old twin girls. They live in a huge, old, 5,600 square foot, four-story, refurbished farmhouse at the end of a long country road, overlooking hundreds of acres of bucolic rolling hills, complete with in-ground pool, humongous barn, and, of course, the family dog, Dim Sum.

How idyllic, you might say. How much closer to Paradise could you get. Not so! Carrie, who works two days at the local hospital, is also in charge of the physical abuse segment of her town's DCF program. Bill, who is in the process of building a successful real estate business, spends his time glued to his cell phone and his Internet site. In spite of the demands of their increasingly stressful professional lives, they are both committed and determined to place their children's lives front and center, making sure that the children are always surrounded and cared for by family members, in particular the grandparents.

Or so they hoped. Everyone had the best of intentions, *but* ... both maternal and paternal grandparents, who live active lives of their own, are only intermittently available—ergo, not very

---

reliable or willing as baby-sitters on a regular basis. And try as they can, in spite of their best efforts, Bill and Carrie cannot seem to establish mutually complimentary schedules, wherein at least one of them is free to remain home with the cherubs, day in and day out.

Enter the solution, in the form of a local newly-retired elementary school teacher Bill and Carrie found through family friends. In return for her spending 20-25 hours per week acting as the children's nanny, Bill and Carrie have provided this senior lady with full-time free room and board. She has total and private access to the entire 4th floor of their home, where she enjoys a 1,000+ square foot large, sunny, apartment, complete with private bath and mini-kitchen, and a huge walk-in closet that she has converted into an office! The one condition to this arrangement—that she plan her 20-25 weekly nanny hours around Carrie and Bill's work schedule, making herself available whenever they are not.

Services Teen through College Students Need

We are all aware of the social pressure brought to bear on pre-teens, teens, and college students. Their needs loom large—academically, socially, and emotionally. Parents acknowledge the fragility and urgency that characterize these age groups. Pre-teens are plagued with all the frustrations and trauma that come with puberty—their bodily changes, their need for social bonding, their process of self-discovery.

High school kids find themselves dealing with the pressures of alcohol, drugs, dating, developing maturity, peer pressure, and academic achievement challenges. They need to come to terms with their passage to adulthood—the "what do I do next?" question emerges all too soon. College? Military service? Vocational training? The work world?

If college is their choice, many young people find they are not ready to handle the freedom and independence college life brings. Many also face financial hardships in the form of student loans and possibly the need to work while in school. The ambiguity of choosing a future career, and the necessity of maintaining a respectable GPA, add stress to the balance, especially when combined with a need to be employed.

What can you, as a self-hiring retired person, offer this group? To start your thinking, some of their needs include:

- after-school supervision
- homework help or tutoring
- after-school music or art activities
- exercise, aerobics, sports or other physical activities
- social networking supervision
- reliable transportation to work, social, school, sports activities
- assistance with academic research and projects
- counseling or mentoring
- summer programs
- part-time employment opportunities

Can you, as a self-hiring retiree, see yourself assuming one of the above roles, providing these services to young people, through either direct or indirect involvement? There are so many ways to be in the company of young people, to give them the opportunity to interact with an experienced member of an older generation, while providing a needed service that you enjoy doing, and that supplements your retirement income! It doesn't get any better than that.

Services Working Adults Need

The entire population of working adults has needs, whether they have children or not. And this is our largest group, comprising more than 63.7% of the total population in 2012, according to the *Bureau of Labor Statistics*.

The opportunities that self-hiring retirees have to work for and with this demographic group are endless—ranging from the mundane to the exotic—from housekeeping to horticulture—from accounting to adventure travel—from home baking to grooming poodles. Whatever you offer to do for this time-challenged group, you can be sure that someone out there, fighting the good fight, climbing the corporate ladder, needs to have it done. All that is needed is for you to find each other and make a match!

Remember what your life was like when you were working full time? All non-work-related chores, tasks and appointments had to be squeezed into your so-called "free time"—those too short lunch breaks, after work and weekend timeslots. There never seemed to be enough hours in the day to do everything you needed to get done.

With your constant juggling and multi-tasking, admit it—sometimes you dropped the ball, threw your hands up in frustration, and ceded defeat! A true confession—I once had to retrace 20 miles and drive back into Charleston because, after leaving my after-job job, to my shame and amazement, I was half way home before I realized that I had forgotten to pick up my children!

During your working years, you were the one who needed any help you could get! Now your role is reversed. You find yourself in a position where you can be the one to alleviate some of the pressure that the working majority faces on a daily basis. *You* can become their hands, feet, brains—their full-service concierge—the very person *you* so desperately needed before you retired—the one whose services you would have been thankful to use, if only you could have found someone reliable, energetic and capable like YOU to help you out.

SNAPSHOT

Dwight worked as a transmission engineer for the phone company for 30 years, then "volunteered" to retire at age 50. He immediately "unretired" and took another job, working for an equipment manufacturer that sold products to his former employers, among others. When this job ended after 6 years, he found himself "really retired" at age 56.

But not for long... Soon he had "unretired" again and taken a part-time job in charge of maintenance for a retirement community in Pennsylvania. Already highly skilled at all things electrical, he now tackled the full range of repairs and tasks—from plumbing to landscaping to carpentry to heating and air conditioning—learning on the job to "fix almost anything."

This maintenance job ended too, when he and his wife moved to North Carolina to be closer to the grandkids. But once they had the move behind them, and Dwight had completed his own long "Honey Do" list putting his own new home in order, he was back to eagerly looking for something useful to do.

Describing himself as a man who "always needs a project," he started working as a handyman—a "guy Friday" to neighbors, friends, and friends of friends who had daunting "Honey Do" lists of their own. These working adults, with their hectic lives, were more than delighted to "share" their fix up lists with Dwight, and to pay him well for his efforts, of course. Word of mouth was all that it took for him to stay as busy as he wanted to be, turning other people's "Honey Do"s into "Honey Done"s.

Tasks that working adults need to have done, include:

- **Mundane tasks—**
  Watering plants; picking up dry-cleaning, mail, drugstore or department store items; maintaining calendars for appointments, children's activities, family functions.
- **Pampering tasks—**
  Providing fresh flowers, maintaining candle scents, gift shopping, organizing and displaying family and travel photos.
- **Domestic tasks—**
  Organizing cupboards, closets, drawers; taking care of gardens, lawns, yards; redecorating; house sitting; home maintenance; home cleaning; shopping and stocking household items; doing laundry, ironing, mending and other routine tasks.
- **Social tasks—**
  Planning, organizing and orchestrating parties (birthday, holiday, wedding, anniversary, family celebrations, graduations); designing and sending invitations; purchasing and setting up decorations; planning menus; providing food; arranging music and entertainment; procuring photographer, favors/gifts.
- **Travel tasks—**
  Making complete reservations, including transportation, lodging, sightseeing, adventure activities, shopping; planning suitcase contents; child-sitting, pet-sitting, plant-sitting, house-sitting, business-sitting, elder-sitting.
- **Food-related tasks—**
  Food shopping; menu designing; planning and executing formal dinner parties or informal meal-centered gatherings; high-quality home-cooked entrées and prepared meals; home baking .

- **Fashion tasks—**
  Shopping for clothes, utilizing the best online clothing sites, including specialty and discount shops and department stores.
- **Petcare tasks—**
  Feeding, walking, cleaning animals and their living environments; arranging for and taking pets to vet appointments.
- **Body-related tasks—**
  Providing massages, personal training, hair, nails, cosmetics products and services. Pedicures.
- **Money and business tasks—**
  Performing personal accounting, tax preparation, checkbook monitoring, and bill paying services; filing and organizing personal documents; completing travel reimbursement paperwork; responding to business correspondence.
- **Large project tasks—**
  Cleaning/organizing attics, basements, garages, file cabinets, closets. Repurposing space for master suites, home offices, home theaters, playrooms, art studios, workshops, home gyms.
- **Maintaining entertainment and technology systems—**
  Ensuring that all video, voice, network, data systems, computers, phones, TVs are in perfect working order. Teaching personal technology use, one-on-one.

SNAPSHOT

Liz spent much of her career in retail sales, culminating in a position where she managed all operations for several stores. She and her husband eventually settled in the lovely North Carolina mountains, where they built a home that provided the best of both worlds—mountain views, yet within a 10-minute drive to downtown Asheville—a colorful, arty city that has become a popular vacation and retirement destination.

Starting as a sideline, Liz and her husband purchased other well-located properties and refurbished them to sell at a profit. Over time Liz became expert at selecting high-potential vacation rental properties from the local real estate market—houses that offered the same perfect "mountain and town" lifestyle she and her husband had created for themselves. Based on her considerable experience, she estimates that properties like these that combine mountain views with close access to town, will yield average rental earnings of $30,000 a year for a two bedroom unit.

Because of the impact the recession has had on owners of vacation properties, many have been forced to sell at hugely reduced prices. And some owners, unable to sell at a price that will satisfy their mortgages, are forced to rent out their properties in order to cover costs. Many, if not most, investors interested in purchasing these highly discounted vacation homes to generate income, are absentee owners who need a responsible, hospitable property manager, who lives locally, to handle their properties for them.

One such investor, a doctor whom Liz had introduced to the high income potential of Asheville vacation rentals, asked Liz if she knew anyone who would be good at managing his first investment property for him. She offered to do this herself, and so it all began. Liz's doctor associate now owns seven such properties, all of which Liz manages. Through friends and word-of-mouth, Liz has added more properties to manage, bringing the total to 14.

Capitalizing on filling the doctor's need led Liz into her current lucrative business, which she enjoys thoroughly. She says: "I have always created my own jobs. If I can do it, anyone can."

Services for US–What Retired People Need

Another group with needs for services is *us*—the ever-growing senior population, ranging from those of us who are newly retired to those who have been retired for a decade or more.

Because Boomers number 77 million, our demands for services are growing at exponential rates, creating a current and emerging target market that holds so many exciting and potentially lucrative possibilities. In fact, we have dedicated the entire next chapter to this group.

Again, the focus of our discussion, both now and later, is "What does this group need?" What kinds of services do people like *you* need that *you* may want to be the one to offer?

Services that retired people need, and will gladly pay for, include:

- Recreational and activity needs
- Intellectual and mental stimulation needs
- Physical and health needs
- Financial and money management needs
- Home maintenance and remodeling needs
- Travel needs
- Transportation needs

SNAPSHOT

Ralph was the town dentist, with his offices on Main Street. So what does a dentist do next after he retires? And what does he do with the Victorian-style home on Main Street that had been the location of his dental offices?

The answer to this question is that he, along with his wife Betty, converted his former dental office into Zazzy'z, a popular and comfortable local hang-out, serving breakfast, coffees, and lunch. And, for those who prefer not to cook at all, Zazzy'z also offers frozen home-cooked entrées to take home for dinner, with delectable options that include: Tidewater Crab Cakes with spicy mustard sauce, rolled in hand-crumbled crackers and lightly sautéed, served with fresh steamed asparagus and white rice. Or Champagne Chicken with artichoke hearts, baked in a champagne cream and served with steamed rice. Or eight other equally amazing-sounding full meals.

Zazzy'z has become a local favorite. Small groups gather in the lounge chairs around a large round coffee table in the bookshop bay window. Repeat customers snag their favorite tables, and settle in. Local artists display their work on a rotating basis, gaining both exposure and sales.

Ralph and Betty started Zazzy'z with the idea of ultimately turning the business over to their daughter and son-in-law. But they drift in and out all day. Betty is also busy finalizing her third published book in her area of expertise, antiques.

> Ralph now has accepted the role of *Director of the College for Older Adults,* operated through the *SWVA (SW Virginia) Higher Education Center* in their small town in Virginia. He also has his own radio show on *WEHC FM* (an NPR affiliate) called "Minding Your Brain," where he offers expert interviews, and his own research-based commentary, on the important topic of *Brain Health.*

You surely can expand on these various categories and lists of services. Where could the reenergized and reinvented YOU and the diversity of needs for services match up? What could you offer to:

1. Capitalize on the talents, skills, experiences and interests that you personally and professionally could bring to bear, and
2. Meet the needs of one or more of the above categories—children, teens through college, working adults and retired people?

Businesses That Meet Needs for Creativity

Returning to Richard Florida's research introduced in Chapter 5, a growing role of creativity in our economy is the fundamental theme that runs through a host of seemingly unrelated changes in American society. The ongoing increase in the options for creative work suggest some excellent opportunities for retirement work that would engage you, and through which you could express your special gifts.

"Creative class" workers are found in a variety of fields, from engineering to theater, biotech to education, architecture to small business. Creativity workers constitute an estimated 40 million individuals who fall into two broad categories (based on the *Standard Occupational Classification System* codes): 1) the *Super-Creative Core*, and 2) *Creative Professionals.*

The *Super-Creative Core* is a group that comprises about 12% of all U.S. workers. This group includes a wide range of occupations (science, engineering, education, computer programming, research), with arts, design, and media workers forming a small subset. Their primary job function is to create and innovate, contributing commercial products, consumer goods, problem solving and "problem finding" (Florida, 2002).

The *Creative Professionals* are classic knowledge-based workers, including those working in healthcare, business and finance, the legal sector, and education. They "draw on complex bodies of knowledge to solve specific problems."

WOW FACTOR

Although creative work makes up roughly 1/3 of total employment, it accounts for more than 1/2 of all wages and salaries in America.

Creative employment has seen relatively low rates of unemployment during the course of the economic crisis, and is expected to account for roughly HALF of all projected U.S. employment growth - adding 6.8 million new jobs by 2018.

How to "Go Creative"

So… What does the "creative class" have to do with you? It has *everything* to do with *you*! The whole purpose and thrust of this book is to address *your* "specialness"—to determine a match between *your* uniqueness, *your* passion, and what needs to be done. This journey of personal discovery may well take you down a new path that culminates in you launching yourself into creative work of some type.

And what would your own creativity work be? You may engage in work that is typical of the *Creative Core*—writing, painting, photography, sculpture, woodwork. Or you may take off in the entirely different creative direction of a *Creative Professional*, engaging in problem solving or even problem finding. You may invent all new products… Or create solutions… Or design better systems… Or otherwise make the world safer, more comfortable, more accessible, more engaging…

SNAPSHOT

While on vacation in Italy, I intended to purchase an authentic cameo ring for myself. As we travelled from town to town, I searched for that perfect piece, confident that I would "know it when I saw it."

As our trip neared its end, I wondered whether I would find that elusive unique cameo. We were on the Isle of Capri when I spot-

---

ted in the window of a small, off-the-beaten-path shop, an unusual cameo ring that featured a cluster of three delicate tiny silhouettes. Wandering into the shop, I found there an older gentleman sitting in the back carving away.

Soon I had learned that this native Italian was retired from his major work as a fisherman. For several years now he had carved cameos as his creative outlet, and even had earned a prestigious certificate that entitled him to teach others to carve.

Leading me to a small display that featured two especially unique rings, he proudly stated that, if I chose to purchase one of them and then later found one similar "in all of Italy," he would gladly refund my cost in full.

He went on to describe in detail how he plied his craft, how many years he had been carving cameos, and why each of his creations was special. His passion, his talent and his work were obviously aligned in perfect harmony. And he was able to earn a respectable supplementary retirement income doing what he loved most.

How About Creative Consulting?

Think about it—for x number of years, you worked within a particular field—as a plumber, a nurse, a truck driver, a financial analyst, a teacher, a chef. Think about the unique experiences you had and what you learned along the way—experiences and knowledge to which only those in your particular type of work have been privy.

You can most certainly parlay that knowledge into offering valuable, revenue-generating advice to others. Consulting is an ideal way to earn a supplemental income. You can work part time, set your own schedule, choose which clients and types of work you want to engage in, and even determine your own salary.

Businesses That Meet Needs Abroad

Since it will be *you* who decides what business you start, whether it offers goods, services or creativity, it also will be your decision to determine *where* it will be located. Here's where it pays to dream big.

International Living Magazine (internationalliving.com) claims that there are appealing places in the world where you can live comfortably on less than $700 a month. Or you could retire like royalty on a $1,600-a-month budget (for a couple) that will "buy you a comfortable home in a beautiful setting, pay for your food, utilities, housekeeper, gardener...and even leave you with money left over for entertainment and travel!"

International Living magazine claims to have been helping readers for over 31 years to "live better lives for less, retire earlier, travel further, have a lot of fun, and even make money—overseas." Many people, including many retired people, are doing just this.

SNAPSHOT

"I get paid to travel the world" says Sandra Kennedy, a retired teacher now turned travel writer. Here is her story:

I stayed at lavish haciendas, ate the freshest foods in Ecuador, got to know the smiling, helpful locals. I went to a Shaman healing ceremony, rode horses in the Andes and learned to weave. Then I sat sipping fresh mango juice, relaxing by the pool. It's hard to believe it costs me nothing to travel like this.

Okay, so I had to take notes and photos along the way and spend a few evenings writing up my impressions while they were fresh in my mind. Back home, I would put them into proper sentences and then three different editors would pay me for them.

I used to think it was too good to be true. But it's the life I lead today. I've always loved travel and photography. And as a retired teacher, I figured I could put a sentence together—though I'd hardly say I have great literary flair.

So a few years back, I attended a travel writers workshop in Buenos Aires to see if I could gather the secrets to getting stories into print and cashing in on some of the perks I knew could come with this line of work. For the workshop's writing assignment, I wrote about renting an apartment to stay in for the week before the event, and "living like a local." "Escape

> *Artist" published it within a few weeks of my return home. I was hooked.*
>
> *Now, five-years later, my portfolio is filled with travel articles and photographs from Chile, Ecuador, Guatemala, Portugal, Uruguay, Argentina, Alaska, Maine, Oregon, and Washington. And many of those articles recounted trips I enjoyed for next to nothing or even for free.*
>
> *It was while exploring the Schist villages of central Portugal earlier this year that I realized just how much my life has changed. I'd retired from teaching and wasn't sure how I'd keep myself busy. But now here I am getting paid to travel, take pictures along the way, and write about what I recommend other people do and see. It's hard to believe it's even a real job! But I'm living proof: It is.*

What Business to Start

It's not surprising that many of us, at one time or another, have given at least a cursory nod to the idea of starting our own business. Sometimes the thought came from reading about someone who had achieved phenomenal success following their passion. At other times, some specific life experience sparked the thought—"I have a great idea that I think could make money, and I would love to try it!" Perhaps now is the time to take that leap of faith into the entrepreneurial pool!

Of course there is no guarantee that if you decide to take steps to launch your own business, you'll soon be featured on the cover of Forbes. But, like many of us, you may have a latent money-making idea that has remained dormant all these years as you carried out the important business of making a living, raising a family, and saving for retirement—an idea that has stubbornly persisted to this day, creating a spring to your step, a sparkle in your eye, and a fire in your belly when you think of the possibility of following through on your dream. The question is, what do you do with it now? And if not now, *when*?

To move ahead towards a plan, or to at least think through the possibilities, here are the three keys:

1. Identify matches between what people need and what you most enjoy doing.

2. Select work that would engage your essential self, including your type, temperament, interests, values, skills and traits.

3. Consider if you may want to partner up.

Identify Matches Between What People Need and What You Enjoy

In our previous lives, we worked and worked, then tried to "fit in" a small packet of fun. Now we find that our whole formula for living has been reversed! We can play and play, then intersperse our leisure with some form of work, if we so choose. How delicious and delightful!

Of course, the question is, "Now that I have all this latitude, precisely what is it that I want to do? What is it that I always look forward to doing—that so consumes me that I lose track of time?

And what if there was a way my natural drive, my creativity, my love for horseback riding or sailing or travel, could become a source of limited, but adequate discretionary cash? Imagine doing something that I am passionate about, that I would want to be doing anyway, for the fun of it, and getting paid for it! What might that be like?

SNAPSHOT

DJ Wika Szmyt, 73, spends her retirement days behind a DJ console, playing music at a club in Warsaw three days a week, and watching people dance to her rhythms. She plays disco, rumba or samba for a mostly older audience, because she feels she is giving them a new take on life. As well as working at the club, DJ Wika has also been involved in other musical projects, including parties where she plays for a younger and more demanding audience.

Clearly, as part of embarking on this "what if I could get paid to do what I already love doing and would do anyway" journey, it is also necessary to ask yourself if anyone needs to have done whatever it is you love to do. Return now to some of the ideas about what people need, and look for items that you do well, and possibly even do for fun.

Read through these areas of need and check those that you enjoy and do well. Then from those you checked, circle the checkmarks of the ones you might consider doing for others—for pay, of course.

What Do You Like to Do?	
☐ **Organizing**: cupboards, file cabinets, drawers, clothes closets, offices, garages, basements	☐ **Yard and Garden**: planting, mulching, weeding, lawn care, hedging, pruning
☐ **Redecorating**: painting, wallpapering, furnishings, functional design, decorating	☐ **Party Planning**: birthday, holiday, wedding, anniversary, graduation, family celebrations
☐ **Sitting Services**: child-sitting, pet-sitting, plant-sitting, house-sitting, business-sitting, elder-sitting	☐ **Food Planning Services**: shopping, menu designing; meal preparation
☐ **Pet Services**: feeding, walking, cleaning animals and their living environment	☐ **Photo Services**: organizing, enhancing, and displaying family and travel photos
☐ **Tutoring**: assisting children who have difficulty learning in the school setting	☐ **Writing Services**: business correspondence, memoires, family histories and stories
☐ **Catering**: formal dinner parties, meal-centered family gatherings, celebrations, receptions.	☐ **Home Maintenance**: painting, repairs, sprinkler systems, AC systems, repairs, shelving
☐ **Travel Planning**: reservations, for transportation, lodging, sightseeing, adventure activities, shopping	☐ **Financial Services**: personal accounting, tax preparation, checkbook monitoring, bill paying
☐ **Major Household Projects**: adding patios, porches, sunrooms, outdoor living spaces; refinishing basements, home offices, art studios, workshops	☐ **Technology Services:** ensuring that video, voice, network, data systems, computers, TVs, phones, are in perfect working order; teaching personal technology use

Select Work that Engages Your Temperament

Returning to the four temperaments (from Chapter 7), one of which defines you—*Guardian, Artisan, Giver* or *Thinker*—whatever business you develop needs to be one where the work you will be doing is work that will engage you over time, given your temperament.

Think through what the actual tasks will be. Then evaluate that option based on the degree to which you will gain satisfaction by completing those tasks over the months and years ahead.

If the major tasks of a goods, services or creativity business do not suit you, and will not engage you long term, that occupation may not be the right type of business or enterprise for you. On the other hand, if some of the tasks of a business do excite you but others do not, this venture may still be a good possibility for you IF you find a partner whose interests and unique abilities balance and complement yours.

If you are a **Guardian** (SJ), with a drive to be useful, your temperament may fit well, and you may be well engaged, by a number of the service business possibilities. Your inclination to seek stability and orderliness, and your underlying capacity to be practical, organized, thorough and systematic, make you a natural for providing many of the types of services that are particularly in demand.

If you are an **Artisan/Experiencer** (SP), with a need to act freely, you may find your best match with either a service or a creativity business that involves action, challenge and resourcefulness. To add to the excitement and adventure of an opportunity, consider shifting the location of your business abroad.

If you are a **Giver** (NF), for whom purpose and personal growth are essential, your best options may be providing services or creating products or solutions that focus on human potential and that bring out the best in others.

If you are a **Thinker** (NT), with a drive to improve, your best selections of possible service or creativity businesses may be ones where you will be adequately challenged. Your ability to see possibilities, understand complexities and design solutions are of considerable value, and will need to be engaged in order that an enterprise holds your interest over time.

Consider Partnering Up: Joint Employment

If the scope of work goes beyond what you can hope to accomplish by yourself, it may make sense to think bigger and consider enlisting a partner. Think about what your full list of collective capabilities would be if you combined what you can do with what your spouse can do. What if you added your son into the mix? And his wife? And your daughter? And her husband? Or what if you went beyond your family and added in your best friend? Or a former colleague?

Pick Your PARDNAH!

If you do decide you would like to partner up with someone, the question arises, "Who?" Start by looking close by, possibly to your spouse. After all, for all these years, you have shared your hopes and dreams with this person. Who better knows your Achilles' heel, your "ups and downs," your "highs and lows"?

Or maybe your best option is your longtime friend and college roommate. You know—the one who was best man or maid of honor at your wedding; the one after whom you named your first-born; the person you always seem to call first in good times and bad.

It might be someone you met recently, brought together by the very business idea you are planning to bring to fruition. You may have met online, or at a conference or expo, or any similar type of venue where people with similar interests, talents, and skills gather to see what's new, to glean ideas for their own projects, and to meet and network with colleagues.

In any of these scenarios, before you even consider the possibility of venturing into a professional working partnership, be sure that:

- there exists a high level of mutual confidence, trust, and respect;

- each partner has a clear understanding of his/her role and is well qualified to perform it;

- the individual skills, talents and strengths of each partner are clearly defined and understood by both parties;

- you have had at least some practical, long-term experience working together on defined projects or activities;

- you share the same vision for your venture and agree upon the strategic direction your endeavor should take;

- you both have clear expectations (both financial and professional) of what each person hopes to derive from the partnership; and

- you have a balance of different skills, talents, strengths and expertise that complement and supplement each other.

Communication Is Key

As with any partnership, including marriage, the importance of communication between business partners cannot be overestimated. A regular "coming together" for reality/progress checks, whether remotely or in person, is absolutely essential and critical to the success of any partnership.

Think about how many personal relationships have disintegrated because of a lack of communication on the part of one partner or the other. In advance, agree upon a means of communicating both formally and informally on a regular and frequent basis, whether these connections are made through:

- scheduled meetings
- informal breakfast/lunch/ sessions
- phone conversations
- e-mails
- annual shared trips or conference attendance
- Skype sessions

In these times of virtual commuting, it is easier and more important than ever to work "side by side" even when you live 500 miles apart.

Partnership Pros, Cons & Potential Minefields

Pause to consider the pros, cons and potential minefields of partnering up before you make the leap. Determine if the *Pros*, in your case, outweigh the *Cons*. And make every effort to avoid the *Minefields*.

Pros

By partnering up, you will:

- Enjoy a partner who complements and supplements your personality, skill set, talents and areas of expertise.
- Get to share the workload. This allows both members to enjoy a vacation period without worrying about "who's minding the store."
- Gain another perspective on your ideas by listening to your partner's point of view.
- Share the financial burden of start-up and maintenance costs.
- Share the risks of failure as well as the joys of success.
- Have someone with whom to commiserate and problem solve when setbacks and unexpected roadblocks appear.
- Share the burden of responsible decision-making.
- Have a partner with whom to discuss current steps and future directions in your business plan.
- Expand your circle of colleagues with two sets of business and social contacts.

Cons

Are you willing and able to work collaboratively, as a member of a team, knowing that sometimes your ideas may need to be adapted to accommodate your partner's perspective? Highly inflated egos can easily jeopardize a potentially healthy partnership. Intelligent compromise, based on objective data, needs to rule the day, rather than emotional attachment to an idea that flies in the face of current conventional wisdom.

Are you ready to take the risk of jeopardizing the permanency and health of the relationship you had with this person before you entered into the partnership? Many a marriage, friendship, and business relationship has bitten the dust because of the partners' failure to resolve conflicts and come to a meeting of the minds. What happens when you and your partner cannot agree on a major business decision that needs to be made? "Irreconcilable differences" apply in business as well as in marriage!

The element of trust must be paramount when it comes to sharing the financial burdens and ramifications of operating your business. You or your partner always runs the risk of bearing the brunt of the other's financial incompetence or possibly even dishonesty.

Don't underestimate the role that money plays in a successful partnership. Having enough money, agreeing on expenditures, determining how much each party will contribute—agreement on all these factors can make or break a successful partnership.

Potential Minefields

If you decide to partner with your spouse, pause to anticipate what this will mean. You already share your bed and breakfast, your mornings and evenings, and all other things domestic, social, and familial, with this person. Think long and hard. Do you *really* want to add to all this time together working with him/her all day, every day?

Similar issues apply when considering a business partnership with a friend. If you value your friendship as a haven from the stresses and challenges of your life, do you really want to load down your relationship with a shared enterprise?

Before you embark on such an expanded commitment, consider, too, your personality similarities and differences. Think about the professional assets and liabilities that each of you would bring to the partnership. Setting emotions aside, do the two of you, combined, possess all the skills, talents, knowledge, and connections that are essential to ensure the success of your proposed business?

A friend of mine jokingly refers to his female partner as his "work wife." The analogy refers to the close proximity that business partners experience, and the fragility of such relationships. Just as seemingly perfect marriages can end in bitter divorce, so too can a business partnership between spouses or best friends end in disaster. At the outset, potential partners need to confront the possibility that joining forces in a business partnership may change forever what is now a special relationship.

And although that person you met at that fabulous weekend expo in Vegas may seem to be *the one*, how much do you *truly* know about this person? In a few days, how much could you possibly have learned about his/her value system, character, work ethic, personality, and actual expertise as it relates to the business you plan to start?

Kahlil Gibran's famous observation that "your joy and your sorrow spring from the selfsame source" aptly applies to the entire gamut of issues to be considered when seeking out that ideal complementary business partner.

First, consider *personality styles and differences*. Should both parties be different or the same when it comes to being—

- laid back versus regimented
- gregarious versus introverted
- task-oriented versus idea-generating
- impulsive (works in spurts) versus structured (adheres to a schedule)
- Concrete/Sequential versus Random/Abstract

Second, examine the importance of *complementary talents and skills*. Who has the greatest strength when it comes to—

- business acumen
- effective money management
- task focus
- technical skill
- interpersonal skill
- marketing/sales experience
- community/social/political connections
- content expertise

Third, consider the *different lifestyles* within the partnership. Is the business relationship jeopardized or enhanced if—

- one member works full time while the other is semi-retired
- one is self-employed, while the other is employed by an organization that makes demands
- one has major family involvements, while the other is free-wheeling and independent
- one has more of a commitment to a hobby or leisure time activity than the other
- one has more volunteer or travel priorities than the other

Hire a Good Lawyer!

So ... now that you have waded through the labyrinth of potential partnership pros, cons and minefields, you are surer than ever that you have the right idea, the perfect partner, and all the stars are aligned in your favor. This is good, but you are not done yet. Next on your list is to get yourself a good lawyer!

Yes, you will need to secure professional help to draw up a legal partnership agreement, *regardless* of who that partner is—faithful spouse, eternal friend, close relative, or newly-found business colleague. In fact, the closer the personal relationship, the more important it is to crystallize any business plan in writing, from startup requirements to an exit strategy. It is in the best interest of both parties to realize that such a strategy provides protection for you both.

Get It In Writing!

Darrell Zahorsky, small business expert and consultant, says that, according to the Small Business Administration (SBA), a good business partnership agreement should include:

- type of business
- amount of equity invested by each partner
- partners' pay and compensation
- how profits and losses will be shared
- restrictions of authority and expenditures
- dispute settlement clause
- length of partnership
- settlement plan in case of death or incapacitation of one partner
- provisions for changing or dissolving the partnership
- distribution of assets on dissolution, including cases in which one partner is obliged to buy out the other's interest —for instance, if one wants to quit the business
- how to assess the total value of the business at dissolution, including who will do the appraisal, using what methodology

How to Start Your Own Business

Once you have identified your business concept, and feel certain that what you will be doing meets your own needs as well as the needs of one or more target groups, move through this six-step process, first mentally (and on paper), then for real.

1. Consult resources
2. Design your business
3. Design your promotional materials
4. Create your business
5. Prepare to launch

6. Launch, market and promote

Now let's discuss each of these in turn, in very general terms, for now. Clearly, it will be necessary to consult resources beyond this book if you do plan to start a business. But this will get you started.

Consult Business Startup Resources

Let's get real! you say. There are so many skills to hone, so many landmines to navigate, so many negative non-believers to avoid, so many dollars to raise, so many details waiting to sabotage my ambition.

Fear not. Don't lose heart. Help is on the way in terms of specific resources designed to help you launch your dream. For starters, explore the links on these five websites:

USA.Gov: *http://www.usa.gov/Business/Self-Employed.shtml*   Provides resources for the self-employed, including financial assistance, hiring, laws, scams and fraud, and taxes.
Business.USA: *http://business.usa.gov/*   Describes itself as "A product of collective thoughts and inputs from agencies ... committed to making this site a one-stop shop for everything related to business in the USA.
Small Business Administration: *http://www.sba.gov/*   A wealth of information on starting and managing a business.
Entrepreneur: *http://www.entrepreneur.com/*   Features "How-To" Guides for starting your own business.
BizFIlings: *www.bizfilings.com/*   Covers all aspects of starting, running, and growing a business. Offers a *Learning Center* to get you up to speed as a business owner, and an easy online incorporation process.

Design Your Business

If you are establishing your own business, take a few weeks to contemplate the "What? Who? Where? When? and How?"

- WHAT will your business be called?

- WHAT will it offer?

  Create a name for your business that clearly describes the services you provide.

- WHO will your business serve?

- WHERE will your business be located?

  Is it your plan to base your business from home? Online? Or abroad? All three? A good means for deciding the *where* is to decide where *you* would like to live as your business evolves.

- WHEN will your business be open?

  Will your business be available full-time? More importantly, how much of the time will you need to be there? Only certain hours of the day? Certain days of the week? Certain weeks of the month? Certain months of the year? If you want your own on-site time to be limited, consider who will serve as Manager-in-Chief in your absence.

- HOW will your business operate?

  Will you operate your business on your own? With a partner? By hiring staff? By hiring a manager plus staff? Consider what you want as a lifestyle, as well as financial limitations and ramifications, then work backwards from these criteria.

Design Your Logo, Promotional Materials & Website

- Select a URL for your business website, preferably one that aligns with the terms your potential clients will use when they search for the goods, services or creativity you provide.

- Set up a simple website for your business, or hire someone to do this for you.

- Create a brochure and business cards for your business, with your Website address and other critical contact and descriptive information clearly displayed.

For a simple business, these tasks will take much less time and will be much less daunting than you may expect, because there are so many productivity tools available to help you get started.

To locate a great URL for your business, go to _Go Daddy.com_ and start searching various combinations of words, phrases and titles until you find a suitable one that is still available. Then click on "Register" and Go Daddy will take care of the rest for you, charging your credit card about $15.

To design your website quickly, you may consider using other products available through Go Daddy.com that allow you to "create your website tonight." This will get you up and running quickly. You can always return later with a more complex website that you design using more powerful tools and templates such as those available from _AllWebCo.com_. Or, for a price, you can elicit the services of a professional to redesign your site for you, or even perhaps hire one of your children (or grandchildren) to accomplish the task.

To prepare your brochures, business cards, and announcement cards, go to _VistaPrints.com_ and start playing with the various design tools. For each of these items, type in some appropriate, relevant words, select various images and colors, and experiment with different fonts. When you arrive at a draft that satisfies you, click it into your shopping cart.

If you avoid all the possible "extras," your brochures, business cards, and announcements will be on their way to you within an hour or so, and without a major outlay of cash.

Later you may come back to VistaPrints for additional products and services, such as:

- mailing lists tailored to your market demographics and location
- postcards for direct mail campaigns
- services to print, address, and mail postcards to your lists of potential and/or current clients
- T-shirts, pens, ball caps, car door magnets and other promotional items carrying your business logo

Prepare to Launch

Next, set a date for launching your business. Let the world know what you will be offering, and otherwise get the word out.

Begin by completing these tasks:

- Announce your business to family, friends, and community;

- Set up Google ads and post on Craigslist to advertise the services you offer;

- Incorporate your business using the business type most appropriate for what you are doing;

- Open a business bank account;

- If you will be accepting credit card payment, select a payment processing service such as Intuit, or plan to use PayPal.

To select what type of business "entity" you want to be, and to carry out your incorporation, begin in the learning Center on the _Bizfilings.com_ website, where you can learn about your choices, and the advantages and disadvantages of each. It is relatively easy to gather enough information about your incorporation options to then move forward with confidence, undaunted by the alphabet soup of types and terms—C Corp, S Corp, LLC, LP, LLP, or PLLC. Once you have made your decision, you can even use the website to guide you through your incorporation process.

Once you have established yourself as a business entity, you will be able to use your business EIN number to set up a business bank account, and even to arrange for a payment processing company (like Intuit) to accept credit card payments on your behalf and deposit the money you earn into your account.

Launch, Market and Promote

Once the date of your launch has come and gone, establish marketing and promotion as ongoing tasks. Follow these and other plans to keep your business in the forefront of the minds of all those potential clients who may need and want your goods, services or creativity.

- Continue your Google ads;

- Continue posting via Craigslist to advertise the services you offer;

- Make presentations to groups that include, or have contact with, your potential clients;

- Promote your Website using SEO (Search Engine Optimization) techniques, or hire someone to do this for you;

- Circulate your marketing materials until you have all the business you want or need.

Even your business bookkeeping becomes surprisingly manageable using a combination of *Quicken* or *QuickBooks* and a payment processing service such as *Intuit*. Go to *Intuit.com* to watch videos and learn how client payments will be processed and how your business accounting tasks be accomplished. Your role will be to set up your list of clients, oversee the invoice and payment processes, then monitor the deposits made to your business bank account.

The short version of this process using *QuickBooks* is:

1. You set up your client information in *QuickBooks*;
2. You invoice your clients for payment;
3. Your client pays by credit card;
4. You accept the payment, and;
5. Money shows up in your bank account.

What once would have required a staff to accomplish, now can be done by you weekly (or biweekly or monthly), in an hour or less. And it can be done at any time, day or night, and from anywhere you happen to be living or visiting at the time.

15 Sample Goods, Services or Creativity Businesses

Consider these sample business ideas to get you started. There are many others you could add. Do not allow these suggestions to limit your creativity, imagination or options.

Scrapbooking

The latest trend among families is to preserve their memories in fancy albums. These memoires make great gifts for any occasion—birthdays, anniversaries, weddings, religious events, and holidays.

An entire industry has arisen around buttons, bows and gizmos to adorn the pages of scrapbooks. For someone who is artistically inclined, scrapbooking is a dream hobby that can turn part-time job if you offer these services to others.

Preparing Home-Cooked Meals

If you like to cook, the armies of working parents who want to feed their families home-cooked meals, but lack the time or energy to do so, would love to meet you. When both Mom and Dad work all day, who is left to prepare a daily feast in time for the family to sit down to dinner together at six o'clock—before or after shuttling the kids around to scouts, gymnastics, karate, band and dance lessons?

Enter *you*, who will do just that, and deliver it ready-to-serve. Move over fattening fast food. Make way for balanced, healthy, nutritious, delicious, freshly home cooked meals, served piping hot and with a smile. Clean-up services included, on request!

Sewing & Mending

You truly enjoy TV, and have a long list of programs that claim you as an avid fan. In fact, you usually schedule your daily tasks and errands around your favorite TV shows. However, you can't just sit idle as you watch the latest edition of Dancing with the Stars or American Idol. Your hands need to be busy ... and you just happen to derive a great deal of satisfaction from sewing.

Enter the need for hems—on skirts, on pants, on slacks, on sleeves! No need for a fancy sewing machine—all you need is a small sewing kit and a few extra-busy clients with fancy wardrobes!

From Whence Did I Come?

You have spent hours on the computer researching your family's lineage, developing trees and charts tracing your genealogical heritage. And your research finds you ever more fascinated with the past.

Why not parlay your experience into a for-profit endeavor? In our age of multi-culturalism, families have developed an ever-growing obsession in knowing about their ancestral roots. This is an interest *you* can satisfy by conducting authentic research, then writing up the findings and presenting them in an appealing graphic format.

Honey-Do List Doer (AKA: "Domestic Peace Keeper")

How often have you been the recipient (or the perpetrator) of your spouse's frustration, disappointment, even sometimes anger, over household chores that have remained undone, and broken things that have remained unfixed? And none of your various excuses (no time, no tools, no skills) have succeeded in mollifying the annoyed, harried, harassed requestor.

Rest assured, you have many fellow "fixers"—some capable, some not—all buried beneath their own "Honey Do" lists that only get longer. Mr. Handyman *you* to the rescue—the hero who gets a high fixing the unfixable. You might as well get paid for the fun you have solving problems. Hearing the sighs of relief and seeing the smiles on your clients' faces is almost worth as much as the money you earn.

If you tackle this as a self-employed fix-it-up service, count on a smorgasbord of odd jobs that range from repairing running toilets to tightening loose door handles. It can be a toss-up of woodworking, plumbing, electrical and even painting projects. There are more structured opportunities in this arena with building owners who hire part-time workers to perform basic maintenance. Pay ranges from $10 to $20 an hour, and up to $50 an hour for certain custom work.

If you are competent in various aspects of home improvement, have your own tools, are self-motivated and have good customer-service skills, this business may be for you. Be sure to achieve a first-name basis with the manager of your local hardware store.

National Geographic, Here I Come

Do you have a photographer's eye, and a passion for photography? While others never leave home without their iPhones and Kindle Fires, is it your camera that has become the extension of your hands? Have old country barns, unusually shaped trees, modern "Madonna with child" images, reflections in still waters become your specialties?

Why not matt your best work inexpensively, and show off your wares at spring, fall, and holiday craft fairs? Or you could sell your best images online.

Lori Allen, in her article about the "math" of stock photography calculates that if you upload your photos to four agencies at the rate of 20 photos per week, and assume that you will earn around $1 per image per month, your photography income will reach over $23,000 within one year, $69,120 by year two, and $115,200 by your third year.

Of course for this to work, you will need to consistently take good photos that sell. And you will need to learn to edit your images in a program like Adobe Photoshop or Lightroom before you submit them to agencies.

Animal Lovers Delight

It seems as though animal owners and animal lovers have taken their relationship with animals to an all new level. We now take our pets to the dentist. Vets administer MRI's. Hotel and motel chains offer "pet-friendly" rooms. Owners arrange for "play-dates" with "compatible" animal friends. Today's pet owners will go to any length, and will spare no expense to assure adequate care and comfort for their pets and animals. Average expenditures are around $13,000 over the lifetime of a small to medium-sized dog and $11,000 for an indoor cat (_petplace.com_).

So, you are someone who prefers animals to people. You are happiest when you are surrounded by these small or large furry creatures. Here's your chance to pet sit, walk, groom, or otherwise cater to, your friends', families', neighbors', community's animal needs.

Pet grooming a pooch or kitty runs the gamut from bathing to nail-trimming to brushing to cleaning ears and clipping coats. Pay ranges are from $7.76 to $17.80 an hour, up to $25 to $30 an hour for an experienced groomer. Pet sitters handle daily exercising, prepare meals and fill water bowls, feed fish, hamsters and gerbils, and scoop out litter boxes—along with spreading around that all-essential dose of special love and attention. The main requirements for this kind of work are a rapport with animals and a reputation for being dependable. The charge for a single visit to a pet can range from $10 to $22 and up, depending on the location, and $45 or more for overnight care.

Dog walkers often walk more than one dog at a time, in all kinds of weather, at least twice a day. Median hourly pay is $8 per dog, up to $37.50 with experience (according to _PayScale.com_).

Calling All Fitness Freaks

Now that you are retired, you still want to retain those firm thighs, that flexibility. In the warm months you are happiest when you are biking, hiking, or swimming. You are familiar with all the best biking and hiking trails within a 100 mile radius. You know their lengths, degrees of difficulty, and how to spot and identify wildlife along the way. In the cold months, you are adept at cross-country skiing, snow shoeing and even sledding. You know which trails are best groomed, how to dress appropriately, how to pace yourself.

Why not become a fitness guide who caters specifically to those in the over-50 crowd who want to stay in shape? Members would pay an annual fee for your "club" membership that features a monthly newsletter of fitness tips, and includes yourself as guide on a range of trips and adventures. Imagine doing what you love, staying fit, sharing your passion with other Boomers, and getting paid in the process.

Flea Market Maniac

Flea markets are "your thing." You truly believe that one man's trash is another person's treasure. In fact, you have finally admitted that your garage is now maxed out housing the goodies you have managed to amass in the short time since you retired, and you are seriously contemplating investing in an outdoor shed to house future acquisitions.

Enter *E-Bay*—the answer to every collector's dream. Wouldn't it be fun to see whether others share your taste in collectables by posting some of your items for sale—that is, if you are emotionally ready and able to "let go" of your flea market finds. Consider this. Every time you make a sale, this will generate a "need" for you to do more shopping!

But let's take this eBay frenzy one step further. Why not become a broker for those hoarders who seek a vending outlet for their treasures, but have neither time nor talent nor inclination to master the E-Bay process? For a percentage fee, you can be the "connector" between buyer and seller. Your task—to photograph, describe, and post product descriptions, photos, selling conditions and prices for your clients' goods. Imagine... Then you could feel perfectly guilt-free when you spend more time surfing E-Bay goodies!

Bartending/Waitressing/Catering

If you are an amiable person, with charm and an uncanny ability to smooth ruffled feathers of disgruntled customers... And if you have patience, a good memory and organizational skills, and can smile though your feet are aching... You may be the perfect candidate for starting a food and beverage service business. These services are in high demand, especially during the end-of-year holiday party season, and for all those special family and social occasions.

Schedules will fluctuate. Nights, weekend and lunch times can peak during the weeks before and during holidays. Median pay for bartending and wait staff services ranges from $7 to $15 an hour, plus tips. Caterers should expect an hourly range between $10 and $20 an hour.

Running a Cleaning Business

Are you kidding?! I *hate* house cleaning! In fact, I'll do anything to avoid it, using every real or imagined excuse to postpone pulling out that vac, managing that mop, dusting those knick-knacks.

But, then again, you might be one of those persons who derive a great deal of satisfaction from all that scrubbing, scouring, and shining, and seeing the immediate and tangible results of your efforts.

The good news—you won't need a great deal of start-up money, nor will you need an advanced degree in Housekeeping 101. Other benefits—because it's a cash only business, you will not need to get involved in billing procedures, or otherwise wait to get paid. And you will be able to work at your own pace, part time or full time.

You may want to specialize—such as vacation rental homes or small local businesses or a specific type of cleaning such as organizing closets and drawers, shampooing rugs, pressure washing patios and decks, or even being the rare individual who *does* do windows.

And if you don't want to dirty your own hands, or you don't have the energy for all that "bend and stretch," you can always hire someone else to do the actual cleaning and pay them an agreed-upon amount, while you spend your time supervising and marketing your business.

Operating a Bed & Breakfast

If, as a couple, your favorite place is your own home and you are happiest when you are there... If you spend most of your financial resources on home improvements, inside and out...A Bed-and-Breakfast might be the ideal way for you to earn extra cash—especially if, as empty-nesters, you have surplus rooms standing empty.

There are a few realities you will need to anticipate and plan for. First, you had better love to cook, because you will need to commit to preparing irresistible meals every morning. Or, of course, you could hire a local to come in to prepare gourmet meals for your guests. If so, be sure to have them prepare enough extra for you and your spouse, and thus enjoy the side-benefit of having a personal breakfast chef.

Then there's the "spotless sunshine" factor. Do you think you'll *really* enjoy cleaning up after strangers...day after day? Of course, these tasks, too, could be "outsourced," possibly relieving you of many of your own household duties. Oh well...

Most importantly, would you welcome the "adventurous" opportunity to meet all types of people from every walk of life? Travelers who choose to stay at B & B's tend to be friendly, gregarious, well-travelled, and laid back. A morning breakfast can easily turn into a two-hour social gathering, with conversation covering a range of topics. As a host, you will need to be interesting and interested, not only in the world around you, but also in your guests.

An ideal location for your enterprise would need to be remote enough to provide peace, quiet and bucolic beauty, but also close enough to one or more cultural, tourist, resort attractions to be an interesting vacation destination. This may require that you move to a more appealing spot, which is not much of a problem, since you will be able to enjoy your new, improved location along with your guests.

Gardening, Lawn Care, & Landscaping

I have a brother who refuses to purchase a power lawn mower. He just loves "the feel" of controlling the mower, and the satisfaction he derives from forming his own mowing patterns crisscrossing his lawn. But mostly, he finds mowing to be an effective way to stay in incredible shape! Luckily, his yard, although quite large, is relatively flat!

No one is suggesting that you would want to go to these extremes to stay in shape. But you may be a person who gains a sense of pleasure and accomplishment when you transform a bland yard, or a wild tangle, into a tidy, aesthetically-pleasing vista.

For this type of business, you will need basic yard equipment similar to what you use on your own property. The difference—you also will need to invest in more and better tools, as well as a means for transporting them.

So you will have the perfect excuse to purchase that edger or pruner or small cultivator that you secretly would love to own and use on your own property. And what about that small (or large) pick-up truck, with trailer-hitch and flatbed trailer? All these may come in handy for your own yard tasks as well as for carting around your equipment to your clients' properties. And all this equipment and transport will be tax deductible, of course, since these purchases are needed to support your business. Being able to purchase plants at wholesale prices will be yet another nice perk!

One caveat... In the summer months, it will be important to avoid the high-noon heat. So you will need to plan your work for early mornings and late afternoons, avoiding the dangerous timeslot of noon to three. Of course, you could always designate the high heat part of the day as siesta time! What a hardship...

Online Store

The idea of launching an Internet business sounds really intriguing to us, you say, but where would we start and what would we sell? Start by taking a minute to think about how you currently spend your time when shopping on the Internet yourself. What could you sell that would appeal to a shopper like you?

Do you spend hours searching fishing-supplies websites to find the latest, greatest lures? Do you surf from one site to another looking for unusual nursery items for your recently-born twin grandchildren? Do you have a passion for collecting a particular type of item? Are you involved in a serious hobby, like crafting or handiwork or restoring classic cars or welding yard art from metal scraps?

If so, your first product may be waiting to be discovered in your garage, attic, workroom, or basement. The sky is the limit in terms of what you may want to sell, how you would present your product, how many hours you would invest in your new venture.

A few caveats... There will be expenses involved to launch your online business. Also, it will help if you have at least some background in sales and marketing. And you will need to be computer savvy.

Teaching Abroad

The advantage of *teaching* abroad lies in the fact that in order to teach abroad, you will need to *live* abroad. This is an ideal way to experience the true ambience and flavor of a foreign culture.

Teaching abroad can take many different forms. Most American military bases employ U.S. educators to teach children of military families. Many American parents living abroad with their families because of business or job obligations, prefer to employ the services of an American educator. Even some foreign families with the financial means, seek to hire American teachers to teach their children in English, rather than in their native tongue. Or you (and possibly your partner as well) may be fortunate enough to secure teaching positions in your content areas in foreign schools.

This type of venture will require unique personalities who are able to adjust to living in a foreign country, and immerse themselves in a culture that is very different from their own. As a couple, you will need to be mature, broadminded, and flexible, with a sense of humor, and the ability to adjust to unexpected, even unusual, circumstances. You may consider offering specialized services such as preparing students attending high school overseas to return to the USA for college.

A Cautionary Note

First, let's not forget where and why you decided to start your newly established "fun and funds" project. Your primary objective is to have fun doing what you love to do—what you would be almost willing to do for free—for the sheer joy of doing it. Do not become so obsessed with your passion that it ceases to be play and instead becomes drudgery.

Secondly, keep the financial rewards in perspective. You may never make a full living "working" at your hobby, on your own schedule, in tandem with your other retirement activities. But at this point in your life, this hopefully is not your sole source of income. And it's not only about the money anyway.

If your goal is to earn supplemental retirement income—enough, perhaps to travel regularly, to upgrade some expensive family "toy" or to indulge some other passion—you are on the right course. You may even make enough to sustain the fun you are having so that you won't need to tap into your basic retirement savings—yet.

Now What About You?

Select three specific actionable ideas for hiring yourself or partnering up."

Record your three top choices here for now, then copy them to the composite of possibilities you began to create in Chapter 8.

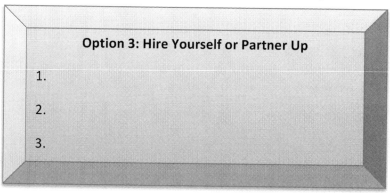

Option 3: Hire Yourself or Partner Up

1.

2.

3.

And So...

You might have found the content of this chapter the most personally attractive, the most relevant of all. This idea of "hiring yourself," and possibly "partnering up," can be very appealing, especially if the business you pursue is something you love anyway. So, if you catch yourself shouting "Yes, I can do this!" and "This is the one for me!"—then what are you waiting for?

After all, you are at that point in your life where you want to do what you want to do. And you may want to spend more time now with your "best friend"—whether that "best friend" be your spouse, your former college roommate, your second cousin, third-removed, or your Zumba companion.

This could mean that the time has come. The stars may now be aligned for you to go forth and tackle, on your own or in collaboration, your new venture—your dreamed-of entrepreneurship—the one final career goal you are destined to make happen as part of your new retirement life.

But first, before your business concept is locked in, read ahead to consider whether you may want to expand or adjust your plans to include us, the 77 million retiring Boomers, among your potential clients. Who better to benefit by serving the needs of this exploding population than someone who is one of us?

CHAPTER 12:
Option #4: Work For "Us"—
Seniors Serving Seniors

"Why would I want to work for or with Seniors as my retirement business?" you ask. After all, I *am* one myself. Whatever I might have to offer older adults by way of goods, services or creativity, may actually be something that I need, too.

You've just identified one of the "why"s for considering a retirement enterprise working for "us." Who better than *you* to know what goods, services and creativity Seniors need and want, since these are things that you may need or want yourself. You will be brilliantly capable of relating to what other Seniors will seek out. And you will understand the relevance, even the urgency, of obtaining it.

Boomers are a Very Large Group

Another "why" for choosing the option of working for "us" is that the retiring Boomer population is a *very large* group, as you have learned throughout this book. The first wave of Boomers reached full retirement age in 2011.

Continuing over the next 20 years, over 77 million Boomers will retire, at a rate of around *10,000 each day*. According to the *UN Population Division*, it is expected that by 2035 one in five people will be 65 or older.

Our group is not only prolific in our numbers, but also in our longevity potential. Dividing ourselves into the subgroups of "Young Old" (ages 65-74), "Middle Old" (ages 75-84) and "Older Old" (ages 85 and above), we anticipate that the growth of each of these subgroups over the next 20 years will be startling, with the "Older Old" subgroup showing the most stunning growth rate of all.

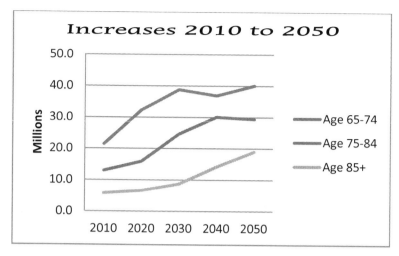

The *Young Old* age group will increase from 21.4 million to over 40 million between 2010 and 2050, according to the *U.S. Bureau of the Census*. This represents an increase of 87%.

The *Middle Old* age group, due to significantly increased life expectancy, will show a steady increase from *13 million to over 29 million* between 2010 and 2050, representing an increase of 126%.

By far the fastest-growing segment of the total population will be the *Older Old*—those 85 and over. This subgroup will *more than triple*, from 5.8 million in 2010 to over 19 million, by 2050, representing an increase of 228%.

This rate of increase is *twice* that of the Young Old (65-74), and almost *four times* that of the total population.

Growth Rates by Subgroup			
	Young Old **Age 65-74**	**Middle Old** **Age 75-84**	**Older Old** **Age 85+**
2010	21.4 million	13.0 million	5.8 million
2020	32.3 million	15.9 million	6.6 million
2030	38.8 million	24.6 million	8.7 million
2040	36.9 million	30.1 million	14.2 million
2050	40.1 million	29.4 million	19.0 million

Boomers Have Resources to Spend

A third "why" for looking closely at the needs and priorities of aging Boomers as an option for your retirement business is that as a group Boomers control a major part of all material resources. They have the greatest buying power in the history of our country, with more discretionary income than any other age group. And they spend more money in proportion to their numbers.

WOW FACTOR

Boomers hold 70% of the total net worth of all American households—$7 trillion of wealth. They own 80% of all money in savings and loan associations.

Even during the recession, *Baby Boomer Magazine* (*http://www.babyboomer-magazine.com*) reported that Boomers were still the largest consumer group in America, accounting for a dramatic 40% of total consumer demand.

As empty nesters, Boomers spend their money on goods and services for themselves. They are Internet-savvy, and use technology for business and pleasure, shopping, communicating and reading online. They own and use the latest technology tools and toys, including smart phones, high-end TV's, and high-tech cars.

WOW FACTOR

While Boomers represent 26% of the country's population, they generate 40% of consumer demand, wielding $2.1 trillion in annual buying power. That's more than seven times Generation X and Generation Y combined. (*MetLife Mature Market Institute*).

Boomers Are Creating New Markets

A fourth "why" supporting the idea that aging Boomers are a market that is ripe with possibility for all manner of goods and services, is that, according to most predictions, Boomers will predominantly choose to live independent lifestyles until late in, if not throughout, their lifetimes. Whole industries are emerging to offer the products and services that will make this prolonged independence possible.

This trend translates into many potential opportunities for you to generate an income stream that supports your own lengthened and more expansive lifestyle, and that also keeps you fully engaged well into the future.

Transgenerational Design

The terms "transgenerational design," "universal design," "design for all" and "human-centered design" have entered the lexicon specifically to address the emerging *practice of making products and environments compatible with those physical and sensory impairments [that are] associated with human aging and that limit major life activities" (http://transgenerational.org/)*.

As the world's population rapidly grows older, businesses are recognizing that it is important to create new products that are easily used by people throughout their lifetimes—whatever their current capabilities or limitations. The *Transgenerational Design* initiative dictates that intelligent decisions be made during a product's design, production, marketing, promotion, and sales processes in order that these products and services may be used comfortably by an aging population with a wide range of abilities.

When applied effectively, *Transgenerational Design* addresses the need for products that enhance the quality of life for users of all ages. When considering common functional limitations and how they could inhibit independence—such as sensory changes, balance and falling, dysmobility, and memory and confusion—the intent and the challenge is to develop products that support and extend independence by accommodating human limitations in vision, hearing, touch, dexterity, and mobility. These types of product *microenvironments* will "enhance the overall quality of life for people of all ages and abilities," according to James Pirkl, author of *Transgenerational Design: Products for an Aging Population*.

As an example, according to Ford Motor's Pete Hardigan, one major trend is to design cars with features that make them safer for aging drivers. Some such features are already available, including *blind spot monitoring* and *lane departure prevention systems* that use cameras and radars to monitor the area around the car. These new systems offer visual and auditory warnings, and intervene if the vehicle starts to drift out of its lane or turns towards a car passing alongside it.

Ford and Nissan have developed special "old age" suits to be worn by their engineers, using a system of straps and braces, that restrict their movement as though they had a decreased mobility condition like arthritis. Sight-limiting goggles do the same to simulate reduced vision. Wearing these suits and goggles, an engineer can get a feel for how to optimize various driving aids to support drivers with slower reflexes, reduced vision, and more limited mobility.

Architects and homebuilders, too, are increasingly attentive to *Transgenerational Design*. As applied to housing, these concepts stress accessibility and comfort for all people, whether young, old, in peak physical shape, or physically challenged.

According to a presentation at the *American Institute of Architects' 2012 National Convention and Design Exposition*, entitled "*Welcome Home*," the aging population in the 21st century will demand design concepts such as:

- main-floor living
- step-free entries and access between rooms
- non-slip flooring
- five-foot turning radii in rooms
- increased daylight or special lighting

Meanwhile, there will be an increasing demand for plaza-style communities that combine housing, shopping, dining and services to accommodate a lifestyle that does not require a car (Taryn Plumb, 2012, in *Worcester Business Journal Online*; *www.wbjournal.com*).

The priority that Boomers place on independent living impacts existing housing as well as new. Dozens of thriving businesses offer various home renovation products to support the continued ability of older people to live in their own homes. Some highly-affordable examples include:

- **Shower roll-in** conversions. Cost: $1200, installed;
- **Bathtub walk-in** conversions. Cost: $1200, installed;
- **Walk-in whirlpool** tub conversions. Cost: $1600, installed;

- **Stair lifts** that provide independence, convenience, and security, as an alternative to selling a multi-level home and moving to a single-level home. Cost: starting at $1900, installed;
- **Dumbwaiters**, to move goods and supplies up and down stairs in multi-storied homes. Cost: starting at $3700, plus installation;
- **Residential elevators**, with rigid guide rail systems that can be installed into a wood framed home. Cost: starting at $16,000, plus installation (*http://www.ameriglide.com*).

Cars and homes represent just the tip of the iceberg in the area of *Transgenerational Design*. With the goal of making independent living and mobility possible longer for more people, society's challenge will be to invent and deliver literally hundreds, if not thousands, of products and services that Boomers will increasingly demand.

Some of these needed products and services to support the burgeoning population of aging Boomers are already known and available. Others have yet to be invented. And all of these products and services offer income potential for you, should you so desire, at any of the key points in the *Transgenerational* process—from invention, to design, to production, to marketing, to advising, to promotion, to sales, to installation, to use assistance.

SNAPSHOT

Shaune, a third grader, was expected to participate in his state's 'Invention Convention,' an annual event sponsored by the state university as an incentive to young people to use their creative imaginations to "improve their community's standard of living and quality of life."

For the past few years, Shaune's grandmother had been confined to a wheelchair, unable to maneuver easily within her own home. Shaune noticed that when she was alone, it was impossible for grandma to reach objects higher than her head. For one thing, she could not easily balance herself when she attempted to get up from her chair; secondly, her arms ached so severely that to raise them above her head was excruciatingly painful.

So Shaune decided to invent "The Grabber" for his grandma—an automatic, battery-powered, extendable pole with a

---

flexible "hand." When squeezed, the "hand" would grab an item up to one pound and thus make it accessible to Grandma.

Shaune's invention was an immediate success. Not only was grandma surprised and grateful, but the *Invention Convention* judges, touched by Shaune's sensitivity to his grandma's condition, and impressed by his problem solving skills, awarded Shaune *First Place!* Proof positive that it's never too early for an entrepreneur to begin serving the Boomer generation!

Meeting the Needs and Wants of the *Young Old, Middle Old & Older Old*

So...on the one hand, we have this ever-expanding group of age 65 and over. On the other hand, Boomers have a great deal of discretionary income to spend on all types of pursuits—intellectual, recreational, professional, personal, physical. And many, if not most, of these aging Boomers have every intention of retaining their independence and mobility as time goes by, and as they advance from one subgroup to the next.

So once again, as Pogo says, "We are surrounded by insurmountable opportunity." When you begin to "match" what you have to offer to those who need it, you may find that your particular talent, skill, product, or service will best serve one or more of these three aging Boomer subgroups.

What Does Each Subgroup Want and Need?

As we study each subgroup, we quickly come to realize each group's uniqueness. While there may be a great deal of overlapping in terms of serving and being served, there are also some important distinctions that present themselves. All of the above provides us, the service/product providers, with myriad opportunities for productive and potentially lucrative employment.

Let's begin by considering some practical scenarios. Members of the *Young Old* and *Middle Old* groups may want to satisfy their recreational and intellectual needs by becoming frequent travelers. They now may have the time and financial resources to attend more performances and to visit more cultural venues and museums. And they may have renewed interest in studying and learning.

Physically, these two subgroups may be seeking ways to maintain a regular regimen of exercise, healthy eating, and daily movement in the form of a exercise or sports activities. Remember that members of this generation have been, and probably still are, avid skiers, golfers, hikers, bicyclers, kayakers, swimmers, and tennis players. As long as their health cooperates, they now have both the time and the financial resources to experience these pleasures more often. And they have every intention of doing so.

When it comes to managing money, members of the *Young Old* and *Middle Old* subgroups may be accustomed to managing their own financial affairs—investments, monthly domestic bills, banking, taxes, and so forth. But now they may prefer to "outsource" these tasks to free up their calendars for more interesting pursuits.

As these members move into the *Older Old* subgroup, their intellectual needs might be satisfied in less vigorous ways—listening to books on tape or watching educational and cultural TV or video programs. But their needs for mental stimulation will persist, as will their needs for social relationships, personal significance, freedom and fun.

And even as *Older Olds* find themselves slowing down physically, they still may be able to, and want to, continue some type of low impact activity such as swimming, gardening, water aerobics, walking, or yoga. But they may be more than happy now to hire someone trustworthy and competent to manage their finances, carry out correspondence tasks, make repairs and help solve problems.

Senior Schizophrenia

By now you surely have thought about the irony of your situation. You yourself probably are an actual member of one of these subgroups. Yet, if you are reading this book, you also may be considering becoming a provider of goods or services to one or all of thm—*Young Old, Middle Old* and/or *Older Old.*

So your role is both reciprocal and complementary. Given the richness of your experiences, talents, skills and interests, you are in an excellent position to earn money by providing products or services, or even by bartering one set of products or services for another.

In fact, as you settle into this new phenomenon of extended and redesigned retirement, you might find yourself (as others have) needing to choose among several appealing ways to earn an income as a senior serving other seniors.

How Can Senior Me Serve Senior You?—10 Ideas

Let's take a look at some practical, meaningful, profitable ways in which *Young Old* or *Middle Old* Seniors can serve Young, Middle or Older Seniors, while generating supplemental income, remaining engaged and purposeful, and also having fun.

1. Medical & Financial Forms Filler-Outer

How many elderly family members and friends do you know who exhibit avoidance behaviors, or even defeat, when they receive complicated, lengthy, ambiguous forms from their medical provider, their insurance company, their attorney, their financial manager, the state and local government, the registry of motor vehicles?

Here's an opportunity to provide a critical service that could prevent serious legal or financial consequences for seniors if paperwork is not completed accurately and submitted on time. Since these tasks can be on-going, it is conceivable that you could develop a cadre of clients who would need your services regularly.

2. Salon on Wheels

Think about how you feel when you walk into your favorite hair salon or barber shop, and what a transformation takes places before you emerge. I always say that I approach my salon feeling like Cruella Deville on a bad hair day, and walk out with a renewed conviction that I do, in fact, have some physically redeeming qualities.

Then there's the growing challenge of giving yourself your own pedicures. It seems that as you gain in maturity, either your legs get longer or your arms get shorter. This typical conundrum provides you the opportunity to offer yet another potentially popular traveling salon service—*"Fingers & Toes."*

Just imagine a roving van, fully equipped as a portable "Day Spa," with all the tools to make "house calls," serving the various neighborhoods and communities where seniors live. Step inside to a menu of options—foot massage, pedicure, manicure, facial, new hairdo, or even a make-up makeover—a virtual, and actual, *"Spa on Wheels."*

3. Thanks for the Memories

You know you can write, and you enjoy it. Biographies have always been your favorite type of reading. When you were young, you eagerly sat at your grandparents' feet as they told the stories of their youth. And you genuinely appreciate, even relish, the ease with which seniors talk about "the good old days."

Here's your chance to do something you love while also providing a service to seniors—preserving their precious personal, family, and life stories—and earn income in the process. What a meaningful way to collect primary source material as history, while preserving the thoughts, stories and experiences of past generations.

Your research and interviews could culminate in a publication for the narrator to present as a family gift to be handed down from one generation to the next. This production could be in the form of a bound book, complete with photos. Or it could be a full multi-media package that combines video, prose, and photography.

What an opportunity to validate the contributions of seniors while preserving their experiences for their children and grandchildren!

4. Not-So-Fast Food Chef

You love to cook ... and to eat! In your former life you were the composite embodiment of Rachel Ray, Julia Childs and Nigella Lawson. But now there is one small problem. All of your off-spring have sprung the nest, and you have experienced major difficulties in your attempts to "think smaller" and cook less. You still cook for six, when in reality there are only two of you still present to partake!

What if you could parlay your culinary talents into an express delivery service of home-cooked meals for seniors who are too busy to cook—or who are temporarily or permanently unable or unwilling to deal with the very idea of preparing meals for themselves anymore.

You could provide your lucky clientele with a weekly menu of lunches and dinners that you will prepare and deliver daily at their designated mealtime. Or you could offer a service to restock their freezers and fridges weekly or bimonthly with a delicious assortment of your home-cooked meals, ready to thaw, heat and eat.

Just think. You could cook to your heart's content, experiment with new recipes, and know that you are providing pleasure, as well as meeting an essential need for your customers—all while earning a supplemental income.

With your own assembly of hungry seniors, you could easily provide a month's worth of meals with no repeat performances. Your clients soon would be begging you to "make that such-and-such" again soon! It doesn't get much better than that!

5. Playmate, Come In and Play with Me!

As seniors age, many can and do choose to remain in their own homes, even as they enter the *Older Old* subgroup, and even after they have become widows or widowers. These seniors can be intelligent, alert, curious, gregarious, and delightful company.

Some become "stay-at-homers" by choice, preferring the comfort and security of familiar surroundings. Others have stopped driving, or have stopped driving at night, and so find themselves confined to their homes for longer periods of time.

Still these *Older Olds* welcome and need the companionship and friendship of others. Some would appreciate having adult "play dates" with someone whose company and presence they can look forward to sharing for a designated period of time each week. After all, seniors can have play dates too, just as their grandchildren do!

Imagine the camaraderie, the laughter, the fun you could share playing cards, board games, or chess—working crossword puzzles, sudukos or cryptograms—cooking or baking together—watching TV or a movie classic—woodworking, scrapbooking or working on crafts projects—reading and discussing favorite books—gardening—surfing the Web or learning how to navigate social networks—e-mailing with family, friends or even pen pals from abroad.

Going on outings together would be additional enjoyable options—to concerts, to shops and cafes, to the movies, or even just to ride around enjoying the flowers blooming in spring, the fall foliage, or the Christmas lights in December.

In fact, you could start your own *"Play Date" Club*. For a monthly fee you would provide transportation, refreshments and an "activity agenda" for a small group of like-minded seniors. Imagine giving and receiving so much pleasure, companionship and joy while also supplementing your retirement income!

6. "Get it Done" Agent

There is a seemingly never-ending list of "to do"s and "fix-it" projects that some retirees never seem to find time, or have the knack, to complete.

The garage needs to be cleaned out. The Christmas lights need to be put up—or taken down. The patio furniture needs to be cleaned and stored. The kitchen cabinets need to be restained. The basement needs to be converted to a home theater or an exercycle hang out, or both. The sagging pantry shelves need to be replaced. The list goes on.

Murphy's Law dictates that, every mechanical or electrical device seems to conspire to take turns becoming inoperable, often at the most inconvenient times! The smoke detectors are beep, beep, beeping again! The weed eater string is used up. The bathtub drains too slowly. The attic fan has stopped working. The doorbell is broken.

However "unhandy" or "domestically and technically challenged" or even just unwilling or unable to climb the wobbly ladder into the attic they might be, many seniors are, like me, compulsive about having everything in perfect order at home.

Enter you, the reliable, honest, competent "handy person" to take charge of that daunting check list and *Get It Done*, performing "miracles" with a toolbox.

7. The Green Thumb

As more and more seniors choose to remain in their homesteads, the ongoing maintenance of their grounds and property can become increasingly overwhelming. Even for the smallest of home yards and lawns, keeping up with nature can prove daunting—a battle that older seniors sometimes prefer to cede to someone else who has more energy—someone closer to nature who enjoys playing in the dirt.

The ordinary home lawn and garden requires planting, pruning, weeding, watering, nurturing, tending, mowing, and raking. Gutters, porches, patios, outdoor furniture and roofs need cleaning. Weeds need whacking.

What a great way to enjoy the outdoors while supplementing your retirement income. And as an added bonus, studies show that landscapers and gardeners find their work to be therapeutic.

8. Field Trip Leader

How often have you heard active Seniors, when talking about travelling within their town, state, and region, make comments like—

"Now that I have the time and money to take day trips, there are so many interesting places I'd like to visit. But I hate being corralled around on a big bus where we never spend enough time in any one place, and we always seem to be getting on and off the bus."

"When I go somewhere for the day, I want to travel at my own pace, and stop wherever and whenever I see an interesting spot, without structure or time limits. What is this, a race to get the trip over with? We can always come back again to do more exploring."

"I don't like travelling in packs, like a member of a herd. I much prefer the company of a few close friends, so that we can engage in one common conversation, agree on destinations that are of mutual interest, and set a pace that is comfortable for all of us."

If comments like these don't sound the call for you to start your own private small-group travel service, what would? For starters, you could pinpoint your geographical location on a map and draw a set of circles 25, 50, and 100 miles from that center point. Then get online and research all the museums, AAA designated scenic routes, historical sites, gardens, lunch spots, parks, inns, entertainment venues, specialty shops, antiques, and theme-related shopping destinations (crafts, sports, glasswork, woodwork) within each of those boundaries.

Undoubtedly, you could offer a trip a week for a full year, and never exhaust your field trip options. Your clients could participate by membership, then pay an additional fee per trip, receiving a quarterly brochure of upcoming outings and adventures. You may consider investing in a comfortable van, or even a limo, to hold six to eight guests—a perfect number for small group travel—so you and your entourage will be able to travel in style.

Another excellent method for gaining clients is to list the "experience" you are offering through *Vayable.com*. *Vayable.com* was created with the revolutionary idea that "by exploring the world, we can better it." Its mission is to "To enable entrepreneurship, cultural exchange, community-building and exploration worldwide by empowering people to share experiences with others."

You could even expand to offering trips abroad, guiding small groups on a riverboat cruise down the Danube from Germany to Hungary or along the rivers of France, or the waterways of Holland to see the tulips in spring. Your guided travel offerings could be theme-based, focusing on music or dance or history or handcrafts or theater.

Think about what a winning proposition this type of business could become. You would be highly motivated to become expert on a particular cultural environment in order to provide enriching travel experiences for an appreciative audience, *and* earn money, too, while having fun yourself.

9. Personal "Pro"

How many times have you heard (or said to yourself) "When I retire, I'm going to learn to golf or cross-country ski or kayak or sail or play tennis or plant an English flower garden. Make your own substitution.

Others are doing this too, possibly in areas where you know yourself to be something of a pro. There may be other Boomers out there who never had the time or opportunity to pursue this interest at which you excel. Why not offer your services to teach your senior colleagues how to enjoy any one of these invigorating outdoor activities?

This concept can be transferred to the world of arts and crafts, as well as to other areas of skill and expertise. There are those who don't know how, but who may be eager to learn from you… how to build furniture… how to quilt… how to speak fluent French or Italian… how to write a memoire. By offering to teach them, you will make new friends, provide companionship, use your expertise to pass on what you know, and earn money in the process!

The added benefit of any of these possibilities is that "to teach is to learn twice," as the saying goes. Through your efforts to help others learn, you will hone your own skills even further. Immersing yourself in activities that you genuinely enjoy yourself is another major plus. And don't forget, you then will be able to claim your related purchases and expenses as tax deductions.

10. Grandma & Grandpa's Closet

As a grandpa, Speedos, tie-dyes, and cut-offs, if ever they were part of your wardrobe, are no longer in your closet or on your radar screen. *But* you still may have closets and drawers full of formal business suits, button down shirts, some still in their wrappings, dress shoes in their original boxes, and high-end luggage you used when it seemed as though you were forced to spend half your life in airports.

As a grandma, you may be nostalgically hanging on to those broom skirts, Kasper suits, and sweater sets, with your walk-in closet still filled to the max with color-coded, coordinated "tops and bottoms." When you were a career professional, you never seemed to have anything to wear! Now, after 12 or more months of retired bliss, it dawns on you that you can't remember the last time you donned even one of those previously essential wardrobe items. You are not alone! Imagine how many Boomers share your situation, with closets full of designer clothes, some hardly worn, or even *never* worn, with their tags still on them to bear evidence.

What about offering a "Closet to Cash" service, clearing out Grandma and Grandpa's closets, then targeting a specific audience of men and women currently in the workforce who would gladly take advantage of the professional wardrobe bargains they'd find—all offered in matched sets—from your own and your fellow Boomers' neglected wardrobe collections?

And once those closets and drawers are starkly bare, possibly for the first time in decades, you could offer to custom design and install their "closet of the future," with racks, shelves, hooks and drawers to hold their new "uniforms"—travel clothes, golf shoes, dress clothes for attending symphony concerts…or for dancing under the stars.

Now What About You?

Select three specific actionable ideas to add to what you will consider later when you "make your match and move." Record them here, then copy them to the composite of possibilities you started in Chapter 8.

Option 4: Work for "Us"

1.

2.

3.

And So...

Who would have thought that you would find your niche serving the very Boomers among whom you are numbered? Yet, if you think about it, who is better suited to cater to the needs of this population than someone who is one of them? Who would be more keenly aware than you are of the social, cultural, and professional needs of your senior colleagues, since you share many of these same needs yourself?

For your entire working career, unbeknownst to you, you have been preparing for this, your re-invented retirement phase. All the skills, experience, and talents you have developed in the course of your past professional life now come to bear upon what, hopefully, will prove to be not only your last hurrah, but your best.

Think about the gratification you will find sharing the fruits of your younger years' experience. Each day you are realizing more and more the expertise you accumulated over your 30+ years in the traditional workforce. It may never have entered the thinking of your younger persona that you would later have so much to offer in terms of the goods and services that your own generation now needs and welcomes.

If serving the needs of the exploding population of retiring Boomers appeals to you, but not as a business venture... Or if you would thrive offering your services elsewhere, but again without the demands of creating your own business... Your future may be better served by considering work as a volunteer. Whatever of value you may have to offer, read ahead to consider whether you may want to expand or adjust your plans to include volunteering, but your way.

CHAPTER 13: Option #5:
Work for Free—But YOUR Way

"Who me, volunteer?" you ask. "I've never volunteered for anyone or any cause, and I'm not about to start now! I have no intention and no desire to volunteer for anything, anytime, for anyone—*ever*!"

There are lots of reasons why you may believe that you are not cut from the volunteerism mold. Perhaps in your former life as a member of a demanding, stressful service profession, you were forced into involuntary pseudo "volunteering" as part of the "do more with less" and "give back to the organization" mantra, and you feel exhausted and depleted by the thought of ever being drawn into doing that again.

Or perhaps you are an extremely shy introvert, who freezes up at the very thought of walking into a room of strangers, or making phone calls to sometimes annoyed and hostile recipients, or otherwise meeting and greeting people you don't know. Or you may just be entering your "me, myself and I" phase, with an aversion to giving away any of *your* time and energy—time that you gained only recently—time that you intend to relish and protect, and to spend on *your* new endeavor, *your* recent idea, *your* current passion.

Possibly your concept of volunteering dates back to an earlier age when volunteers were mainly recruited to do the mundane, unappealing tasks that none of the employed staff wanted to do themselves—tasks that required no intelligence or skill—tasks that anyone could do with their eyes closed and their brain on standby. Address these envelopes. Sit by this phone. Lick these stamps. Fill up these boxes. Peel these potatoes.

In any of these cases, think again. You may come to view volunteerism differently once you have had the chance to understand how volunteering has changed, and, in particular, how and why it is that volunteering now can be highly fulfilling when it is personalized to your own unique capabilities, purposes and interests.

You may not be willing to volunteer to do just any old thing, at the whim of some organization. But you well may be interested, even intrigued and eager, when you consider involving yourself in some of the volunteering options now available. What if you could find a volunteer placement that is engaging, fulfilling, challenging and fun? What if you could volunteer *your* way?

SNAPSHOT

After retiring from a lifelong career in education, Ted fulfilled a long-standing dream of purchasing a house in the mountains. Initially he went there to write, but soon found himself going into the little mountain town and frequenting its art galleries and family shops and restaurants for his afternoon breaks. As he became involved in this small but creative community, he learned that, as with many such communities, although their economy flourished during the spring and summer months, businesses languished when winter set in.

He began to volunteer his time working with the local business leaders and Chamber of Commerce, contributing effort according to his own design. With his highly developed technology and communication skills, and 40 years' experience as a learning expert and instruction design professor, Ted made a range of appealing offers to the business leaders of the little town— and all of these were projects that he would find stimulating and fulfilling.

First, he would design and present training to the local business leaders and owners, focusing on the economic development of their town. Secondly, he would work with business owners to increase their web presence and thereby reach a broader base of customers to sustain them in the lean months between their thriving summer seasons.

Thirdly, he would lead an effort to seek small town economic development funding that would enable the town to support

---

small but promising projects that held promise and would increase the economic vitality of their community.

Through these offers, Ted donated considerable time and effort, as well as his particular expertise and enthusiasm, while doing work that he found to be highly engaging and satisfying.

Volunteerism is Growing Rapidly

In recent years, volunteerism has increased dramatically, particularly among older Americans. Why is this? What has changed about the perceived benefits of volunteering? What is transformatively different about the potential for the volunteer work itself to be more fulfilling?

Higher income levels, along with greater educational achievement among older Americans, may help to explain some of the increases in the rates of volunteerism among older Americans. So... is there a correlation between a more educated, more affluent Baby Boomer group and the degree to which this generation is willing and/or able to volunteer?

The research seems to indicate that such a correlation does exist. In 2010, *9.2 million older adults* dedicated *1.7 billion hours of service* to communities across the country (*VolunteeringInAmerica.gov*).

WOW FACTOR

Over 46% of older adults each volunteer 100 or more hours per year, according to the Corporation for National and Community Service. This proportion is higher today than it has ever been before.

As an example, in 2010-2011 more than 330,000 Americans aged 55 and over participated in three programs alone—*RSVP*, the *Foster Grandparent Program,* and the *Senior Companion Program* (according to the *Corporation for National and Community Service*).

RSVP volunteers recruit and manage other volunteers, participate in environmental projects, mentor and tutor children, and respond to natural disasters. They provided 60 million hours of service on 685 projects in 2010/2011, mentoring 80,000 children, including 16,000 children of prisoners.

Foster Grandparents serve one-on-one as tutors and mentors to young people with special needs, working for 15 to 40 hours a week, providing loving and experienced support in schools, hospitals, drug treatment centers, correctional institutions, and childcare centers. Among their other activities, *Foster Grandparents* review schoolwork, reinforce values, teach parenting skills to young parents, and care for premature infants and children with disabilities. In the 2010/2011 timeframe, *Foster Grandparent* volunteers served a total of 24 million hours, working with 232,300 young people, including 7,000 children of prisoners and 2,250 children of military families.

Senior Companions, serving 15 to 40 hours a week, help frail seniors and others maintain independence, primarily by attending to clients in their own homes. Volunteers typically divide their time among two to four clients, assisting with daily living tasks, such as grocery shopping and bill paying, and providing friendship and companionship. They alert doctors and family members to potential problems, and offer much-needed respite to family caregivers. In 2010/2011, *Senior Companions* served 60,940 clients for a total of 12.2 million hours.

WOW FACTOR

A total of 8.1 billion hours were contributed by volunteers of all ages in 2010, valued at an estimated $173 billion. Over 20% of these hours (1.7 billion) were volunteered by older adults, with a total estimated value of $34.6 billion.

Benefits of Volunteering

Clearly communities and other causes receive major benefits from the billions of work hours contributed by volunteers, including the significant portion donated by Boomers. But beyond these benefits, research has shown that the volunteers themselves reap significant rewards.

Most startling is the fact that individuals who meet the volunteer "threshold" of at least one or two hours a week are more likely to live longer. Furthermore, those who engage in volunteer activities are less likely to suffer from ill health later in life, and instead are experiencing a positive reinforcing cycle of good health and future volunteering.

States that show higher volunteer rates are more likely to have lower mortality rates and lesser incidences of heart disease (as reported in *"The Health Benefits of Volunteering"* published by the *Corporation for National & Community Service*).

These health benefits are more pronounced for older than for younger volunteers. This is in part due to the fact that, by volunteering, older individuals are provided a purposeful social role that otherwise may be missing in their lives. In addition to providing health benefits, volunteer activities can strengthen the social ties that protect individuals from isolation during difficult times. Also, the experience of helping others leads to a sense of greater self-worth.

If you need any added impetus or encouragement as to how and why *you* should strongly consider devoting some of your new-found freedom to volunteering for a cause of your choice, these research findings may be something to consider.

Oh, one last thing—did you know that you can claim your volunteer time as a tax deduction? And your expenses and gas mileage? Just another added bonus for doing what you love while helping humanity in the process!

Volunteer Where, With Whom, Doing What?

But, you say, "Where would I volunteer?" and "With whom?" and "Doing what?" All valid questions.

Options for volunteering abound, some that you already may have encountered some of these opportunities, but many others that may be entirely new to you. What will almost certainly seem new is the matchmaking process, made possible by the Internet that can, and will, bring you together with your optimum volunteer placement.

In the past you may have been limited in your volunteering options, dependent on a traditional set of organizations and agencies—political, social, medical, church-affiliated, educational—where you would be assigned traditional types of volunteer tasks—clerical, telephone-based, fund-raising, mail-outs, food or clothing distribution.

This is no longer the case. Now volunteering options, like the paid work and business options discussed in earlier chapters, have been transformed through the connectedness made possible by the Internet.

Entire websites are devoted to matching up those who want to offer their services with those who need their unique abilities and help.

On these websites, agencies post full descriptions of what they need, as they need it. Then potential volunteers are able to search through the countless volunteer opportunities available to identify those to which they are best suited, in terms of the:

- cause or issue that matters most to them;
- skills and abilities needed; and
- types of work activities involved.

These websites thus become powerful connecting tools that enable agencies and volunteers to find each other.

Using the Internet to Find Your Ideal Match

Discovering your own best volunteering match—whether it reflects your past work or involves branching out into something entirely different—starts, as with any meaningful search for work, with your knowing yourself well. What do you most care about? What will best engage your mind as well as your energies, your assets, and your special talents? The more you know about what you want to do, the more valuable you will be to the organization you join as a volunteer.

As a volunteer, you will have the freedom to experiment with new activities as well as to do work that calls upon skills that you developed throughout your working career.

Is there something you wish you had had the opportunity to learn? Some organizations will gladly assign you to work as a "beginner" because they know you will be motivated by learning something new. Many agencies provide training to enable you to learn new skills, develop fresh talents, and otherwise be more effective as a volunteer.

Expanded Options Made Possible by the Internet

Not only does the Internet make it possible for you to locate an ideal volunteering match, it also expands the options available to you far beyond your own locale. Many volunteer tasks and projects actually can be done by working online or by phone, with no necessity that you travel or meet face-to-face.

This means that you are no longer limited to volunteering in your own area of the country—or even in your own country. Online volunteer work abroad can be done from your home as readily as online work in and for your own neighborhood.

A Sample Online Volunteer Matching Service

Smart Volunteer is one example of an online service that matches needs with volunteers (*SmartVolunteer.org*). This service allows you to search for volunteer opportunities by type of agency, such as: arts, children and youth, community building, energy conservation, family and parenting, women's issues, wildlife and animal welfare. You will be able to select the type of work that interests you, and refine your list according to whether you wish to volunteer locally or "virtually."

Some skill categories listed on the *Smart Volunteer* website are:

- arts/creative
- business development
- child advocacy
- board participation
- counseling
- writing/editing
- videography
- event planning
- research

Some of the volunteer options listed on *SmartVolunteer.org* are one-time projects. Others are ongoing. Some activities are to be carried out locally. Others may be done online, from any location where you have access to a computer and an Internet connection.

As an example of the many types of interesting volunteer project matches available through this website, a search in the *Arts and Creative* and *Hospitality* categories yielded options that included:

- **Design a logo for *Green Africa***

   Green Africa (*http://www.greenafricafoundation.org*) is an African organization focused on capacity development of African communities through life skill training, promotion of good health and peace within communities, and advancement towards sustainable livelihood and environmental conservation.

- **Create a T-shirt for *Voice for Earth International***

  Voice for Earth International (http://www.voiceforearth.org/) is a non-profit organization that supports a "just, healthier and more sustainable society, irrespective of color, caste, creed or race, in any part of the human world" by meeting basic needs for food, water and shelter for all.

- **Develop instructional materials for *Jumpstart***

  Jumpstart (http://www.Jstart.org/) is a national early education organization that helps children to develop the language and literacy skills they need for school.

- **Teach beginning crochet** for a Seniors Center;
- **Teach art** two Wednesday evenings a month;
- **Help with the silent auction** at a *Lifestyle Film Festival*;

These *SmartVolunteering.org* lists of needs for volunteer effort go on and on, and change continuously. Possibilities vary according to where you live, your preferred type of agency, and what you want and are able to do. Another similar matching service is *VolunteerMatch.org*. This site supplies links to a full range of opportunities for volunteers. Type in your location, and review the list of opportunities near you. Some examples include:

- Become a mentor, imparting your lifelong experience to guide college students in your field;
- Refurbish donated bicycles or help with an "Earn a Bike" program, where 10 to 15-year-olds learn bike repair and maintenance while earning a bike for themselves;
- Mentor high school exchange students;
- Conduct a weekly bilingual story time to engage Spanish-speaking families in a "fun and energetic learning environment, while promoting early literacy, and strengthening the connection between parents and their young children."

Select Work that Engages Your Temperament

Let's consider the increased range of volunteering options, as well as the powerful means now available through the Internet to match yourself with an opportunity that ideally suits you. The volunteer work that you select should and must be work that will excite and engage you, taking into account your special gifts, interests and temperament—*Guardian, Artisan, Giver* or *Thinker*.

Consider what the actual tasks of a volunteer work opportunity will be, then evaluate that option based on the degree to which you will gain satisfaction by engaging in that work over the months and years ahead. If the major tasks of a volunteer opportunity you are considering are ones that do not suit you, and that will not engage you long term, then keep looking. You may not yet have found your volunteer niche. The better you are able to define exactly what you *uniquely* want to and are able to offer, the greater the likelihood you will find your optimum volunteer placement.

Here are some examples of volunteer work that may best suit you, depending upon your innate temperament. There are many other possibilities, but here are some models.

If you are a Guardian (SJ)

If you thrive on nurturing others and being useful, your temperament may fit well, and you may be well engaged, by volunteering to...

Provide Protection as a Guardian Ad Litem

A volunteer Guardian ad Litem is appointed by the court to advocate for a child who comes into the court system, primarily as a result of alleged abuse or neglect (*http://guardianadlitem.org/vol_faq.asp)*. The task of a volunteer Guardian ad Litem is to:

- Advocate for the child during court hearings.

- Protect the child's inherent right to grow up with dignity in a safe environment that meets that child's best interests.
- Ensure that the child's best interests are represented in the court at every stage of the case.

As a volunteer Guardian ad Litem, you will be required to successfully complete 30 hours certification training plus 6 hours annual recertification training. Work requires 10 hours per month on average.

If you are an Artisan/Experiencer (SP)

Your need for action and challenge to engage your innate capacity to be resourceful may find a suitable outlet when you...

Dream Green

Consider working for an environmental or animal welfare agency committed to the protection and preservation of resources, natural areas, and wildlife in your community, nation or world. One source of environmental volunteer projects is *The Nature Conservancy* site at *http://www.nature.org* where you can learn of opportunities in your own state...or in another state where you would like to spend time.

Another example is *Together Green,* a national organization that organizes hundreds of Volunteer Days at Audubon Centers across the country, engaging thousands of volunteers in tens of thousands of volunteer hours of effort: *http://www.togethergreen.org.*

When you visit the *Together Green* website, click on the map to find a location near you and to see a complete list of events and programs. Or you could select a location where you would like to spend time, and explore your volunteering options there. Types of volunteer activities listed by *Together Green* include:

- habitat and trail restoration
- river and lake clean-ups
- invasive species removal
- nest-box building
- wildlife and plant surveys

SNAPSHOT

Yvette brought to her volunteering activities years of experience working in the non-profit world. So she knew how to

---

"do a lot with a little by reaching out to the community and its resources to get more and do more." Her business background and consulting experience, combined with her passion for the environment, animals, and waterways, pointed her in the direction of focusing her efforts on environmental education.

Among the groups she supports are the *Talkin' Monkeys Project* (a project that provides a healthy, safe, lifelong home for apes and monkeys taken from private homes or released from medical labs), *OneLightBulb.org*, *Pooches for the Planet*, and the *Tampa Bay & Sarasota Bay Estuary Program*.

She says: "I feel really good getting the educational message across and promoting environmental welfare and conservation... the environmental movement is trying to move in a positive direction and I'm glad to be a part of it."

Or "Dream Green" Abroad

To increase the excitement you need as an *Artisan/Experiencer*, you may consider volunteering abroad. Agencies like *ProWorld Volunteers* (*proworldvolunteers.org/*) match volunteers to communities that need help in Latin America, Asia and Africa, with opportunities in 14 countries, including:

- *Belize*
- *Brazil*
- *Costa Rica*
- *Ecuador*
- *Ghana*
- *India*
- *Mexico*
- *Morocco*
- *Nepal*
- *Panama*
- *Peru*
- *Philippines*
- *South Africa*
- *Thailand*

As a volunteer you would be matched to a "high-impact project" in your area of interest, including:

- **Construction:** build a school, a cleaner burning stove or a shelter for animals; help locals construct more sustainable buildings.
- **Community Development:** support community centers and fair trade initiatives; preserve history and encourage sustainable development through local team projects.
- **Education:** teach local children, women's groups or community courses in English; assist at primary schools and nurseries.
- **Environment:** clean hiking trails; monitor invasive species; plant organic seeds; help local farmers thrive in a global economy.
- **Health:** work in local and rural clinics, helping to immunize, diagnose and treat patients; combat HIV/AIDS through public health education programs.
- **Women's Development:** nurture microfinance and entrepreneurial initiatives for women; support fair trade of women's crafts.

Another major agency matching volunteers with environmental programs abroad is *United Planet* (*http://www.unitedplanet.org*), committed to a variety of environmental awareness projects around the world. Volunteer-abroad opportunities available through this agency are called "United Planet Quests," and include short-term and long-term, professional and non-professional assignments where "volunteers make a critical difference worldwide."

Short-term Quests (1–12 weeks), in countries like Costa Rica, Italy, Ghana, Nepal, Romania, Ecuador and Peru, involve a wide range of projects that support essential community development work, such as orphanage care, teaching English, environmental work, or healthcare.

Volunteers are 100% immersed in the local culture through cultural activities, excursions, and host family stays. They are asked to pay a modest fee to cover preparation and training before departure, food and lodging in the host country, air transportation, emergency medical insurance, on-going support and supervision, as well as language lessons, cultural activities and excursions. As a sample, the fee for an

8-week "Quest" in Italy is $2515. The charge for a 6-week Quest in Tanzania is $2195; a 4-week Quest in Peru, $2190; a 2-week quest in Mexico, $945.

If you are a Giver (NF)

Your *Giver* temperament makes it essential that your work be meaningful and that it contributes to your own personal growth. You thrive by focusing on human potential and bringing out the best in others, providing services, products or solutions that...

Change the World, One Relationship at a Time

Child mentoring programs enlist volunteers to create a positive, supportive, one-on-one relationship with a child, by participating in everyday activities together such as playing basketball or going to the beach, and otherwise by contributing to the child's achievement of personal, social and educational growth.

Time commitments start at a few hours per week, and span a full school year. Mentors meet with "their" child for one or more hours a week for the duration of the school year, playing games or helping with homework. Some mentors are assigned to children in foster care, with the goal of providing consistent adult role models to help the child handle the challenges of their foster care environment.

A search on *Volunteer Match* (*http://www.volunteermatch.org*), yielded 6,780 mentoring opportunities in the US.

Another large mentoring organization in the US is *Big Brothers Big Sisters* (*http://www.bbbs.org*), matching at-risk youths with caring, adult role models in communities across the country. A nationwide study showed that children in the *Little Brothers and Little Sisters Program*, as compared to those not in the program, were:

- 46% less likely to begin using illegal drugs;
- 52% less likely to skip school;
- more confident of their performance in schoolwork;
- better able to get along with their families.

Volunteering as a Big Brother or Big Sister is an opportunity to help shape a child's future for the better by empowering him or her to achieve. The mentoring provided by Big Brothers and Big Sisters has a long-lasting, positive effect on a child's confidence, grades, social skills, and life. According to an imact survey, 81% of former "Littles" reveal that their "Big" gave them hope and changed their perspective of what they thought possible.

Big Brother/Little Brother and Big Sister/Little Sister teams keep a consistent schedule of outings, meeting together on a regular basis for a few hours several times a month. They decide together what they want to do, and obtain parental approval. Activities and outings vary— playing sports together, going on a hike, reading books, attending cultural events. By keeping a consistent presence in the life of their assigned child, "Bigs" have natural opportunities to provide guidance, advice and inspiration, and otherwise to have a life-changing impact, one child at a time.

Currently there are more than 21,000 boys and 10,500 girls ready and waiting to be matched with Big Sisters and Big Brothers across the country—twice the number of boys than girls.

If you are a Thinker (NT)

With your drive to learn, achieve, and continuously improve, your best volunteer options are those where you will be adequately challenged, possibly by being the one to take on the design and leadership role of initiating suitable volunteer opportunities yourself. Your ability to see possibilities, understand complexities and design solutions can best be engaged when you...

Take Volunteerism One Step Further

The volunteer project where you could best contribute may not exist...yet. In fact, your efforts may serve a greater good, and your particular gifts be more fully engaged, if you establish and operate a volunteer program or change initiative of your own. Although other potential volunteers may be "actors in search of a play," you could be better suited to be the play's author.

Possibly you have already identified a viable organization in your community that could use the services of a vibrant, dedicated corps of volunteer workers, with you in the lead. Or you may have become aware of a problem that needs to be solved...a current situation (or place, or group, or opportunity) that could and should be better, broader or more accessible, or otherwise restored, improved, rescued or preserved. What seems to be lacking is the organizational structure—the ability to perceive and work with the "big picture." What is lacking is YOU.

If you have the time, the energy, and the leadership skills, what organization would not welcome you into their sphere of influence? And if the organization within which your efforts would fit does not exist—yet—who better than you to invent it yourself?

Go for it! Use your Google and amazon.com skills to find the many resources you can use to get the help you need. Also, you will find that sites such as *ServiceLeader.org* will provide you support and guidance for the process of "Developing and Implementing a Volunteer Program." You might also choose to use as a model a volunteer initiative from elsewhere in the country, and take the lead to apply the same concept in your own locale.

For example, the *Parks By You* effort in Houston, Texas has set out to connect the city of Houston through a series of linear parks along the bayous and to improve existing neighborhood parks throughout the city. The vision is to engage local volunteers and neighborhoods to create a "park by you," so that the majority of the citizens of Houston will live within 1.5 miles of a park or green space.

You could set in motion a similar vision in your community.

SNAPSHOT

Wesley, whom we met in an earlier Snapshot, was eager enough to volunteer his services after he retired. But he had never been one to just accept the status quo. He was willing to volunteer, but only if he could do it HIS way.

One of his prime causes was both personal and environmental. His home in Bellaire Beach, on the Tampa Bay side of a narrow barrier island, was vulnerable, as were those of his neighbors, due to severe beach erosion that had removed the beach completely. There no longer *was* any beach. At high tide the Gulf of Mexico lapped against the sea wall, and during heavy storms, the entire island disappeared underwater.

Wesley tackled this problem from every direction, beginning by approaching the Town Council, meeting with town leaders and

---

seeking out other associations, including condo HOAs, whose members had personal and financial interests in the problem.

He quickly discovered that any and all efforts to restore the beach, and thereby to protect the island and its inhabitants, had been brought to a firm halt. The obstruction was a small contingent of Gulf-front home owners who selfishly, and unwisely, had exerted pressure to keep the ocean views in front of their multi-million dollar homes *exclusively* for their eyes only, even if this meant putting the entire island in jeopardy.

With this discovery, Wesley's "volunteer" efforts kicked into high gear. Soon he was authoring a weekly environmental science column for the local paper, "teaching" the community the how's and why's of environmental conditions and beach erosion, and how these factors would play out over time if no action was taken.

He created a "Photo Montage" that vividly showed the devastating impact of one heavy storm that had covered the island in water. Then he nudged and prodded until he had obtained permission to display his montage on the walls of City Hall—in the conference room where the City Council met regularly.

Wes came to be seen as a visionary and leader by some, and a major nuisance by others. He attended every City Council meeting, where he was outspoken, and sometimes even volatile, on the subject of beach erosion and the undeniable necessity for beach renourishment. Using his career-long experience writing formal proposals for funding, complete with budgets, timelines and detailed plans, he led efforts to seek and obtain federal funding for a beach renourishment project to replace the beach.

The outcome of all of this... The beach was saved. The sand was restored. The island was preserved. His legacy... Both now and for generations to come, a full diversity of people are once again able to enjoy the beauty, and the protection, of what is now a broad expanse of white, sandy beach.

But Where Do I Start?

Although you may have friends and family who have made volunteering a permanent, meaningful, important part of their lives... And although you suspect that a serious, long-term commitment to some type of volunteer service could produce a positive lasting effect in your life ahead... You still may be at a loss as to where to begin.

Begin by considering your SELF. What in your own view is the most worthy cause for you to support? What project, activity or cause would most engage your authentic commitment and enthusiasm?

Once you have some ideas in mind, write them down. Then follow through by taking the following eight actions to propel you in the direction of your own best volunteer engagement.

Action #1: Explore Online

We already have talked about a number of websites where you can begin your quest. Look back in this chapter to locate them, and add them to your URL notebook as websites you will want to explore fully and to consult frequently.

Some additional sites to visit include:

VolunteerMatch.org (_www.volunteermatch.org_)

This site offers you the opportunity to explore volunteer options by geographic location and/or by keyword topic search.

Volunteers of America (_www.voa.org_)

With offices throughout the US, the _Volunteers of America_ site is searchable by zip code. Links for veterans are included.

Experience Corps (_experiencecorps.org_)

This site, sponsored by AARP, emphasizes working with children in schools on literacy, reading, and tutoring.

National Park Service

(_www.nps.gov/getinvolved/volunteer.htm_)

Check the "Get Involved" section.
Points of Light (*http://www.pointsoflight.org/*) Search by location and type of work.
VolunteerGuide.org (*http://www.volunteerguide.org/*) This site offers *Volunteer On Demand* options, catering to "busy people who want to make a difference" even if you have an unpredictable schedule. Volunteer projects are grouped into those that can be accomplished in 15 minutes, in a few hours, or during a "volunteer vacation," and include causes such as animal welfare, children's issues, community concerns, global warming, health care, and poverty.

Action #2: Research Your Options

Spend time learning about the causes or issues that are important to you. Look for a group that deals with topics about which you feel strongly. Start reading magazines, articles, and other publications related to the type of organizations for which you are interested in becoming a volunteer.

The more you know, the more meaningful your decision will be. The first and most important thing about volunteering is to become involved with an organization that correlates with your particular values. If you choose a cause that you strongly believe in, you will find the time to commit, and, as a result, you will derive a sense of fulfillment, while making a significant contribution.

Action #3: Find That Life-Style Fit

At the outset, before you finalize any commitments, do a "lifestyle check" of how you want to structure your retirement.

- Are you planning to do a serious amount of travelling? Do you want to protect your flexibility? If so, you probably will not want to volunteer for tasks or projects that require a daily or weekly commitment.

- Are you a morning person or a night hawk? There are still many volunteer opportunities for those of us who like to live on an "off-beat" schedule.

- Are you a "gregarious Gregory," or do you prefer working on your own or one-on-one?

- How do you react to older people? Young people? Sick people? Problem people? Or do you just prefer animals?!

SNAPSHOT

When Jason retired from the Navy as a corpsman in his early 40's, he had planned to seek employment in the public or private sector in some aspect of the medical field. But soon after retirement, he developed a generic eye disease that classified him as legally blind, and unable to work in his desired field.

An avid fisherman and hunter in his younger days, Jason began chatting with a neighbor who belonged to the local game club. Before long, he found himself heavily involved in every aspect of the club—from raising game birds, to cooking for large outdoor gatherings, to property maintenance.

The game club became not only his primary source of social activity, but more importantly, gave him a renewed sense of purpose outside himself. His disability became a non-issue in this environment. Although he could no longer legally hunt, he continued to be an avid fisherman, while making a meaningful contribution to the efficient operation of the club.

Action #4: Think Outside the Box

Many community groups that are looking for volunteers, such as neighborhood watch programs, prisons, disaster relief organizations, youth organizations, intergenerational programs, and park services, may not have occurred to you, but could just be the perfect fit.

Schools, hospitals, nursing homes have countless opportunities and critical needs for quality volunteers. Don't forget your local church organization, food pantries, and homeless shelters, as well as your local drama or theater group, and community music, library, museum, parks and recreational organizations.

Action #5: Make That Call

Sometimes the hardest step is the first one. Pick up that phone and punch in that number! Making that first point of contact will impel you to continue your new journey. Your phone conversation will probably result in an initial introductory meeting that you should approach just as you would a job interview. Be ready to describe your interests, qualifications, and background. Use this time to learn as much as you can about the organization, how it operates, what benefits it offers volunteers, and how you will (or will not) fit within its structure.

Action #6: Show Up

Once you have found your perfect fit, establish yourself by providing a regular reliable presence at the organization or activity. This will indicate that you are truly committed to your chosen cause, and that you can be counted on to make a positive, consistent, substantive contribution. The quality of reliability cannot be underestimated or over emphasized. Others are counting on you for your presence on a regular basis. Don't disappoint them.

Action #7: Use Your Skills to Take On a Project

Don't wait to be asked. Offer to provide a specific, tangible service, to lead an activity, to participate in a program. You could initiate a fund-raiser, plan a basket raffle, chaperone a field trip, do accounting, develop a newsletter, update a web site. Once you achieve success on any one of many projects, you can be sure your services will be appreciated and called upon again and again.

Action #8: Have Fun

Volunteer work may be called "work," but it also should be fun—something you enjoy doing—something that adds a spring to your step, recharges your energy battery, and gives balance and perspective to your life. It should provide you with an outlet to do and to try things that you may have never had the time to experience before—even things that you never thought you could do or accomplish!

And it should make you feel engaged. Along with your time, you optimally will be donating your spirit as well. If the work feels like drudgery, you will not have much to offer. So call a halt and look elsewhere. But if the work does engage and excite you…if it provides you with a sense of purpose and connection…you will put your heart into it as well as your hands. And that will make all the difference.

Now What About You?

Select three specific actionable ideas for working "for free, but your way." Add these to what you will consider later when you "make your match and move."

Record your three top choices here for now, then copy them to the composite of possibilities you started to create in Chapter 8. Of course, if you wish, feel free to note more than three…

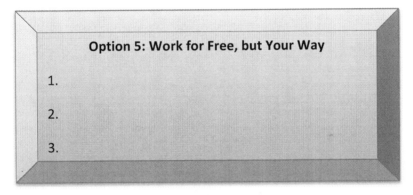

Option 5: Work for Free, but Your Way

1.

2.

3.

And So…

Throughout this book, we have explored our unique selves, determining who we are psychologically, and where we have been professionally. We know what unique strengths and personal passions we bring to bear on the types of causes we want to support.

As this chapter shows, whatever your temperament, your age, your background, there is need and opportunity galore for you to volunteer your services, according to your personality, interests, talents and time availability. Organizations near and far, serving every type of need, seek competent, reliable, volunteer talent to supplement and complement their paid employees. There never seem to be enough hands and heads to fill society's ever-increasing needs and demands for social services.

Did you want to become a veterinarian, but not have the financial resources to pursue the extensive demands of this profession? Now you can volunteer at your local animal rescue facility, or within a vet's office. Was your dream to enter a branch of the armed services, but a slight physical disability prohibited you from doing so? Now you have unlimited opportunities to work with veterans of all ages, as well as their families, assisting them with those physical and mental disabilities and limitations that resulted from their military service.

Were you a member of the medical profession, working in an enclosed antiseptic, environment, but longing for the great outdoors? Your timing couldn't be more opportune, with society's new awareness about the fragility of our planet. So many organizations promoting ecological environmental causes would welcome your participation and enthusiasm to work outdoors, close to nature's flora and fauna.

Did you lack the maturity and perspective in your youth to realize that you had a particular gift of relating to children, yet throughout your working life in the business world, often wish you could work directly with kids? Now is your chance. This chapter cites numerous venues for doing just that.

Perhaps it's an appropriate and fitting reward that, for our life's last passage, we find ourselves positioned to do exactly what we want to do, when and where we want to do it. In fact, even if during our prime working lives we were not able to pursue our lifelong career goal, now is the time we can do exactly that.

CHAPTER 14:
Parting Words

We hope you have experienced your own unique "happening" as you have journeyed through the chapters of this book. Wasn't it awesome, and even daunting, to remind ourselves of who we are as a generation in terms of what we have accomplished... advancing the fields of technology, business, medicine, and education... transforming the political, social, economic, intellectual, and technical landscape of the second half of the 20th century... And, in the process, becoming the most educated, affluent, healthy generation in US history.

This is the legacy that we now find ourselves in a position to leverage as we "shift gears" into a new life phase. But even more daunting is the conviction and determination that we are not finished—yet! We have saved the best for last!

The realizations and the inspirations you have experienced through your reading hopefully have generated your "new birth," the re-invented, re-energized you who knows that this is just the beginning of what is, no doubt, the final chapter of your biography. Determine to make this next phase your best. Your happiest. Your most gratifying. And, yes, even your most productive.

Armed with the tools, strategies, and connections (both tangible and virtual) that you now have at your disposal, you can and will accomplish what you set out to do—next.

You know where you've been—your past accomplishments. You know who and where you are—your current self-awareness and self-assessment. And you know where you are going next—your new life paradigm, with career options galore. Hopefully, you also now know how to get there, or at least where to start. So what are the operative concepts that should prevail in this glorious next period of your life? We leave you with these six treasures.

Savor the Richness in Full

Whether we remember or acknowledge it or not, we have spent too much time in the past "short-cutting" so many of those small, but important, "minute vacations."

Now is the time to retire the "I'd like to, but I don't have the time" mantra in favor of "Yes, I can indulge—in that second glass of wine, that lengthy, somewhat frivolous phone call, that "chick flick" or "action movie" matinee, that extra round of golf, that beer or coffee and cake break with my friend, that no-buy (or buy-buy!) shopping spree.

Whenever you are tempted to by-pass a "carpe diem" moment, ask yourself: "If not now, when?" Then tell yourself: "I deserve it now!"

Frivolity Is a Luxury You *Can* Afford

Who said you are too old to ride that Zip Line across the Costa Rican rain forest? Where is it written that you are beyond the "adolescent phase" of taking an impulsive skinny dip in that mountain lake, or getting that tattoo of a phoenix rising from the ashes? And, no, it is not too late to buy that Harley that you have secretly coveted, along with the black leather jacket, to complement the tattoo!

Maybe, just maybe, blending into the crowd, acting with proper decorum, and always dressing, speaking and acting "appropriately" are conventional wisdoms that are outworn and overrated.

As Boomers, haven't we earned the right to "loosen up and live a little closer to the edge"? So...go put on those Nikes or buy that mountain bike or take up line dancing. Just do it!

Live In The Moment.

My very dear friend, who happens to be a Quaker, once shared with me a basic precept of this gentle sect—"Be where you are." I can't tell you how many times I have applied this wisdom in my own personal life—in mundane as well as complex situations.

When I was frazzled and frantic in an endless, seemingly unmoving line at the supermarket checkout, in five o'clock rush hour traffic, or on overload with job projects... When I was in the middle of housework or cooking—both chores that I abhor—or stuck in an airport after missing my flight, and facing a night attempting to sleep upright on a plastic seat... After my mental and emotional hysteria subsided, "be where you are" always came to the rescue, providing me with a sense of calm, sanity and perspective. "Be where you are" has become for me the psychological equivalent of "take a deep breath."

As Boomers, we have seen our share of tragedies and triumphs. We have learned the sobering lesson that often in life waiting is the hard part of any experience, and waiting for clarity is the hardest. Whether in good times or bad, we also have come to know the meaning of "this, too, shall pass"—whatever the "it" was. And in time it did.

Living in the moment has been one of the most ignored habits we haven't mastered. Now is the time to become experts at it. Because, in reality, the moment is all we are assured.

Be True to Yourself

However accustomed you have become to doing, doing, doing for others—caring for them, working for them, raising them, being their spouse or their friend—the time is now to break free and learn to be true to yourself. Shakespeare had it right when he wrote, "This above all, to thine own self be true. And it must follow, as the night the day, thou canst not then be false to any man."

Give yourself permission, immediately, to take charge of your own life and to speak up for yourself. After a lifetime of effort to avoid being "selfish," or otherwise putting your own self first, this is the time that you have been waiting for. Now it is your turn.

Move forward, firmly, with no regrets from the past, into the future. Find your own way—your own work—your own legacy. Surprisingly, you will be of more value to the others in your life when you are acting as your own true self than you ever were when you were attempting to put your own self—your wants, enthusiasms, passions and purpose—on hold in favor of accommodating others, or otherwise setting yourself aside.

Revise the Revisions

As a Boomer, it may not seem all that long ago that you heard Arlo Guthrie's mishap while singing "Alice's Restaurant." When he got into a tangle, and missed some of the words, he just kept on playing, saying "That's alright. It'll come back 'round again..." And it did come back 'round again, at which point he went on to sing the rest of the song.

So, too, will your Next Phase life "come back 'round again." If you find that your first set of plans and directions do not suit you after all, just come at it again from another direction.

Considering how dramatic and deep your life changes may be at this point, and how eager you may have been to choose your next direction, any direction, and end the suspense... you may find yourself heading off, energetically and with great speed, down the wrong path. If so, the faster you go—the harder you push down on that pedal—the further afield you will find yourself before you finally do call a halt, put on the brakes, and turn around.

You may find that you have made too many compromises, possibly in your attempt to align your Next Phase goals and plans with those of your spouse...or a close friend...or your children and their children. Perhaps you have made compromises that are too extreme, or have allowed your next life to choose you instead of you choosing it. As with most things, "not to decide is to decide."

A sign that may indicate you have "veered off" in a direction that is not optimum for you, is the sense that you are waking up into someone else's life. If this should happen to you, the heart of the matter, most likely, is that your concept and sense of your true self, in all its uniqueness, has somehow been sidetracked. Your most essential self may be telling you that you are not there yet.

If so, like Arlo, just "let it come back 'round again"—your retirement life, that is. Revise the revisions until you are on the right course for you... And you know you are on the right course... And you know that you know.

Now Pass It On: Your Legacy as a Role Model

You already may have embarked on your new life's adventure before you connected with this book. If so, your reading may have enhanced, enriched, and given added impetus to your new career, providing you with new connections, perspectives, and strategies.

Or you may be embracing this book at the very beginning of your "re-invention" stage. If so, we hope our words have proven to be an effective, inspiring and empowering "yellow brick road" to help you expand your thinking, find your way, and reach your own intended destination.

In either case, now we ask that you "pay it forward." Share your own Senior Snapshot—your new adventure—with your fellow Boomer colleagues who may still be in search of their own next lives. And, when possible, help them through the process of clarifying their own journeys—but their way.

We welcome you to post the story of your journey on our book website at _http://BoomerRetirementLifeandWork.com_. After all, the greatest legacy we can leave each other is the camaraderie and confidence we share by showing fellow Boomers "how we did it," and cheering them on to do the same.

May the wind be at your back.

TABLE OF URLS

Although we have done our best to assure that our list of websites is up-to-date and accurate, be aware that sites change frequently, both in title, content and in web location. Also, our list is not meant to be all-inclusive. Rather, we hope you will use these sites as springboards to other equally valuable Internet resources that you will then share with all your other Boomer friends.

Category	Web Name	URL	Chapter
Career Opportunities	Bureau of Labor Statistics	http://www.bls.gov	8
Entrepreneuring	Crystal Underground	http://www.crystalunderground.com	4
Entrepreneuring	Money US News	http://money.usnews.com	5
Entrepreneuring	ABC Go	http://abc.go.com	5
Entrepreneuring	Chord Buddy	http://www.chordbuddy.com	5
Entrepreneuring	Rent–A-Grandma	http://www.rentagrandma.com	5
Entrepreneuring	Vayable	http://www.vayable.com	12
Event Management Jobs	Convention Net	http://www.Convention.net	10
Event Management Jobs	SMG World	http://www.SMGWorld.com	10
Freelance Networks	eLance	http://www.elance.com	9
Freelance Networks	Freelancers	http://www.freelancers.net	9
Freelance Networks	Freelancer	http://www.freelancer.com	9
Freelance Networks	All Freelance	http://www.allfreelance.com	9
Freelance Networks	V Worker	http://www.vworker.com	9

Category	Web Name	URL	Chapter
General Research	Amazon	http://www.amazon.com	5
Health	American Heart Assoc.	http://hyper.ahajournals.org	1
Health	Arthritis Foundation	http://www.arthritis.org	10
Health Careers	Ace Fitness	http://www.acefitness.org	8
Help for Entrepreneurs	USA Gov	http://www.usa.gov	11
Job Newsletters/ Newsgroups	Bassador Company	http://bassador.com	9
Job Newsletters/ Newsgroups	Home Job Stop	http://HomeJobStop.com	9
Job Newsletters/ Newsgroups	Career Builder	http://CareerBuilder.com	9
Job Newsletters/ Newsgroups	I-Hire Accounting	http://IHireAccounting.com	9
Job Sites For Boomers/Seniors	Work Search	http://foundation.aarp.org	10
Job Sites For Boomers/Seniors	World Force 50	http://www.workforce50.com	10
Job Sites For Boomers/Seniors	Internet Senior Success	http://www.internetseniorsuccess.com	10
Job Sites For Boomers/Seniors	Now What Jobs	http://www.nowwhatjobs.net	10
Job Sites For Boomers/Seniors	Future-Jobs-O-Matic	http://www.marketplace.org	10
Job Sites For Boomers/Seniors	Retirement Jobs	http://www.retirementjobs.com	10
Job Sites For Boomers/Seniors	Senior Job Bank	http://www.seniorjobbank.com	10
Job Sites For Boomers/Seniors	Retire & Consult	http://retireandconsult.com	10
Living & Working Abroad	International Living	http://www.internationalliving.com	11
Market & Survey Research Jobs	Casro	http://www.casro.org	10

Category	Web Name	URL	Chapter
Market & Survey Research Jobs	Market Research Assoc.	http://www.mra-net.org	**10**
Newspaper Online Classifieds	Aspen Daily News	http://www.AspenDailyNews.com	9
Newspaper Online Classifieds	Daily Camera	http://www.BoulderNews.com	9
Newspaper Online Classifieds	Denver Post	http://www.DenverPost.com	9
Newspaper Online Classifieds	Denver Rocky Mountain News	http://www.RockyMountainNews.com	9
Newspaper Online Classifieds	Durango Herald	http://www.DurangoHerald.com	9
Newspaper Online Classifieds	Steamboat Pilot	http://www.STMBT-Pilot.com	9
Networking	LinkedIn	http://www.linkedin.com	8
Online Classified Ads	CraigsList	http://Craigslist.com	9
Online Classified Ads	Oodle Market-place	http://Jobs.Oodle.com	9
Online Classified Ads	Jobvertise	http://Jobvertise.com	9
Online Classified Ads	Job Factory	http://www.jobfactory.com	9
Online Employ-ment Agencies	Assist U	http://www.AssistU.com	9
Online Employ-ment Agencies	Cyber Secretaries	http://www.YouDictate.com	9
Online Employ-ment Agencies	Desktop Staff	http://www.DeskTopStaff.com	9
Online Employ-ment Agencies	Hire Me Now	http://www.hiremenow.com	9
Online Employ-ment Agencies	Electric Quill	http://www.Electric-Quill.com	9
Online Employ-ment Agencies	Executary	http://www.Executary.com	9
Online Employ-ment Agencies	HireAbility	http://www.HireAbility.com	9

Category	Web Name	URL	Chapter
Online Employment Agencies	Vworker	http://www.vworker.com	9
Online Employment Agencies	Freelancer	http://www.vworker.com	9
Online Job Boards	Genunine Jobs	http://www.genuinejobs.com	9
Online Job Boards	Hot Jobs Yahoo	http://hotjobs.yahoo.com	9
Online Job Boards	Quintessential Careers	http://www.quintcareers.com	9
Online Job Boards	Guru.Com	http://www.guru.com	9
Online Job Boards	Employment 911	http://www.employment911.com	9
Online Job Boards	Jobline International	http://jobline.net	9
Online Job Boards	Home Job Stop	http://www.HomeJobStop.com	9
Online Job Boards	Home Workers	http://www.Homeworkers.org	9
Online Job Boards	2 Work At Home	http://www.2Work-at-Home.com	9
Online Job Boards	JuJu	http://www.job-search-engine.com	9
Online Job Boards	Employment Spot	http://www.EmploymentSpot.com	10
Online Outsourcing	oDesk	http://www.oDesk.com	5
Online Outsourcing	eLance	http://www.eLance.com	9
Online Outsourcing	Click-N-Work	http://www.clicknwork.com	9
Online Outsourcing	Prime Outsource	http://www.Prime-Outsource.com	9
Online Outsourcing	AccounTemps	http://www.AccounTemps.com	9
Online Outsourcing	AB Global Translations	http://www.abglobal.net	9

Category	Web Name	URL	Chapter
Online Outsourcing	VIP Desk	http://www.VIPDesk.com	9
Online Outsourcing	Balance Your Books	http://www.BalanceYourBooks.com	9
Online Outsourcing	Outsource Your Books	http://www.osyb.com	9
Online Staffing Services	Global Staffing	http://GlobalStaffing.com	9
Online Staffing Services	Staffing Services	http://StaffingServices.net	9
Online Staffing Services	Professional Support Service	http://ProfessionalSupportService.com	9
Online Staffing Services	Binary Anvil	http://VStaff.com	9
Online Staffing Services	B&V Staffing	http://bvstaffing.com	9
Online Staffing Services	Virtual Office Temps	http://VirtualAssistantJobs.com	9
Online Staffing Services	Virtual Corporation	http://www.Virtual-Corp.net	9
Online Staffing Services	Virtual Staffing	http://VirtualStaffing.com	9
Online Staffing Services	Monster	http://www.monster.com	9
Online Staffing Services	Career Builder	http://www.CareerBuilder.com	9
Online Staffing Services	Jobs	http://www.jobs.com	9
Online Staffing Services	Outsource 2000	http://www.Outsource2000.com	9
Online Staffing Services	Flex Jobs	http://www.FlexJobs.com	9
Online Staffing Services	Workaholics 4 Hire	http://www.Workaholics4Hire.com	9
Public Education Jobs	National Education Association	www.nea.org	10

Category	Web Name	URL	Chapter
Public Education Jobs	National Substitute Teachers Alliance	www.nstasubs.org	10
Resources for Entrepreneurs	Swilt	http://www.theswilt.com	5
Resources for Entrepreneurs	Readerest	http://www.readerest.com	5
Resources for Entrepreneurs	Meet The Blanks	http://www.meettheblanks.com	5
Resources for Entrepreneurs	Vista Print	http://www.vistaprint.com	8
Resources for Entrepreneurs	Business USA	http://business.usa.gov	11
Resources for Entrepreneurs	SBA Gov	http://www.sba.gov	11
Resources for Entrepreneurs	Entrepreneur	http://www.entrepreneur.com	11
Resources for Entrepreneurs	Biz Filings	http://www.bizfilings.com	11
Resources for Entrepreneurs	GoDaddy	http://www.GoDaddy.com	11
Resources for Entrepreneurs	AllWebCo	http://www.AllWebCo.com	11
Resources for Entrepreneurs	VistaPrints	http://www.VistaPrints.com	11
Resources for Entrepreneurs	Intuit	http://www.Intuit.com	11
Resources for Entrepreneurs	Pet Place	http://www.petplace.com	11
Résumé Services	Microsoft Office	http://office.microsoft.com	8
Résumé Services	JobBank USA	http://www.jobbankusa.com	8
Résumé Services	Super Writing Services	http://www.SuperWritingServices.com	8
Security Services	Scam.Com	http://www.scam.com	9

Category	Web Name	URL	Chapter
Self-Discovery	Personality Pathways	http://www.personalitypathways.com	6
Self-Discovery	Type Logic	http://typelogic.com	6
Self-Discovery	Human Metrics	http://www.humanmetrics.com	6
Self-Discovery	Similar Minds	http://similarminds.com	6
Self-Discovery	Career Zone	http://www.cacareerzone.org	7
Self-Discovery	University of South Dakota	http://people.usd.edu	7
Statistics	Demographics Now	http://www.DemographicsNow.com	1
Statistics	Life Goes Strong	http://www.lifegoesstrong.com	1
Statistics	ChildStats.Gov	http://www.childstats.gov	11
Statistics	Money CNN	http://money.cnn.com	11
Statistics	Pay Scale	http://www.PayScale.com	11
Statistics	Baby Boomer Magazine	http://www.babyboomer-magazine.com	12
Statistics	Retail Traffic	http://www.retailtrafficmag.com/	12
Technology Use	Elder Gadget	http://www.Eldergadget.com	2
Technology Use	National Association of Home Builders	http://www.nbnnews.com	2
Technology Use	Varsity	http://www.varsitybranding.com	2
Transgeneration-al Design	Transgeneration-al	http://transgenerational.org	12
Transgeneration-al Design	Worcester Business Journal	http://www.wbjournal.com	12

Category	Web Name	URL	Chapter
Transgeneration-al Design	Ameriglide	http://www.ameriglide.com	12
Travel	Road Scholar	http://roadscholar.org	5
Travel	Smithsonian Journeys	http://www.smithsonianjourneys.org	5
Travel	National Geographic Expeditions	http://www.nationalgeographicexpeditions.com	5
Tutoring/Test Preparation Jobs	Tutor	http://www.Tutor.com	10
Tutoring/Test Preparation Jobs	SmarThinking	http://www.SmarThinking.com	10
Volunteering	EzineArticles	http://EzineArticles.com	5
Volunteering	Volunteering & Civil Life In America	http://www.VolunteeringInAmerica.gov	13
Volunteering	One Light Bulb	http://www.OneLightBulb.org	13
Volunteering	Smart Volunteer	http://www.SmartVolunteer.org	13
Volunteering	Green Africa Foundation	http://www.greenafricafoundation.org	13
Volunteering	Voice For Earth	http://www.voiceforearth.org	13
Volunteering	I Start	http://www.istart.org	13
Volunteering	Volunteer Match	http://www.volunteermatch.org	13
Volunteering	Guardian Ad Litem	http://guardianadlitem.org	13
Volunteering	Nature Conserva-tory	http://www.nature.org	13
Volunteering	Together Green	http://www.togethergreen.org	13
Volunteering	Pro=World Volunteers	http://www.proworldvolunteers.org	13

Category	Web Name	URL	Chapter
Volunteering	United Planet	http://www.unitedplanet.org	13
Volunteering	Big Brothers Big Sisters	http://www.bbbs.org	13
Volunteering	Volunteers of America	http://www.vog.org	13
Volunteering	Service Leader	http://www.ServiceLeader.org	13
Volunteering	Experience Corps	http://www.experiencecorps.org	13
Volunteering	National Park Service	http://www.nps.gov	13
Volunteering	Points of Light	http://www.pointsoflight.org	13
Volunteering	Volunteer Guide	http://www.volunteerguide.org	13

REFERENCES

Florida, R. (2004). *The Rise of the Creative Class: And How It's Transforming Work, Leisure, Community and Everyday Life.* Basic Books.

Harris, D. J. (1983). Psychological Aspects of Retirement. *Canadian Family Physician. 29,* 527-530.

Holtzman, E. (2002). Emotional Aspects of Retirement. *Amherst College Faculty And Staff Assistance Program.*

Jones, L. Y. (2008). *Great Expectations: America and the Baby Boom Generation.* New York: Ballantine Books.

Kauffman, E. M. (2013). *Retiring Outside the United States: A Special Report: How Grown-ups Run Away from Home. Kansas City, Mo: Ewing Marion Kauffman Foundation.*

Kubler-Ross, E. & Kessler, D. (2013). *The 5 Stages of Loss and Grief.*

Merrill Lynch (2012). *Affluent Insights Survey: National Fact Sheet.* Bank of America Corporation.

MetLife Mature Marketing Institute (2003-13). *Retirement.* New York: Metropolitan Life Insurance Company.

Moeller, P. (2013). The Best Life: Success And Happiness In Older Age. *U.S. News and World Report.*

Peddicord, K. (2010). "On Retirement: How To Retire At Any Age." *U.S. News And World Report.*

Smith, C. (1990). "The Long Weekend: Transition and Growth in Retirement." *NIU Annuitants' Association.*

Smith, J. W. & Clurman. A. (2007). *Generation Ageless: How Baby Boomers Are Changing the Way We Live Today . . . And They're Just Getting Started.* New York: HarperCollins Publishers.

INDEX